On the Creation of a Just World Order

PREFERRED WORLDS FOR THE 1990's
Saul H. Mendlovitz, General Editor

On the Creation of a Just World Order: Preferred Worlds for the 1990's
edited by Saul H. Mendlovitz

Footsteps into the Future: Diagnosis of the Present World and a Design for an Alternative
Rajni Kothari

A World Federation of Cultures: An African Perspective
Ali A. Mazrui

A Study of Future Worlds
Richard A. Falk

The True Worlds: A Transnational Perspective
Johan Galtung

A program of the World Order Models Project. Sponsored by The Institute for World Order, Inc., New York, New York.

On the Creation of a Just World Order

Preferred Worlds for the 1990's

edited by Saul H. Mendlovitz

THE FREE PRESS
A Division of Macmillan Publishing Co., Inc.
NEW YORK

The Free Press
A Division of Macmillan Publishing Co., Inc.
866 Third Avenue, New York, N.Y. 10022
Collier Macmillan Canada, Ltd.
First Free Press Paperback Edition 1976
Library of Congress Catalog Card Number: 74-28937
Printed in the United States of America
printing number
   2   3   4   5   6   7   8   9   10

Library of Congress Cataloging in Publication Data

Main entry under title:

On the creation of a just world order.

   (Preferred worlds for the 1990's)
   "A program of the World Order Models Project."
   Includes index.
   1. International organization--Addresses, essays,
lectures. 2. Peace--Addresses, essays, lectures.
I. Mendlovitz, Saul H.   II. World Order Models
Project.
JX1954.053   341.73   74-28937

ISBN 0-02-920900-5
ISBN 0-02-920910-2 pbk.

*The publication of this volume has been made possible by collaboration
among the following publishers:*

The Free Press
A Division of Macmillan Publishing Co., Inc.
New York, N.Y.

Ghana Publishing Corporation
Accra, Ghana

North-Holland Publishing Company
Amsterdam, The Netherlands

Orient Longman Limited
New Delhi, India

CONTENTS

INTRODUCTION

Scholars and intellectuals, like human beings in other walks of life, are attempting to interpret and come to grips with the crises plaguing the contemporary global political and social system. Indeed their obligation to do so may be a particularly special and important one. They are, or are supposed to be, able to discern trends, detect signals warning us of emerging social problems, to think seriously and critically about alternative solutions and possible future worlds, as well as recommend strategies for achieving those solutions and worlds. One would think that this somewhat crucial albeit relatively precious sector of the world's population, more than others, is capable of avoiding too firm an anchor in the particulars of what is. "Reality" may, for a number of reasons, constrain and overwhelm the thinking and imagination of those who have to struggle for daily existence. But surely professional thinkers and analysts have a mandate to look beyond the obvious, the immediate, and to see the possibilities open to enlightened and compassionate people who seek to reform and improve upon what prevails.

For reasons that I suspect to be familiar to most of us, social scientists are yet to adequately meet this challenge. There is initially the bias in the social sciences against work that explicitly utilizes preferences and values as a way of defining problems to be investigated, and as a standard to be used for what will be considered an adequate solution to the problems. Research that deviates from the confines of a perspective that is viewed by its adherents as empirical and scientific, is either dismissed as ideological or as being an exercise in wishful thinking. In this view, description is a proper social science concern, while prescription is not. Second, the same tradition's narrow sense of realism and empiricism operates quite decisively to inhibit futuristic thinking and orientation. If one wants maximum certainty and minimum speculation, concern with what prevails is preferable to what might or will be. If those who subscribe to the dominant thrust of social science manage to get over their reluctance to engage in futuristic thinking, their work generally confines itself to relatively simple extrapolations of current trends. The future then becomes a mere extension of the present, as though humankind has little or no ability to shape the future in preferred directions.

Two additional factors are also to blame for the lack of creative thinking about the contemporary world order system and its major crises—e.g., war, social injustice, widespread poverty, and ecological imbalance and alienation—as well as alternative systems more compatible with a humane and just world order. All these crises are global in scope, yet most social scientists who pay attention to them are wedded to an analysis in which the nation-state system informs their definitions and solutions to global problems. At the same time it is becoming increasingly clear that most of the major problems confronting humankind defy national solutions and perspectives, and are generally aggravated if not directly caused by the imperatives of national sovereignty.

Finally, creative thinking about the globe, its crises, and future is hindered by an element which is inherent in the nature of social knowledge itself and the extent to which it is culture-bound and geographically circumscribed. Even the most sympathetic and globally-minded scholar can only perceive the world from a particular angle and perspective; his (or her) roots in a particular nation, race, or class help determine and shape the choice of the problems—and the proposed remedies to them—that concern that person. Certain cultural assumptions, values and concerns may sensitize a person to some problems at the same time that they cause the individual to neglect a number of different problems that other people in other places deem important. Then too, the same global problem or phenomenon is frequently interpreted in different ways by observers from different cultures. Given the global dimensions of our major world order concerns, these truisms of the sociology of knowledge recommend in favor of transnational and cross-cultural perspectives being brought to bear upon the questions and problems that concern us. In short, it speaks against ethnocentric knowledge and research. While this point has long been well known, there has been much too little social science research carried out in this fashion, and collaborative research across cultures and worldviews is yet to be widely practiced.

On the Creation of a Just World Order is one volume in the series, "Preferred Worlds for the 1990's," resulting from a transnational research enterprise, the World Order Models Project. Because the World

Order Models Project (WOMP) is likely to be the forerunner of many more such transnational and global enterprises, it seems appropriate to say something about its genesis, development and future.

WOMP was initially conceived in response to pedagogical needs related to the study of the problem of the elimination of war as a human social institution. It was originated in the early 1960's by a small number of U.S. citizens who wished to introduce the subject matter of war prevention within formal academic environments. The individuals involved at the outset of this program brought to it a seriousness one associates with those individuals and groups who between the eighteenth and nineteenth centuries advocated and participated in the global movement to abolish slavery, or with those persons in this century who have been participating in the dismemberment of colonialism and imperialism.

To put the matter forthrightly, it was a conscious "political" act, based on a theory of social change, taken for the global social movement pursuing the eradication of war, which reasoned that most individuals in the globe, including, perhaps even especially, political leadership were encapsulated in a view of the world in which war, while perhaps unfortunate, was a necessary and permanent ingredient of human society. Thus the decision to enlist the energies of educational structures throughout the globe was based partially on the notion that the seriousness of the idea might be legitimated if the academic community throughout the world were to give it the status of a subject matter of discipline, or at least admit it was the kind of social problem which was amenable to rational analysis. Concomitantly and certainly as important as legitimation was the possibility of enlisting the talent and skills of the academic community in the research and education necessary for a successful global peace movement.

And so it was in 1966 we began to examine how to establish an educational effort that would get serious attention by scholars and educators throughout the globe. WOMP emerged as an answer.

The notion which we began to pursue was that if we were to get outstanding scholars as well as thoughtful individuals throughout the globe to become involved in the problem of war prevention, it would be necessary that they contribute in an active way in the inquiry. We hit upon the idea of asking groups of scholars in various parts of the world to direct nationally or regionally based inquiries into the problem of war prevention. We did not proceed very far in our recruitment of individuals for the project when it soon became clear that the subject matter would have to be expanded to include the related problems of economic well being and social justice, if we were to generate a world interest in this inquiry.

There were two reasons advanced for the inclusion of these problem areas. To begin with, there were many persons who argued that it was impossible to deal adequately with war prevention without taking into account poverty and social injustice; that as an empirical matter, these matters were so inextricably interwoven, they should be seen as part of the definition of the problem of war prevention. More importantly however, it became increasingly clear that while peace, in the sense of the elimination of international violence, might have a very high priority with individuals in the industrialized sector of the globe, economic well being and social justice received a much higher rating in the Third World. When we discussed these three problems, war, poverty and social injustice, as they persisted in national, regional and global contexts, and proposed examining them in the light of the next three decades, with particular reference to the countervailing values of peace, economic well being and social justice, virtually all the scholars we approached agreed to participate in the project.

We held the first meeting of the World Order Models Project in New Delhi in February 1968. At that time five research groups had been organized, representing West Germany, Latin America, Japan, India and North America. Groups representing Africa, the Soviet Union, and a non-territorial perspective, joined in subsequent years. More recently we benefited from the critical reflections on the project of a Chinese as well as a Middle Eastern scholar. One meeting was held with a group of economists organized by Jagdish Bhagwati of M.I.T. This resulted in the first WOMP book, *Economics and World Order: From the 1970's to the 1990's* (Macmillan, New York, 1972). A second book, *Africa and World Affairs* (the Third Press, New York, 1973), edited by Ali Mazrui and Hasu Patel, resulted from a conference organized by the African research group. All together some nine meetings have been held in various parts of the world, India, Japan, East Africa, Western Europe, United States and Latin America.

The results of this nearly-seven years of individual and collaborative work are only partially represented by this and the other volumes in the "Preferred Worlds for the 1990's" series. We set out to create the basic instructional materials needed for a worldwide educational movement whose ultimate thrust would be global reform. No one is more aware than we are today of how many additional and different materials still need to be created and disseminated. We set out to do normative social research that was at one and the same time oriented to the future, interdisciplinary, and focused on the design of social change actions, policies and institutions. No one realizes more than the WOMP research groups how difficult it is to do this task with minimal competence, much less with true imagination and intellectual power.

The project has fundamentally affected the personal and professional commitments of virtually everyone who participated in it. It is fair to say that what started out for almost all the participants as a short term and secondary interest has now become a life-time scholarly and political vocation. At a meeting of the Directors of the World Order Models Project in Bogota, Colombia over the New Year's period in 1974, the group decided to collaborate on a series of enterprises which they hope will continue to promote research, education and a genuinely transnational social movement to realize the world order values of peace, economic well being, social justice and ecological stability. The first of these ventures will be a transnational journal, *Alternatives,* of which Rajni Kothari will be editor, with a distinguished editorial board of some two dozen scholars throughout the globe.

Second, a number of the individuals associated with WOMP have assumed the responsibility for issuing an annual State of the Globe Message. This Message will attempt to evaluate local, regional and global trends, rating the extent to which the world order values have been diminished or realized during the preceding year, and to make recommendations as to what ought to be done in the coming years. The State of the Globe Message, issued by a group of transnational scholars independent of any formal structures of authority, will complement the messages which now come from such formal sources.

Third, we have embarked upon a modest but increasingly significant world order value indicator research project, which we hope will support the State of the Globe Message and provide alternative ways for social scientists to think about and measure the quality of social life. In addition, there will be a series of transnational seminars for scholars, public figures in all professions, expanded formal educational programming, and the beginning of a mass public education movement on a global basis. All of this programming has already been undertaken in some form and we hope will involve constructive criticism, support and participation by many people throughout the globe.

The world order images and change strategies presented in these essays (and in the companion volumes of the "Preferred Worlds for the 1990's" series, which are much more detailed attempts) are strikingly diverse, reflecting the different methods, intellectual styles and cultural/political backgrounds of their authors. Although we were able to agree on a way of stating world order problems, and establish a framework of value criteria for what we considered to be appropriate solutions, as well as devise a common methodology, it certainly would be premature to attempt to provide a consensus statement for these various volumes. There were, however, a set of guidelines which were stated with some precision early in the project. Despite repeated critical examination and elaboration, these have remained essentially intact, and it therefore seems appropriate to summarize these guidelines so that the essays might be read in their proper context.

WOMP was not principally a "utopian" undertaking, despite our refusal to succumb either to a complacent or a doomsday view of reality. Where our thinking is utopian, it advances what we call *relevant utopias,* that is, world order systems that make clear not only alternative worlds but the necessary transition steps to these worlds. In fact, each author was asked to attempt a diagnosis of the contemporary world order system, make prognostic statements based on that diagnosis, state his *preferred future* world order and advance coherent and viable *strategies of transition* that could bring that future into being. A stringent time-frame, the 1990's, served to discipline and focus thought and proposals.

This set of steps impose severe demands on our methodological and creative capacity. It is probably fair to say that we discovered more methodological problems than we were able to solve to our satisfaction. Some of these problems are associated with how to do each of the steps, while others arise from trying to link different steps and to integrate the normative, descriptive and theoretical modes of thought. In the end, most of the WOMP research groups chose to adopt the more traditional analytic interpretive style of research, rather than the more methodologically sophisticated behavioral science approach. The reasons for this choice varied from outright rejection of the presumed conservative biases of strictly data-based methods, to pragmatic considerations of limited time and resources. In essence we decided it was more important at this time to prepare full world order statements involving an integrated treatment of all the steps, than it was to do a more rigorous investigation of only one or two of them.

It might be useful if I were to outline here the major problem areas and some questions that arose in the course of our investigation. Let me begin, however, by reiterating that we were able to agree that humankind faced five major problems: war, poverty, social injustice, environmental decay and alienation. We saw these as social problems because we had values—peace, economic well being, social justice, ecological stability and positive identity—which no matter how vaguely operationalized, we knew were not being realized in the real world. Our task then was to develop an analytic frame of reference that would provide us intellectual tools for coming to grips with these problems so as to realize our values, which are termed world order values.

There was also general agreement that we should go beyond the nation-state system, at least in terms of the traditional categories applied to it, namely the political, military, economic and ideological dimensions of foreign policy. Instead of asking how states manipulate their foreign policies along these four dimensions, or even, how they might move the present system to a world order value system, there was general agreement that we would have to use a much broader range of potential actors, including world institutions, transnational actors, international organizations, functional activities, regional arrangements, the nation-state, subnational movements, local communities and individuals. Even here, however, each of the groups placed different emphases, diagnostically, prognostically and preferentially on the roles of this range of actors.

Far more effort than I anticipated was put into clarifying the values implied by these problems and into making some ordered value agenda from which operational strategies or policies could be formulated. Among the points to emerge from these efforts are: the crucial importance of developing global social indicators or operational definitions of value goals; the difficulty and necessity of preparing a set of decision-making rules for dealing with value conflicts; the need for a unified approach to these problem/value areas and for more data and theory on the interrelationships among them; the extent to which one's personal position on the value questions influences every other aspect of the world order research process; and the importance of maintaining a tension between some operational notions of "world interest" and the deeply-felt value agenda of one's particular social group and geographic region.

A number of issues not associated with standard empirical research emerged because of our emphasis on constructing preferred worlds. In this connection it should be noted that the term *preferred world* came to have a relatively rigorous meaning. Building on the concept of relevant utopia stated above, a preferred world is an image of a reformed world stated in fairly precise behavioral detail, including a behavioral description of the transition process from the present to the new system. Since it is possible to depict a range of reformed systems and transition paths, a preferred world is the relevant utopia selected by a proponent because it is most likely to realize his or her value goals. Each of these issues that arose in this context requires separate examination, conceptual and methodological advances, and the testing of a variety of integrated research strategies before we will really be able to move systematically through the steps of world order research to preferred world statements that meet rigorous tests of workability and feasibility. To illustrate:

(1) What are appropriate criteria for evaluating workability and feasibility and what are the appropriate testing procedures for each?

(2) Notions of time and time horizons are critical to both feasibility and workability, yet both are far more complicated than the simple notion of years and decades. Assumptions about time seem to play a critical role in one's optimism or pessimism about the possibility of fundamental change. Also, time as a key variable is surprisingly easy to forget or discount when thinking about such things as value and attitude shifts, or reorientations in bureaucratic objectives and procedures.

(3) Equally perplexing is the problem of adequately defining the relevant environment and its dynamics within which one's desired changes must take place. The tendency is to define the environment as the nation-state system itself, and to ascribe relatively little destabilizing or fundamental dynamics to it. As noted earlier, this can severely restrict creative thinking about alternative futures and transition processes. But it is not easy to come up with equally detailed and useful alternatives to the nation-state image, so rooted is it in our consciousness. To really examine this question is to open oneself to the most fundamental philosophical and methodological search.

(4) On a more mundane level, the presentation of a preferred world in a way that is compelling and persuasive is far more difficult than it might appear. Like good fiction or poetry, utopia writing is an art attempted by many but achieved by few. It involves crucial choices of style and form. For example, how much and what kind of behavioral detail should be used to describe the workings of the preferred world? What are the differences between revolutionary and reformist rhetoric, and, more importantly, what bearing does this answer have on concrete strategies and programs? How much attention is paid to immediate public issues and how are they made to relate to the preferred future, to explicate the method and perspective of the author?

Finally there was a set of issues which arose from my instructions that each of the groups be as explicit as possible about the kinds of authority structure, about the formal constitutive order of the world community, that would be needed and preferred, both during the transition period, as well as at the end of this century. That is to say, there was a distinct weighting of institutional/constitutional issues and approaches in my original definition of our task.

I emphasized this approach—despite the obvious dangers of legalism and formalism—essentially for three reasons: first, a constitutional/institutional approach requires a high degree of specificity and precision and focuses attention on procedures as well as principles; second, this approach leads readily to statements in the form of models with all that that implies for comparability across models and manipulation of parts within them; third, as a form of presentation, constitutional/institutional models can be easily, even powerfully, communicated. In this connection I should like to formally acknowledge my debt to the book *World Peace Through World Law* (Harvard University Press, 1956, 1962, 1966) by Grenville Clark and Louis B. Sohn. My use of this book as an instructional model and as a source of research hypotheses leads me to conclude that many social scientists, as well as lay people, underestimate the extent to which formal constitutional models can lead to clarification of issues, and perhaps even more importantly become a mobilizing instrument for social and political action. I remain convinced of the value of this way of thinking about world order, but the extent to which this view has been resisted, revised and ignored by the WOMP groups will be apparent in these volumes.

Within this context, it should also be noted that the individual authors resolve the actors-levels-authority process questions differently. Some of the issues that surfaced during our discussions in this context included:

(1) The extent to which an institutional or single actor-oriented conception of the world political system is useful either for understanding how the system operates, how it might be made to change, or how it could or should operate. Such conceptions seemed to some to stultify imaginative thinking about alternatives and to mask important change potentials in the current system.

(2) In thinking about transition, some argued for the "primacy of the domestic factor," i.e., fundamental reform in national societies, particularly within the major countries, preceding global social change. Others argued for the primacy of the global agenda and the critical role of transnational functional and political movements and institutions. This debate identified two further issues needing more attention:

(3) Which problems require policy making and review at what level

of social organization from the individual to the global? How much centralization and decentralization was appropriate in various substantive arenas? What are the relevant criteria for deciding the appropriate level or mix of levels?

(4) What are and what might be the linkages between these levels for purposes of analysis, policy making and practical implementation?

Finally, I wish to state my own personal view as to the significance of these essays and of the larger, companion volumes. As I see it, it is necessary to accept seriously not only the rhetoric but the reality of the term "the global village." The fact that the overwhelming majority of humankind understands for the first time in history that human society encompasses the entire globe is a phenomenon equivalent to humankind's understanding that the globe is round rather than flat. This knowledge is having an enormously dramatic impact on the images and attitudes we have with regard to the authority structures of the international community, as well as those of our domestic societies. I should like to state here a conclusion, for which I will not fully argue, but which I believe needs to be articulated for an understanding of the significant global political processes that are now taking place.

It is my considered judgment that there is no longer a question of whether or not there will be world government by the year 2000. As I see it, the questions we should be addressing to ourselves are: how it will come into being—by cataclysm, drift, more or less rational design—and whether it will be totalitarian, benignly elitist, or participatory (the probabilities being in that order).

Since the so-called "age of discovery" (a Eurocentric concept which sorely needs modification in this global community), three major historical processes, or if you will, revolutions, have propelled humankind towards global community, and now towards global governance. These processes are the ideological revolution of egalitarianism, the technological and scientific revolution and the closely allied industrial-cybernetic revolution. It might be noted in passing that of these three, the egalitarian revolution has been least appreciated in recent times, but in fact may account for much of the disorder, dislocation and social tensions throughout the globe.

These three processes or revolutions have converged in such a fashion that war, poverty, social injustice, ecological instability and alienation, or the identity crisis, have emerged and are recognized as having a global scope. It is now generally understood by policy elites and observers of world community processes generally, that these problems are closely interrelated and that "solutions" in one area affect the other four areas. Furthermore, despite gross inadequacies—if not outright failure of the recent conferences organized by the United Nations around the issues of environment, economic order, ocean, food, and population—it is now obvious that governance processes and structures at the global end will become increasingly a focus of international and global politics.

In short I believe that global community has emerged and global governance is not far behind. To my mind, this book and the other volumes in the "Preferred Worlds for the 1990's" series is a contribution to the serious dialogue about what will be the normative basis and the constitutive structure of the global community. Hopefully this set of essays will contribute to the creation of the social processes necessary for a just and peaceful world order.

November 1974

> Saul Mendlovitz
> Director, World Order
> Models Project

Acknowledgments

The preparation of this book received the support and encouragement of many people. I am indebted to all of the Directors of the World Order Models Project for their participation in this program and more importantly for their friendship. I should also like to thank the staff of the Institute for World Order, all of whom have contributed to this book at one time or another.

There are two people to whom I am most especially grateful. Ian Baldwin, Jr., who contributed a great deal of time, patience and work to this volume and rightfully should have been co-editor but, at his own decision, chose not to. And my deepest gratitude to Harry B. Hollins who originated the idea of the World Order Models Project, and for whose continuing support and encouragement I will always be thankful.

I would also like to thank the Carnegie Endowment for International Peace and the Rockefeller Foundation for the support which they gave to specific research within the World Order Models Project.

And in the spirit of dedication, I wish to mention my children— Jessica, Michael, Jamie, John and Martha—and all other children, not wishing to impose this work on them but in the hope they will find it of some value.

List of Contributors

Ali A. Mazrui—D. Phil (Oxon), Professor, Political Science, The University of Michigan, Ann Arbor, Michigan, U.S.A.

Rajni Kothari—Director, Centre for the Study of Developing Societies, New Delhi, India; Editor, *Alternatives.*

Gustavo Lagos—Professor of International Relations, University of Chile, Santiago, Chile.

Carl-Friedrich von Weizsäcker—Director, Max-Planck-Institut zur Erforschung der Lebensbedingungen der wissenschaftlich-technischen Welt, Starnberg, Germany.

Johan Galtung—Professor of Conflict and Peace Research, University of Oslo, Oslo, Norway; Director, Inter-University Centre of Post-Graduate Studies, Dubrovnik, Yugoslavia.

Yoshikazu Sakamoto—Professor of Law, Faculty of Law, University of Tokyo, Tokyo, Japan.

Richard A. Falk—Albert G. Milbank Professor of International Law and Practice, Center of International Studies, Princeton University, Princeton, New Jersey, U.S.A.

Paul T. K. Lin—Professor, Director, Centre for East Asian Studies, McGill University, Montreal, Canada.

WORLD CULTURE AND THE SEARCH FOR HUMAN CONSENSUS

Ali A. Mazrui

What is the relationship between cultural integration, which is the sharing of values and moral perspectives among peoples, and political violence? In that question lies a major crisis for world order.

My earliest encounter with the tensions of cultural integration came with a small incident when I was a little boy. We lived in Mombasa, and World War II had just broken out. When an Italian bomb fell on the tiny town of Malindi, less than 80 miles north of Mombasa, a feeling rapidly spread that the war had come to our part of the continent. Memories of the First World War, when the Germans occupied Tanganyika next door and the British occupied the rest of East Africa, were still fresh to some of the older people, and stories about modern warfare were quick to spread.

It was partly this which led to a decision among families in Mombasa to evacuate their women and children, at least until the implications of the Italian bomb on Malindi had been analysed more fully.

My mother, sisters, and a number of other female relatives and children boarded a ship for Zanzibar. Curiously enough, the ship we boarded was Japanese. At that stage Japan had not entered the war. We were therefore able to sail openly, lights ablaze in spite of the policy of general blackout among some of the other vessels in East African waters. My father and the other men of the families remained in Mombasa, awaiting an Italian invasion that never came.

In my own way as a seven-year-old I was experiencing the kind of anxieties generated by modern warfare. I was passing through a major event in the world, involving perils between big nations situated thousands of miles away, yet quarrels which were beginning to disrupt fundamentally the lives and ways of people in Africa in a bewildering manner.

And then, while I was in Zanzibar, another incident occurred, fundamentally different from being collectively evacuated from Mombasa to Zanzibar, and yet capturing another aspect of the crisis of human relations. This incident was trivial in many ways. We were indeed in Zanzibar, enjoying this refuge from the perils to which Mombasa as a major port was exposed. Some mattresses from our house were put out in the sun to dry, and to enable the heat of the day to frighten away the bedbugs. I was playing nearby, amusing myself. I was not ten. Suddenly I caught sight of another little boy, jumping around on the mattresses. The little boy was evidently a stranger and had no business playing on our mattresses with his dirty feet, or so I calculated. There was a small and thin fragment of a branch nearby, with a few leaves on it. I got hold of the branch, gave a warcry, and made for the little intruder. I believe the little boy was too fast for me, and my weapon probably just grazed him in one mighty throw as he disappeared in a cloud of dust.

Panting and a little frustrated, and yet still congratulating myself for having chased him away from our mattresses, I resumed my quiet game. I played a little longer before I heard voices. When I turned round I saw a crowd of women, shouting and complaining in anger, coming towards our house. They were still some distance away from the house, and so was I, but in a different direction. My mother appeared in the doorway and gave a shout of desperation, ordering me to run back to our house. I was totally bewildered. But I responded and ran straight into the house before the army of invading women got to the door.

My mother and the other women from our house stood across the doorway while someone took me away to hide in another room. The women who had just come shouted and ranted indignantly. They said I had chased their little boy like a dog and was going to "whip him like a slave." Some of the Zanzibari women of our household were arguing back, but my mother was the supreme conciliator. She conceded that I was guilty, and she promised with Allah as witness that she would thrash me for my aggressive games. Gradually the visiting women were mollified and departed with a sense of satisfaction that justice would be done. I do not know whether justice was done, but my mother certainly thrashed me.

The importance of the incident in my evolution as a political observer lay in what at that time I only imperfectly understood but later assumed a meaning deeply relevant to problems of world order. I came to learn later that the family I was living with in Zanzibar was one of Swahilized Arabs and that the child I chased from our mattresses was from the Arabized Swahili. The indignation of the invading women did not stem from a simple case of one child fighting another or chasing

2

another with a branch of a tree. The fundamental factor of tension lay in this clash, incredible in many ways, between an Arab population in Zanzibar that had acquired Swahili as its mother tongue and become substantially Africanized in certain aspects of culture, and the Africans of Zanzibar who also spoke Swahili as their mother tongue, also accepted Islam as their religion, and had acquired certain aspects of the Arab life-style but who still regarded themselves as a group apart.

Underlying this phenomenon was the historical fact of the Arab slave system, once accepted as a matter of course on the island but now a memory of bitterness and humiliation.

Yet these two peoples had biologically and culturally interpenetrated. Intermarriage between Arabs and Africans was part of the very fabric of Zanzibari society. These people had the same staple diet, the same language, and many of the same jokes, and prayed at the same mosques. If countries become more peaceful as cultural integration becomes more complete, Zanzibar should have lived up to that old image of the Isle of Peace. But we now know that a more tragic fate awaited Zanzibar later in the century.

In spite of what appear to be the lessons of Zanzibar, a major premise of our approach to world reform is that a substantial measure of global cultural integration is a precondition for positive change. We will explore this premise in this chapter.

Our approach rests on two major theories—a theory of *normative convergence,* intimately related to cultural integration, and a theory of *dependency.* We accept as a premise that the world needs to be reformed in the direction of three basic values: maximum social justice, more widely distributed economic welfare, and reduced violence, whether actual or imminent. How do we get there? The answer needs a theory of normative convergence. It also needs a theory of dependency as a map to avoid some of the pitfalls that may lie on the way.

Purposeful world reform is a quest for the realization of new *values.* It is a question of defining *new moral preferences.* The question therefore arises: Under what conditions do people begin to share values and moral preferences?

To have new values accepted is, by definition, a problem of mobilizing *consensus.* We must therefore begin to understand the nature of consensus and the conditions that make it possible.

Our position is that consensus on a specific set of reforms can best be obtained where people share a framework of social reasoning and social calculation. To convince another person of a new idea requires a common universe of discourse. Persuasion is the art of exploiting mutually familiar predispositions.

3

To get mankind to agree to a new world system, we need to give it that shared framework of social reasoning and social calculation. Consensus behind three world values will need consensus behind many more supporting values and perspectives. To get Americans to agree to sending children away from neighbourhood schools in order to accomplish racial balance in all schools, one needs prior agreement on a number of other values as well.

In summary, we see world reform as a problem of mobilizing consensus, we see consensus as a problem of building up supporting values and we see this latter as an outgrowth of cultural convergence. That is why, in spite of the paradox of Zanzibar, the search must continue. Values are inseparable from culture. Indeed, what is culture but a system of interrelated values and social perspectives, active enough to condition the behaviour of its adherents?

World Government versus World Culture

A postulate of our approach is that the transmission of ideas and their internalization are more relevant for world reform than the establishment of formal institutions for external control. In other words, when members of World Reform enterprises talk in terms of disseminating their proposals to the reading public they are nearer to the heart of the issue than when they discuss what type of security council or what type of agency for environmental control the year 1990 ought to have.

Thus, even though the transmission of ideas may require some institutions, it is more concerned with *process* than with structure. When we talk of transition stages, we should be thinking of stages in the evolution of human values and human opinion rather than stages in the evolution of human organization.

The main ambition should be to promote the right values and consolidate the right inhibitions in the behavioural orientations of human beings. The controls we should be aiming for are internalized controls emerging from new human inclinations, rather than external controls applied by organizational mechanisms.

This is where the whole concept of *cultural engineering* looms into relevance. Engineering connotes an enterprise of building up new structures, but in this case not structures of external coercion but structures of internalized constraints. The aim should not be a world government but a world culture.

At first sight, the evolution of a world culture seems to be even more distant than the evolution of a world government. But a closer look at human history dispels this misconception. In reality, we are no nearer a world government than we were a century ago, but we are much nearer a world culture. Today there are more independent governments in the world, fewer empires, and a wider distribution of formal jurisdiction on the international scene. It is even arguable that since World War II we have moved further away from a world government than we were before. The disintegration of empires has multiplied sovereignties. It is true that we have something called the United Nations, but even this body has declined in power as it has increased its membership. The UN at the end of the 1960s was in some ways a less powerful and less influential organization than it was at the end of the 1950s. The influx of large numbers of small countries, exercising parity of voting in the General Assembly and activated by issues not always understood by the bigger powers, has created a credibility gap between UN resolutions and UN performance. If the weakening of the UN is an indication that we are moving away from world government, it must be concluded that we are further away in the 1970s than we were in the 1950s.

If we turn our eyes to look not at institutions designed for external coercion but at the phenomena of cultural dissemination and internalized cultural constraints, the picture is very different. We are definitely nearer to a world culture in the 1970s than we were in the 1940s. The spread of literacy, the role of technology in affecting life-styles, the acceleration and facilitation of international travel, the international distribution of books and newspapers, the emergence of television programmes and films distributed on a world scale, the impact of the radio and the consolidation of external broadcasting services to other parts of the world as an aspect of foreign policy have all combined to introduce the beginnings of shared values, shared tastes, and shared images.

This is no more than an initial phase of global cultural convergence. At one level the homogenization manifests itself in the cruder forms of pop culture. Certain American singers and musicians are heroes to teenagers in Iboland, Hong Kong, Bombay, Mombasa and Rio de Janeiro. In other words, certain tastes in music, films, sports, and magazines have become almost global.

But there is another area of cultural convergence more directly political in its implications, the area of shared political emotions, prejudices, and sensibilities. The American war in Vietnam illustrated this political commonality at its most dramatic. Protest against the war came from people of diverse cultures and in different parts of the world. Anger at some of the events of the war has had a wider distribution on the globe than anger about any other war in human history. Never has a war in one part of the world been more widely reported in other parts of the world. Many of those who protested may not have known all that much about the background of the war, or about the issues involved, or about the actual unfolding of the conflict; but that so many knew about any part of the war is an indication both of the communications revolution in the world and of the resultant rudimentary homogenization of political sensibilities.

It is true that we still have wars and the threat of war in interstate relations. It is true that we are nowhere near controlling man's capacity to prepare for destruction. It is true that we are nowhere near an international police force strong enough to keep the Americans out of another Vietnam or the Russians out of another Czechoslovakia, or even the Israelis out of Arab lands. But it would be a mistake to conclude that just because there are no external mechanisms of coercion with global authority in the international system, there are no internalized mechanisms of constraint. And the mechanisms of constraint in the behaviour of the big powers, fallible as they are, are an index of the beginnings of political integration in the world. But the integration is at the level of values and their acceptance as a basis of inhibition, rather than at the level of organizational structures.

It is out of this recognition of the critical relevance of cultural convergence for world reform that we seek to propose cultural engineering as the most promising approach towards that reform.

It was Kenneth E. Boulding who once argued that the people whose decisions determined the policies and actions of nations did not really respond to the objective facts of a situation but to their image of that situation.

> It is what we think the world is like, not what it is really like, that determines our behaviour.... We act according to the way the world appears to us, not necessarily according to the way it "is." Thus in Richardson's models it is one nation's image of the hostility of another, not the "real" hostility, which determines its reaction. The "image" then, must be thought of as the total cognitive, affective, and evaluative structure of the behaviour of the elite, or its internal view of itself and its universe.[1]

Boulding emphasises the phenomenon of the psychological accumulation of impressions and its relevance for the evolution of world views of individuals. Images grow, get modified, interconnect with other images, but in any case often have deep roots in the earlier history of the mind.

[1]Boulding. "National Images and International Systems," *The Journal of Conflict Resolution,* Vol. III, 1959. Pp. 121–122. For a fuller exposition of the theory see Boulding, *The Image* (Ann Arbor: University of Michigan Press, 1956).

It is always in some sense a product of messages received in the past. It is not, however, a simple inventory or "pile" of such messages but a highly structured piece of information-capital, developed partly by its inputs and outputs of information and partly by internal messages and its own laws of growth and stability.[2]

Because of such considerations, mechanisms of socialization have become important aspects of national perspectives on world affairs. The process of such socialization has intimate conditioning implications. To move from national to global perspectives requires in turn a globalization of the processes of socialization and cultural convergence.

Towards Global Integration

Normative convergence entails interaction between groups. The convergence in norms is part of a broader process of integration, which in this regard would involve four stages of interrelationship between diverse racial, national and cultural groups in the world. The minimum degree of integration is a relationship of bare *coexistence* between distinct social identities. Such groups need not even know of each other's existence. Even within single countries in the African continent, for example, there are tribal communities that have no idea where the boundaries of their country end, which other communities are their compatriots, and which are not. Their coexistence with a number of other groups in the same national entity is not always a conscious coexistence. But it exists.

On a world scale, bare coexistence is of course an even more striking phenomenon. Africa and Latin America, for example, though very similar, know very little about each other. Such countries share a world, but not a consciousness of that world's extent.

The second degree of interrelationship between social groups is a relationship of *contact*, which means that the groups have at least minimal dealings with each other or communication between each other. These groups need not be on friendly terms. Tribes or nations at war are often in a relationship of contact, and in spite of the war they are at a higher stage of integration than groups that are barely coexisting.

A third degree of integration between social groups is a relationship of *compromise*. By this time the dealings between the groups have become sufficiently complex, diverse, and interdependent to require a climate of peaceful reconciliation among the conflicting interests. The groups or nations still have clearly distinct identities, as well as distinct

[2]*Ibid.*

7

interests. But the process of national integration has now produced a capacity for a constant discovery of areas of compatibility.

Between this stage of compromise and the fourth stage of *coalescence,* the process of convergence starts. From a cultural point of view convergence is a process that either creates or discovers a growing sector of shared tastes, emotions, images, and values. Cultural convergence need not result in the total coalescence of previously distinct systems. Convergence may combine cultural diversity with cultural sharing. But when convergence goes beyond a certain point, the stage of coalescence is reached.

What should be borne in mind is that whereas coexistence, contact, compromise, and coalescence are stages in the process of integration, convergence is the subprocess that takes groups or systems from the stage of compromise towards the stage of coalescence. This last stage is a coalescence of cultural systems or ethnic identities, rather than a merger of economic interests. The diversity of interests continues. Indeed, should the society get technically complex and functionally differentiated at the same time as it is getting culturally integrated, the diversity of interest would increase as the distinctiveness of group identities becomes blurred. Capacity for compromise would still be needed at the stage of coalescence. But the conflict of interest is no longer a conflict between total identities or autonomous cultural systems but between identities that have gone far in the process of interpenetration.

But by what mechanism does the process of integration move from stage to stage? Two factors are critically important—one is *conflict* and the other is *mobility.* Let us take each of these in turn.

A relationship of bare coexistence has little conflict potential. Somehow contact has to be established with other groups before conflict situations can seriously arise. The move from coexistence to contact might be caused by a number of different factors. Among the most important is simply the factor of mobility. Migrant trade, or movements of population, or a newly built road can convert bare coexistence into contact. It is mobility rather than conflict that initiates the process of integration.

Conflict as a mechanism begins to assume its relevance once the relationship of contact has been established. Conflict plays a crucial part in the movement from a relationship of contact to a relationship of compromise, and then from compromise to coalescence. It is the cumulative experience of conflict *resolution* that deepens the degree of integration in a given society. Conversely, unresolved conflict creates a situation of potential disintegration. The groups within a society then

8

may move backwards from a relationship of compromise to one of hostile contact.

At what points in this four-stage process of integration is violence at its most pronounced? There are occasions when violence erupts at first contact, as when a tribal community feels imperilled by the arrival of foreigners and proceeds to take violent steps for defense. But the move from coexistence to contact need not be accompanied by violence, though it sometimes is.

It is the move from contact to a relationship of compromise that almost invariably entails an intervening period of violent confrontation. Much of the inter-ethnic and even international violence in recent human history has occurred between the stage of contact and the stage of compromise. Political analysts have sometimes assumed that racial intermingling would itself reduce racial tensions. In fact, such intermingling on a large scale increases tension before it finally reaches a plateau of normalization and ultimate ethnic integration. Social scientists often underestimate the tension-generating effects inherent between the stage of contact among groups and the future stage of compromise capability.

Yet the four stages of coexistence, contact, compromise, and coalescence do not operate in precisely the same way among nation-states as they do among ethnic groups. The factors that initiate change from one state to another are different in a multistate region from what they are within a single territorial state. Whereas in relations within a single country it is the stage between contact and compromise that has a high potentiality for conflict among compatriot ethnic groups, in relations among nation-states it is very often the stage between compromise and coalescence. In other words, the subprocess of convergence is precisely the stage that carries both the greatest promise and the highest tensions. It is not without significance that the two most ghastly wars experienced by the human race started as European wars. Of the three older continents of the world—Africa, Asia, and Europe—Europe is the most deeply integrated, even more deeply than Latin America, in spite of the greater diversity of languages in Europe than in Latin America. Yet from within the tensions of this very integrated continent, with hundreds of years of interaction and compromise, major conflagrations have erupted.

The factor of *stratification* is important, and stratification is what *dependency* is all about. Europe has until recently lacked an adequate consensus on the legitimate grounds of stratification, both within a state and sometimes in terms of which particular state should enjoy preeminence among the European states. The whole strategy of bal-

9

ance of power in European history has been an attempt to deal with the dangers of international stratification within that region.

But here mobility comes into play again. The most mobile people in the world in terms of crossing their borders into other countries are Europeans. On balance Europeans cross each other's borders more often than do citizens of any other cluster of states. It is in Europe that we can begin to sense the implications of mobility as a device for growing interpenetration, and the growing interpenetration as gradually both a factor that could lead to war as in the past and a factor that could lead to the formation of new regional organizations as in the case of the European Economic Community. Conflict and mobility once again play their parts in the integrative process.

But at the same time there is a growing cultural core of values about how best to resolve conflicts in the future. Mobility creates not only physical interpenetration between groups but also interpenetration of ideas. The constant search to solve problems between groups consolidates one aspect of culture—the aspect concerned with the norms of handling disputes.

Ultimately the basis for a world of social justice, economic welfare, and minimal violence must be a cultural core of such shared norms. The world must find a way to facilitate the process of convergence towards a shared human culture.

The Tensions of Cultural Coalescence

Are we sure that even the achievement of cultural coalescence would minimize violence, let alone extend the boundaries of social justice and economic welfare? World history reveals not only the tensions of cultural differences but also the tragedies of high cultural convergence.

The worst domestic sin of Hitler's Germany was the genocide of the Jews. Yet the German Jews were the most culturally assimilated to their immediate society of almost all Jews in the West. They were deeply German, and a large proportion of them no longer practised the Jewish religion. Hitler did not care whether a Jew was a Christian or still went to the synagogue. German Jews who were no longer Jews by religion should surely have been deemed to be more German than ever if one insisted on viewing Judaism as non-Germanic. Yet clearly not even the adoption of German Christianity saved the cultural aspirants.

As we have intimated already, Africa too has had examples of cultural convergence accompanied by violent tensions. The two most convulsive social revolutions in Africa took place in the two relatively homogeneous little states of Zanzibar and Rwanda. The degree of brutalization in both Rwanda and Zanzibar was greater perhaps than that experienced anywhere else in modern Africa. Yet these two countries were also culturally among the most deeply integrated of all the new states on the continent. Arabs and Africans in Zanzibar shared a language (Swahili), a religion (Islam), and other aspects of culture. They had also intermarried considerably.

The Tutsi and Hutu of Rwanda also shared a language, a religion, and other important aspects of culture. They too had intermarried. They too had difficulty quite often in drawing a line between where a Hutu ancestry ended and a Tutsi descent began. The two communities had experienced biocultural assimilation.

Yet in 1959 in Rwanda an uprising of the Hutu occurred with devastating consequences for the Tutsi. This was before independence, which was finally granted on July 1, 1962. For Zanzibar it was granted in December 1963. In January 1964 both countries almost simultaneously experienced further agonies of convulsive acculturation. In Zanzibar the Arab Sultanate was overthrown at a cost of thousands of lives, as yet only vaguely calculated. In the same month several thousand Tutsi were massacred by the Hutu in Rwanda, and an exodus of yet another 12,000 Tutsi joined the ranks of the 150,000 refugees already scattered among Rwanda's neighbours.

Burundi, a third East African country with considerable cultural integration, for a while experienced intra-Tutsi violence as the different ruling clans of the Tutsi competed for authority, and later the Republicans finally succeeded in deposing the Mwami from his throne.

But in 1972 Burundi too experienced its hour of convulsion. Amid mutual recrimination about who started the massacres, there seems little doubt that many thousands across the country were butchered, the majority of them Hutu. In spite of a shared language, a shared culture, and significant racial interpenetration, Burundi joined Zanzibar and Rwanda in the worst brutalization in the recent history of East Africa.

Does the experience of these countries indicate a logical validity to the policy of apartheid in South Africa? Apartheid is an elaborate attempt to prevent cultural integration. The Bantustans as an idea, the establishment of "native universities," and the discouragement of cultural as well as racial interaction are all ultimately designed to avert cultural convergence. Would this avoidance of cultural convergence also delay the moment of violent explosions? I now believe that the experience of Zanzibar, Rwanda, and Burundi does lend a respectable logic, though not a respectable morality, to what the racist regime in South Africa is trying to do. Given that the white people want to remain in power unchallenged, the pursuit of cultural and social distance makes sense as an aspect of strategy for the time being.

If the aim of the white people were simply racial harmony, this could be acquired through economic justice and social equality. But economic justice and social equality cannot ensure that the whites will remain privileged. Can the whites remain privileged and still pursue a policy of cultural contact, or meeting at sherry parties, or educating Africans in westernized schools and universities? Is racial privilege compatible with cultural integration?

The experiences of Burundi, Rwanda, and Zanzibar were emphatically negative. These countries sought to maintain some degree of racial privilege (for the Arabs in Zanzibar, for the Tutsi in Rwanda and Burundi), accompanied by considerable cultural integration. The cultural integration simply accentuated the later violence. Because these peoples were so much alike, they were the more brutal against each other.

Yet this whole essay arises from the premise that the ultimate solution to problems of world order is the promotion and consolidation of a shared culture for the human race. How can a shared culture be desirable on a world scale if it has led to such convulsions in smaller societies?

Consensus and Stratification

Assuming that a desirable world is a world of social justice, economic welfare, and minimal violence, the search for such a world is bedevilled by two crises—the crisis of dissensus and the crisis of stratification. For our purposes dissensus is the negation of consensus, and consensus is defined in the following terms:

> Consensus exists when the members of social systems are in a state of affirmative agreement about normative and cognitive matters relevant to their action towards one another, towards the central persons or roles in the system, and towards persons, roles, and collectivities outside the system. Consensus is, then, agreement about the rules which should govern their conduct concerning the goals of the system and the allocation of roles and rewards within the system. There is another element present in consensus: this is a solidarity formed by a sense of common identity arising from ties of personal affection, of primordial (ethnic, kinship, or territorial) characteristics, of a shared relationship to sacred things, of a membership in a common culture or in a common civil community.[3]

[3]*A Dictionary of Sociology,* edited by G. Duncan Mitchell (London: Routledge and Kegan Paul, 1968), pp. 40–43.

It would be premature to think of the whole world as a social system in this sense, but there is little doubt that a viable world order that could guarantee economic welfare, social justice, and minimal violence would indeed require consensus on a wide range of values.

Consensus has been known to grow out of the experience of shared fear. Consensus on the preconditions of such a viable world order can only be obtained either through fear or through a shared culture. But basing a new world order merely on fear would not only make that order more fragile and possibly transient; it would also distort the quality of human life. Even the fear of world destruction as the sole basis of a new world order could not be sustained without psychological costs to man.

Shared culture is then the only effective alternative to shared fear. Culture thus becomes an infrastructure for consensus. Consensus on fundamentals needs the foundation of a shared outlook on a number of other issues. Consensus in a void is a contradiction in terms unless it is exacted by brute force. Yet our experience in a culturally homogenized Europe, Zanzibar, Rwanda, and Burundi tells us explicitly that a wide area of shared values is not by itself adequate as a safeguard against large-scale violence.

What might be needed therefore is a further analysis of the problem of consensus in relation to social and political change. It is clear in some fundamental sense that the human community needs new types of policies. Yet consensus on policies is secondary consensus, subject to fashionable fluctuations. Primary consensus, on the other hand, is consensus behind a new system of stabilized values from which policies may be derived or on which social action may be based.

Even primary consensus appears inadequate to avert convulsion. What should a people in a social system be especially agreed upon? In order to avert violence, it is ultimately imperative that they be agreed on criteria of *stratification*. The world of a shared culture has to include within it a shared consensus on what would constitute legitimate stratification.

Stratification in our sense is that part of the social system that allocates differential rewards and distributes power and influence hierarchically. A stratification system includes both the Marxian class system and the Weberian status system. It encompasses castes as well as estates. In the words of Talcott Parsons, social stratification is "the differential ranking of the human individuals who compose a given social system and their treatment as superior and inferior relative to one another in certain socially important respects." Dependency is the quality of being under the oppressive weight of an otherwise benevolent stratification system.

The most basic fundamental of a social system concerns the criteria of stratification. Karl Marx was right in assuming that social inequalities have a propensity towards producing social antagonisms. But he was wrong in assuming first, that all class differences imply class inequalities and, second, that class inequalities always erupt into class struggle. A propensity towards struggle is not the same thing as the realization of that struggle.

We know only too well that systems of gross social inequalities have often lasted much longer without tension than systems of relative egalitarianism. A good deal may depend upon the degree of consensus behind the inequalities rather than the degree of the inequality itself. The Hindu caste system, because of the sanctification and legitimacy it derives from sacred validation, has survived longer without widespread challenge than some of the more minor inequalities between groups in modern Europe. Even more startling is the almost universal inferior status of women as compared with men through much of human history. Both the Hindu caste system and the relative subordination of women owe their long durability to the consensus behind them. The majority of both privileged and underprivileged groups have for very long accepted the legitimacy of the criteria of stratification.

It is when that legitimacy begins to be eroded, and in the face of considerable shared values in other spheres, that the moment of violent challenge may indeed be at hand. The Arabized Waswahili and the Swahilized Waarabu of Zanzibar indeed shared a language, a religion, and a style of life—but the criteria of stratification in Zanzibari society then began to undergo a process of erosion. The relatively privileged position of the Swahilized Arabs within the system was no longer accepted as fully legitimate by the Arabized Waswahili in spite of the fact that the Waswahili had once accepted the legitimacy of Arab preeminence.

Similarly in Rwanda and Burundi the Hutu, who had for a long time accepted Tutsi preeminence, were no longer convinced of its legitimacy. In a situation of widespread shared perspectives on other issues, dissensus on stratification carries heavy possibilities of violence. On occasion a ruling group that is completely foreign and distinctive can command easier submission than a ruling group that is otherwise too intimately linked to the ruled. Certainly the white man in Africa, by the mystique of the very distance culturally and pigmentationally between him and his subjects, confronted less compulsive challenges to his legitimacy than the white man's indigenous black successors in the new African republics. The problem of political legitimacy in Africa is partly a problem connected with power in the hands of an elite too close ethnically and culturally to the masses and yet deprived of the sanctity of validated stratification.

The issue of the precise relationship between consensus and stratification has direct bearing on problems of containing violence, promoting social justice, and enhancing economic welfare. The stratification system colours conceptions of social justice and when challenged begins to demand a redefinition of that form of justice. Social stratification as a system of differential allocation of rewards also affects differential allocations of economic welfare. Where the criteria of stratification are still widely accepted, violence can be minimal even though economic welfare is not widely distributed. But where those criteria are undergoing the pressures of a new scepticism, violence may rise. A stage is then reached of rebelling against dependency.

Social justice as an ideal is more relativistic, more culture-bound, than either economic welfare or the question of what constitutes a reduction of violence. It is relatively easy to get people from different cultures to agree on what sorts of services or facilities would constitute improved economic welfare. Incomes can be assessed, protein can be measured, housing can be evaluated, and medical facilities computed. Economic welfare in this sense is quantifiable.

Quantifiable also is violence to a considerable extent. Casualties can be counted, riots tabulated, and the destructive power of weapons measured.

It is when we come to the ideal of social justice that a new problem arises. How do we measure social justice? How do we get agreement on such issues as women's rights, polygamy, attitudes to foreigners, and attitudes to other races? All such rights and attitudes are circumscribed by traditions and cultures. Within each culture the concept of social justice may change from generation to generation. The militant scepticism in Zanzibar concerning the legitimacy of Arab dominance was in part a call for a new definition of social justice.

Yet, in a sense, social justice is prior to economic welfare and the minimization of violence. Welfare will not be equitably distributed nor violence averted unless justice is done or is in prospect.

From the point of view of evolving a more desirable world order, this basic clash between the primacy of social justice as a value and the extent to which it is culturally relative must be resolved. As it is not possible to divorce social justice from culture, the only solution lies in making culture itself less relative. In short, the solution lies in promoting some degree of cultural homogenization on a world scale, with a system of stratification capable of yielding both widespread economic welfare and widespread retreat from violence.

A Eurocentric World Culture

Fortunately, we are not starting from scratch. A world culture has already begun to emerge. International law itself is a piece of world culture, consisting precisely of those shared values designed to handle disputes. Starting as a system of rules to govern relations between European states, international law has since been virtually globalized as a diplomatic code.

We might therefore place international law alongside such phenomena as the Bible, computer technology, the plays of William Shakespeare, the music of Mozart, the modern school, and Scotch whisky as elements which have entered the mainstream of world culture.

But here we must distinguish cultural convergence from cultural conquest. Convergence implies a "marriage of true minds," some minimal mutual borrowing between cultures. But the trouble with world culture as it has so far evolved is that it is disproportionately Eurocentric, Western-derived. International law itself heavily bears the marks of its ancestry. Its very name manifests the original European preoccupation with nation states as the ultimate units of diplomatic restraint. "Aggression" under that law became virtually definable as the wanton violation of the sovereignty of another *state*. The idea of committing aggression on another race or another tribe was somehow remote from the canons of international law.

For a while this code even worked, as the basis of stratification in terms of ruling races and subject races, and had yet to feel the full challenge of the scepticism of the underprivileged. Even as late as the 1960s India's military action in Goa was denounced as aggression against Portugal. A well-meaning and otherwise broadminded Adlai Stevenson denounced this action passionately in the UN as a violation of the principles of sovereignty and aggression. The fact that the Portuguese presence in Goa might itself have been a violation of the racial sovereignty of the Indian subcontinent seemed quite incomprehensible to Western critics.

It was Krishna Menon who denounced colonialism itself as "permanent aggression." New definitions of aggression were being sought in the 1960s, partly because the older international law was too protective of both colonialism and racism and regarded both as fair game provided that the sovereignty of no nation state was violated.

Clearly international law as a piece of world culture needed to be reexamined so that the overwhelming preponderance of Western norms could be diluted through the introduction of a few of the more passionately held principles of the Third World.

The global cultural scene contains a hierarchy of cultures, with Western culture enjoying preeminence. In literature as in international law, there continues to be a disproportionate Western presence in the shared global pool. Western literary classics are read throughout the world, but Asian and African classics tend to be limited to their own regions. No Asian or African author can ever hope to be a world literary figure unless he makes a particularly strong impact on the West. But a Western writer can shoot into world fame before a single Indian, Chinese, or African reader has seen a single work of his.

Even the world prizes for excellence are Western-based and Western-awarded. The Nobel Prize winner for the non-Western world is by definition someone who had first to convince a collection of North Europeans, usually of Nordic stock, of his worth.

In Africa, a head of state, Nyerere of Tanzania, has translated two of Shakespeare's plays into Swahili. These are *Julius Caesar* and *The Merchant of Venice.* It would be staggering if a British Prime Minister were ever to be interested in translating into English the much shorter poetic work *Utenzi Wa Mwana Kupona.*

Another African head of state, Obote, when President of Uganda, gave himself the first name of "Milton" out of admiration for the author of *Paradise Lost.* No British politician in the foreseeable future is likely to adopt a name from Uganda in admiration of an African poet. No king or premier would be so enthusiastic.

These examples bring out in their very hyperbolic dimensions the sharp contrast between Britain on one side and the whole of Africa on the other as contributors to world culture as so far evolved. Instead of genuine normative convergence, we continue to have cultural imperialism.

Moral relativists have observed often enough that the ideas of righteousness are not stationary but capable of endless expansion, that "men may get scruples in the future that they have no thought of now." Certainly many men in Africa and Asia today are getting scruples now that they or their parents had no conception of in the past. What must be emphasized is that it would be naive to attribute this merely to some metaphysical force called "moral progress." In the final analysis, the relative and gradual standardization of ethics in the world is to be at-

17

tributed to the political and technological impact of the West. With that impact have come new ways of looking at things, new perspectives, new intellectual horizons, new values, and new types of jealousies, including those arising from Western concepts of sovereignty and Western definitions of territorial jurisdiction.

John Plamenatz, the Oxford political philosopher and historian, once observed that "the vices of the strong acquire some of the prestige of strength." The vices of the West have certainly acquired some of the prestige of Western power. We use the term "West" in the older sense of "the Occident"—including not only North America and Western Europe but also Eastern Europe. Marxist communism itself becomes a branch of Western intellectual tradition, to be distinguished from oriental and Afro-Asian indigenous traditions.

The influence of Western civilization on the lives of peoples very far from the fountain of that civilization brings us to the second major theory underlying much of this essay. Alongside the theory of cultural convergence in relation to *consensus* must be placed the theory of cultural convergence in relation to *dependency*.

The phenomenon of dependency may itself be further divided into two dimensions, *structural dependency* and *cultural dependency*. Structural dependency concerns the organizational aspects of political, economic, and technological imbalance. A lack of symmetry in power relations, captured in an institutional framework, lies at the heart of structural dependency. The phenomenon of multinational corporations constitutes one recent structure of dominance emanating from the Western world and operating elsewhere. Financial institutions and certain types of technological transfers, as well as large-scale military alliances involving major powers, are all forms of dependency structurally defined.

Much of the recent discussion in the Third World concerning dependency has in fact been an analysis of structural dependency. Preeminent among the tools of analysis have been Marxist concepts and techniques of interpreting social and international phenomena. Much of the work within the Third World has been done in Latin America, but theories of structural dependency have been emerging elsewhere as well. Those addressing themselves primarily to African conditions include Samir Amin, Justinian Rweyemamu, and Walter Rodney.

What has been grossly underestimated has been the phenomenon of *cultural dependency*. This latter phenomenon affects two areas of human behaviour especially, motivation and social stratification. What people aspire to in the Third World, what tastes they develop, what expectations they begin to have, and what aversions they manifest are all areas of response greatly conditioned by cultural variables. The impact of the West on the motivational patterns of the peoples of the Third World is a major dimension of dependency. The structural analysts often refer to interlocking elites between the developed and the developing world. What they do not always realize is that these elites, which identify with metropolitan countries and reinforce dependent structures, have been captured *culturally* by the West. The nature of their ambitions, the directions of their aspirations, and the boundaries of their tastes and desires are important factors behind their entire behaviour. Their ambitions and aspirations have to undergo a change before they can evolve the *will* to break the structures of dependency.

A major stumbling block in the way of Third World assertiveness is the absence of the political will for change. The absence of that political will is substantially attributable to normative and cultural conditioning.

The other great domain of cultural dependency concerns domestic stratification within Third World countries. In much of Asia and Africa credentials for leadership and qualifications for becoming a national decision-maker have to include competence in certain Western metropolitan skills. In Africa there is in fact a high premium on Western literary and verbal skills. The first wave of great African leaders consists disproportionately of people who have acquired verbal or literary skills in either English or French. Kwame Nkrumah, Nnamdi Azikiwe, Julius Nyerere, Tom Mboya, Jomo Kenyatta, and Hastings Banda are all people who could demonstrate literary and verbal skills in the English language. In French-speaking Africa the same phenomenon is observable with regard to competence in the French language as a precondition for political success. Members of parliament in most African countries need competence in a Western language to be eligible to stand for election at all. Alien linguistic requirements are demanded of those who want to represent their people. But almost no electoral code in Africa stipulates that a member has to be able to speak at least one indigenous African language.

Access to political careers means access to other privileges. People become not only powerful by virtue of the office they hold but also rich by virtue of what they have acquired in addition. Nkrumah once urged: "Seek ye first the political kingdom, and all else will be added unto it." He meant that nations should first seek the political kingdom; but it was even truer that individuals who first acquired power within the political kingdom succeeded in having "all else added unto them." Literary and verbal skills borrowed from the West became necessary for attaining the commanding heights of the polity, which in turn helped the new elite to share the commanding heights of the economy. Structures of dependency were reinforced by a system of domestic stratification that gave special advantages to those who had been culturally Westernized.

The avenues of European culture infiltration into Africa were: first, modern education; second, metropolitan languages, with special reference to English and French; third, Western religion, primarily Euro-Christianity; and fourth, demonstration effected through Western control of mobility and communications.

The modern school in Africa became a major carrier of Western values as well as techniques. The skills acquired from these schools became credentials for entry into the arena of national competition for privilege. Especially important among the skills acquired from schools was the metropolitan language. Political stratification in the country became profoundly conditioned by linguistic considerations of alien derivation.

Education, language, and communications all facilitated the urge to imitate. Religion reduced any inclination to rebel. The kind of Christianity that came into Africa made a virtue of obedience, urging the colonized people to give unto Caesar that which was Caesar's and sometimes also that which was God's.

At a time when the West itself was becoming secularized, and its religion less self-righteous, missionaries in Africa were propagating a form of Christianity already anachronistic in Europe. "Shut your eyes and pray," "Turn the other cheek"—these were doctrines of "pacification" in Africa, designed in part to end the warrior tradition and encourage subservience to the new white Caesar. The missionaries became important allies of the colonizers. The stage was set for cultural dependency.

Regional Autonomy and World Culture

This essay is caught up in what appears to be a contradiction. On the one hand, there is the view that a consensus for much-needed world reforms is impossible without substantial cultural convergence on a global scale. Yet the cultural convergence the world has so far attained carries with it the evil of dependency. A global stratification system is maintained partly because Europe and her extensions have created relationships of structural and cultural dependency with other sections of the human race. The world needs to reaffirm the need for cultural parity as a basis for mutual respect. The trend towards the emergence of a world culture has to be maintained, and yet solutions have to be found for the accompanying problems of dependency. The principle of regional autonomy here asserts its relevance. At its most obvious this autonomy is political and diplomatic. International law as it now stands seems to be intended to govern relations between states in general and makes no coherent distinction between continental locations of states. But in politics African diplomacy so far has recognized two levels of law. One level is indeed that of international law to govern relations between nations. The other level is a kind of Pan-African law to govern relations among African states themselves. This law is still much less codified than traditional international law, and its future is less assured. So far the ultimate documentary expression of Pan-African law is the charter of the Organization of African Unity (OAU). Yet, as in the case of traditional international law at large, documents normally emerge essentially as confirmation of a preexistent consensus on canons of interstate behaviour. Not all rules supposed to govern inter-African relations are as yet documented. Nor is the fact that such rules are not always obeyed evident that they do not "really" exist. Just as a recurrent violation of traditional international law by Western countries did not completely deprive that law of some kind of a role in Western diplomacy, so repeated violations of the Pan-African code of interstate behaviour has not entirely deprived that code of political significance in Africa. Such a code provides African states at least with a frame of reference for their complaints against each other. Sometimes it provides the basis for mediation by other African states to ease tensions between diplomatic or military combatants.

The central principle is that of *continental jurisdiction,* which simply asserts that there are certain African problems that should only be solved by Africans themselves. Africans in this instance are definable as citizens of countries that are members of the OAU. The principle of continental jurisdiction concedes legitimacy to continental supranationality.

To a certain extent this concept does sound like an African Monroe Doctrine, but it should be noted that the analogy is with the Monroe Doctrine as it was intended to be, which was to exclude intervention from outside the Americas, and not as it came to be, which was to legitimate U.S. intervention in Latin America. There is an important difference between the original Monroe Doctrine and the principle of continental jurisdiction as espoused in Africa. From an African perspective the trouble with the Monroe Doctrine in the Americas was that it was hemispheric. It gave the colossus of North America jurisdiction over the affairs of the rest of the hemisphere. In African diplomatic thought there is something unnatural in hemispheric jurisdiction. It would make better sense, in African terms, if the unit of noninterference was not a hemisphere but a continent. Therefore the Monroe Doctrine would have made better sense to Africans if it had tied Canada and the U.S. together instead of tying the U.S. with Latin America. The individual American is indeed a foreigner both in Canada and in Latin America, but when all is said and done he is more conspicuously a foreigner in Latin America than in Canada.

By implication American interference in Latin America must also be more conspicuously foreign interference than a similar activity in Canada. We are not recommending American interference in Canada; we are only defining different levels of foreignness, different levels in intervention of externality.

The cultural convergence that has taken place between Canadians and Americans is an important aspect behind the emergence of North America as a coherent cultural entity. The cultural convergence of Latin America, a result especially of the impact of the Spanish and Iberian cultures, has also been a major defining characteristic of that area as a coherent entity. Continental jurisdiction can help to consolidate cultural interaction within those areas.

In the case of Asia the approach has to be subcontinental because of the sheer size of the land mass and its millions of peoples. The Asians themselves will have to define which regions make the best cultural sense. Problems of overlap are inevitable whenever limits of human organizations are specified.

In the case of Africa, the overlap is particularly significant in relation to the Middle East. North African states are members both of the Arab League and of the OAU. How much interplay there ought to be between the Middle East and Africa politically is something which is already part of practical politics. The readiness of the OAU to appoint a special committee on the Middle East and attempt to find the elusive breakthrough that would end the Arab-Israeli impasse was one manifestation of this interaction. In the course of 1972 and 1973 more than two dozen African countries broke off relations with Israel. More immediately, the Middle East crisis overflowed into the Nile Valley, intermingling with the problem of Southern Sudan, Uganda, and the separatist movements in Eritrea.

It may well be that one day Africa and the Middle East could constitute one region. This may be a happier situation for a country like

22

Israel than to belong to a formally sovereign region in which almost everybody else is an Arab. Though Israel has critics and enemies within Black Africa itself, she also has more friends among Black Africans than she can claim among the Arabs. A merger of the two regions would not only ease the problem of dual loyalties in North African states but also mitigate Israel's isolation.

But that is a matter for the future. For the time being a more strict continental jurisdiction makes better sense for Africa. Regional African autonomy, with limited interference from beyond the continent and certainly from the major powers, would help to provide a climate for both cultural and structural independence in the years ahead.

Such continental independence would provide an infrastructure for autonomous cultural experimentation. Yet, while that may help regional cultures to be more autonomous of Europe, how can those regional cultures proceed to be better represented in the global pool of man's heritage?

A World Structure of Five Languages

Henry Kissinger once envisaged a five-sided structure of peace involving the United States, the Soviet Union, China, Western Europe, and Japan.

Our own structure of peace will be based partly on five languages —English, French, Russian, Arabic, and Chinese. We have in these five a combination of two types of languages. First, there are those which have already fulfilled the criteria of a world language. English and French already have well over the definitional minimum of one hundred million speakers, have already been adopted as national languages by more than ten states, and have extended well beyond their continent of birth.

The second category is of languages which are not yet world languages but deserve to be promoted and developed for such a role in the near future. Russian, Chinese, and Arabic fall into that category.

The case for promoting Russian further is partly derived from the sheer exigencies of power. The Soviet Union is already one of the two super giants of the twentieth century, with immense power and influence in Eastern Europe and parts of Asia. The country has made remarkable progress in certain areas of technological and organisational innovation, and some of its models of social and economic organisation are influential and have entered the stream of world culture. The Russian language is already the mother tongue of more than the minimum of one hundred million speakers and has been adopted as at least the second language of education and culture by nearly ten states.

In some ways, Spanish is more of a world language than Russian, at least in terms of its adoption by many more states than Russian as the *first* language of national business. Spanish has also spread beyond its continent of birth and has more than the minimum of one hundred million speakers.

But precisely because Spanish is a Western European language in a world already heavily Eurocentric in a western sense, and because we have already adopted two other Western European languages as world languages, the case for Spanish is weaker than that for Russian. Russian—though also a European language—comes from a significantly different cultural tradition. And a World Federation of Cultures has to take pluralism, as well as convergence, into account. In our new world Spanish would have to be demoted into a regional language.

The case for elevating Chinese to a world language is perhaps even more obvious. The very fact that one out of every five human beings speaks Chinese is a major consideration. The language is not widespread and has certainly not crossed continents except with overseas Chinese and some western scholars. But the sheer weight of the number of those who speak Chinese—greater than the numbers of those who speak English and French put together—makes the case for making Chinese one of the world languages of tomorrow irresistable.

There are additional considerations in favour of such a move. One concerns China's past contributions to world culture, ranging from Chinese science and philosophy over several hundred years to Chinese cuisine today.

Third, there is the People's Republic of China as a major model of political and cultural engineering, with all its potentialities as a whole new civilisation in the world. For the time being communist China's experiment still shows Eurocentric intellectual dependency. Marx and Lenin are revered, whereas China's own greatest philosopher, Confucius, is militantly denounced. European-socialist masters are worshipped, while the population is urged to curse its own cultural heritage. The Chinese communists are caught between genuine innovativeness and residual intellectual dependency.

But in this ambivalence they are no different from much of the rest of the Third World. What is more significant and distinctive is China's determined attempt to transcend many of its problems through the energies of its own people and to mobilise a fifth of mankind in the quest for new social directions. The Chinese language deserves to be elevated to a world language partly in order to make this monumental experiment more accessible and more comprehensible to the rest of mankind.

As a candidate for elevation to a world language Arabic is less obvious. But among Third World languages Arabic has special credentials. The development of Arabic into a world language would partly be in recognition of its dual identity as a language of both Asia and Africa and partly in recognition of the impact of the Middle East as a whole on world culture. As we have indicated previously in this book, the Middle East played its part in the evolution of a world culture partly through the emergence of universalistic religions and partly through the impact of Arab scientists and mathematicians on the eve of Europe's emergence.

Both Christianity and Islam were born in the Middle East. Had Hebrew been as widespread as Arabic in the modern world, perhaps Hebrew would have had a stronger case than Arabic for elevation to a world language. Much of the spiritual universe of mankind owes something to the impact of Hebraic values and systems of thought. Even Islam bears the marks of Hebraic and Judaic influence. But given that Hebrew today is the mother-tongue of little more than two million people, its case for global status is much weaker than that of Arabic, with more than a hundred million speakers spread over a much larger area.

Moreover, both Islam and the Arabic language are Afro-Asian cultural phenomena—whereas the great majority of Christians and Jews are part of the already dominant European civilisation. If our world federation of culture is partly a quest to reduce the Eurocentrism of today's cultural arrangements, the language of Islam has a stronger case than the language of either Christianity or Judaism.

From Africa's point of view, Arabic has additional attributes worth taking into account. The majority of Arabic-speakers are part of the African continent and are represented as members of the Organisation of African Unity. Although technically Arabic is not an indigenous language of Africa, it is the mother tongue of millions of indigenous people in the continent from the Sudan to Mauritania. The great majority of African Arabs are not immigrants from the Arabian peninsula but indigenous people who have been assimiliated into the Arabic language and culture.

Linguistic Representation of Cultures

A primary problem to be resolved in devising world institutions based on cultures is to devise an appropriate method of representing cultures. The distinctiveness of our perspective on world order is not in the

25

nature of the institutions devised, but partly in the functions served by those institutions and partly in the principles of composition and membership of those institutions.

During the twenty-first century, transformed global institutions would emerge such as the General Council for Security and Political Affairs (a transformed United Nations' Security Council), Agency for Migration and Economic Opportunity, and Central World Assembly. But particularly relevant to the new world culture would be the transformation of UNESCO. We propose several electoral colleges or General Assemblies, five of which would be founded on the basis of language and the others on the basis of regional geography, of whose primary functions in the next thirty years would be to send representatives to the new World Council on Science and Culture. One of the main aims of this WCSC would be to aid in the interpenetration of cultures and the achievement of parity of esteem through egalitarian dissemination and widespread opportunities for mobility.

We propose therefore that at the global level of a World Federation of Cultures representation should be not only on the basis of nation states but also on the basis of allegiance to a particular world language and on the basis of regional location. A combination of *linguistic, national,* and *regional* principles would constitute the basis of representation at the global level of our institutions.

We must distinguish among four categories of language. A world language is one which, first, has today at least a hundred million speakers; second, is the official language of at least ten states; and third, has spread beyond its own continent in a major way. Of all the languages of the world, only English, French, and Spanish meet these three defining criteria of a world language. But, for reasons already given, Spanish should be demoted to a regional language. The minimum number of speakers for a world language may have to be subject to a periodic review until the population of the world is stabilised.

The second category of languages is regional languages, which are international but not intercontinental. The greatest of the regional languages are Chinese and Russian. But these will be developed as world languages, as we indicated. Other regional languages include German, Arabic, and Swahili.

The fourth category would be communal languages, like Tamil, Gujarati, Luganda, and any of the languages of the Amerindian populations.

In our new world we would require that every child in the world should learn three languages—a world language (e.g., English or French), a regional language (e.g., German or Swahili) and *either* a national language (e.g., Swedish, Persian) *or* a subnational language (e.g., Gujarati or Luganda).

Those countries in the world which for the time being have not adopted English, French, Russian, Chinese, or Arabic for any official purposes domestically would have to declare their allegiance to at least one of them. This would be important from the point of view of their educational system and the degree to which they promote that language in their schools. But it would also be important because their representation on world bodies would be partly by reference to their being within the global territory covered by a particular world language.

It is an assumption of this model that sharing a language helps to reduce the culture gap among a people. When for example Russians are called upon to learn Spanish as their choice of a regional language, and a growing number of Russian children emerge from schools equipped with skills in Spanish, it may be presumed that Russian sensibilities to the problems of Spanish America would enter a more sophisticated phase.

Spanish Americans need not choose Russian as their own world language in reciprocity. They may decide to adopt another world language like French. That would be up to them. If they did adopt Chinese or English or French or Arabic, Spanish Americans would be no better informed about Russians than they are at the moment, but the Russians would be growing more familiar with Spanish America than they are at the moment. The process of comprehension would by no means be symmetrical, but it would still serve the purpose of our World Federation of Cultures. If Spanish Americans were busy learning a little more about the Middle East after adopting Arabic, for example, or about France and French-speaking Africa after adopting French, the cultural order of the world would be served even if they remained as ignorant of the Soviet Union as they had been before.

Each world language would have a General Assembly. The General Assembly for French-speakers would serve certain functions to promote intellectual, technological, and educational collaboration among the countries that have adopted French as their world language. But in addition the General Assembly of French-speakers would serve as an electoral college to elect delegates of the French-speaking World Community for the global institutions at the center of our Federation. The members of the General Assembly of French-speakers would be elected on a national basis, preferably by a popular vote. Each country would have, say, one member for every 10 million of its population. Countries with less than 10 million will have only one member.

On bodies as varied as the General Council for Security and Political

Affairs and the Agency for Migration and Economic Opportunity, representation would in part be by this global linguistic affiliation.

At this initial stage no choice of a world language need be definitive. Brazil and others would have time to rethink by the end of the century. Firm commitment to a world language would not be required of any country until the year 2000.

The United States would now have to seek admission into what has so far been the British Commonwealth. Again the Commonwealth would now constitute the basis of the General Assembly of English-speakers, as a transitional stage. George Bernard Shaw's play, *The Apple Cart,* published in 1929, anticipated the thesis of the United States seeking readmission into the British Commonwealth. The King of England was appalled and frightened by the prospect, according to Shaw.

The original Gaullist idea of the French Community, and the subsequent Senegalese notion of *Francophonie,* would in turn form the nucleus of the General Assembly of French-speakers.

The distribution of the five world languages for the time being would itself offer special opportunities for studying the interaction between regionalism and linguistic affiliation.

The Arab League might form the nucleus of the World Assembly of Arabic-speakers and COMICORN the nucleus of a World Assembly of Russian-speakers. A new body would have to come into being as the global forum for Chinese-speakers.

French provides a special relationship between Africa and Europe. The majority of *individual* French-speakers are in Europe; the majority of French-speaking *countries* are in Africa. The transitional General Assembly of French-speakers would, in the initial stages, be overwhelmingly Afro-European. This would afford special insights into a new interaction between Europe and Africa, hopefully more egalitarian than the original French version of "Eurafrica" as symbolised by the associated territories of the European Economic Community under the original Treaty of Rome.

It is the General Assembly of English-speakers which would be from the start the most ecumenical—absorbing diverse representatives from Europe, North America, Africa, Asia, and Australasia.

Also in the transitional phase pending the end of the century should be a dramatic reform of the functions of UNESCO. Each of the five General Assemblies of World Languages should be sending representatives to this World Council on Science and Culture. The principle of membership of UNESCO, its scale of operation, and of course its resources will have to be drastically transformed if UNESCO is to serve as the transitional mechanism for the promotion of a more symmetrical world culture. The details of this transformation can be worked out only after consultation with the new General Assemblies of the five languages. In other words, the Assemblies have to be brought into being before their precise relationship with a transformed and radically elevated UNESCO can be worked out. In the words of a recent report by a consultative group which met in Paris in December 1972 to review and appraise UNESCO's contribution to the second United Nations Development Decade:

> The present work of UNESCO in the cultural field focusses on three areas: cultural studies, cultural development and cultural heritage. Each plays a part in the general process of development. There is, moreover, an interplay between the national and international aspects in each of these cultural fields. A world culture is emerging in our time, but it is a world culture which is overwhelmingly Euro-centric. Europe's predominance during the last historical period combined with Europe's expansion to the Americas and her annexation of large parts of Africa and Asia, have resulted in an imbalance in *cultural dissemination.* The rest of the world learns European languages, sings European songs, debates about European ideologies, reads European books in a manner which is not reciprocated. And "Europe" in this cultural sense includes Europe's extensions, the Americas.

The report of the UNESCO-sponsored consultative committee then refers to the need for a new emphasis in the acculturation process:

> The right approach to the cultural problems of the world is not to attempt to keep Western influences out, but to help create parity of esteem between cultures. And parity of esteem requires reciprocity of influence.

The report then confronts the issue of the role of UNESCO. Some of the work done by UNESCO—from its eight-volume project on the History of Africa to its promotion of technical assistance—clearly has a bearing on the wider enterprise of seeking cultural parity. But the Report of the Consultative Committee still had to pose the questions:

> Should UNESCO play a greater part in redressing the balance? Should UNESCO play a bigger role in making available to Europe and the Americas the cultures of the rest of the world? UNESCO has started this work but should the scale and the skills needed now be expanded?

This author—who was a member of that consultative group—certainly believes that there is room for a vast expansion of UNESCO's activities if the world we have in mind is to be realized. There is also room for expanding UNESCO's own concept of culture in the direction of emphasising its interrelationship with UNESCO's other endeavours in the scientific, technological, and educational fields.

Actors and social reformers who could be mobilised in support of such changes include many of those who sympathise with UNESCO's aims in cultural dissemination and educational reforms. Educators are particularly relevant here. Other potential actors behind a movement for such changes would include those who sense a profound unease about the phenomenon of international dependency in this northern-dominated world and are groping for ways of reducing the weight of inequality and imbalance.

In the meantime consideration would need to be given to the role of the other bodies of the United Nations, including the Security Council, the General Assembly, and the Economic and Social Council. But the most drastic transitional transformation within the world body would hinge on a redefinition of the role of UNESCO as a mechanism for educational change, dissemination of science, and promotion of a world culture based on egalitarian principles. This would become the World Council on Science and Culture.

Regional Representation of Cultures

The second principle of representation in the world bodies would be by regions. Of course geographical contiguity does not mean cultural congruence. Some regions are more clearly culturally determined than others. On balance, for example, the Middle East has a massive regional identity either by reference to Islam, which would include Turkey and Iran in the Middle East, or by reference to the Arabic language.

Western Europe is also culturally homogeneous to some extent, though not sharing one language. On the other hand, the African continent is not culturally homogeneous if countries both north and south of the Sahara are included. A good deal of attention might have to be paid to the problem of defining regions. The problems can in some cases be very difficult. But they need not be insurmountable. There may be occasions when a particular country might be given a choice in a national referendum to determine whether it belongs to one region or another. For example, North African countries might have to decide whether they belong to the Middle East or to the African continent for the purpose of this representation. It would be conceivable for some of them to regard themselves primarily as African, while others opted to join the ranks of fellow Arabic speakers elsewhere in the area. Irredentism on a regional scale or secessionism on a regional scale, as particular countries seek to change their regional affiliation, might be a recurrent issue. But the World Federation of Cultures might simply have to decide on periodic referenda—possibly every twenty-five years—for those who are ambiguous or ambivalent in their regional affiliations. The issue would simply have to be resolved by resort to a popular decision in the ambivalent country.

The regional principle is chosen partly because the spread of cultures is affected by geographical contiguity. There was a time when culture, like water, flowed downwards—from the dominant group to the dominated group. We referred earlier to the cultural imbalance in the world, with the heavy weight of European civilization in the central pool of the human heritage. One purpose of the new restructuring of institutions in the world is to negate the proposition that culture flows downwards along the political slope, as inevitably as water does.

In reality, as we have indicated elsewhere, there have been cases when rulers have been acculturated to the values of the ruled, rather than the other way around. The case of the Romans gradually imbibing Greek civilization is noteworthy. The Swahili language in Zanzibar was well on the way towards conquering the ruling Arab elite. Turkish and Islam were adopted by the invaders who descended on Anatolia. We might therefore say that culture, unlike water, is capable of flowing upwards—from the politically lower groups to the politically dominant. What the new Federation of Cultures would have to seek is an arrangement whereby the economically and politically less powerful sectors of the world might help to facilitate the flow of cultures towards the common pool of humanity.

Their say in issues concerning education in English or French would itself be a process of decolonizing these languages and making them more responsive to the contribution of users distant from the originators of the language.

In addition the representation of these groups by regions would increase the impact of their values and perspectives on policies which determine the direction of the world. There is therefore a case for suitably modifying and strengthening such organizations as the Organization of African Unity, the European Union and European Assembly, the Arab League, a new organization for the Indian subcontinent and Ceylon, and perhaps even a Sino-Japanese complex. Canada, the United States, and the non-Latin Caribbean may also form a new region.

The three world order values of maximization of welfare, maximization of social justice, and minimization of violence are themselves values which are subject to modifications according to the cultural perspectives of those seeking to realize them. We have mentioned before that the most culture-bound of all these values is the value of social justice. What is social justice to a German in Bonn need not be social justice to a Karamajong in Moroto; what is social justice to an American Indian in Peru need not be social justice to a Korean peasant.

But economic welfare is more easily shared as a value. And both the Korean and the Peru Indian may know the difference when they have more to eat, or newer clothes to wear, or a better house to live in. The quantification of economic welfare is a more manageable ambition than the quantification of social justice.

Violence also is a concept subject to some extent to ideological and cultural differences. Concepts like structural violence have already entered even into the general discourse of the existing world languages. What is violence? The answer varies to some extent according to the ideological position of the person defining it. Ideology is an aspect of culture or subculture.

The central World Assembly may need a new principle of membership. Each region would have a minimum number of seats *as a region*, chosen by the regional organization like the Arab League or the European Union. Additional seats would be allocated on the basis of population in each region. But these seats would rotate among member states of each regional organization on a three-year basis.

National Representation of Cultures

The nation-state would not disappear in the global federation of cultures. Some countries in the Third World need to consolidate both their nationhood and their statehood if they are to realise the values of reduced violence and enhanced welfare and justice. Such nations are sometimes threatened by excessive cultural diversity at the domestic level, and their primary quest is for a new collective national culture. Many individual countries in Africa need a domestic federation of cultures. They already have multiple tribal cultures. What they lack for the time being is a coherent federal level of national culture.

Our blueprint for a new cultural world must therefore give recognition to nationhood as a unit of culture, real or prospective. Representation of regional institutions should be on the basis of nation-states. In addition, global institutions should also find ways to combine national representation with linguistic and regional credentials.

The emergent national cultures should be guided in their evolution by world-order values. A principle of kinship culture especially relevant to world-order values may be the status of women. The national unit of culture would have special responsibility in handling this kinship factor, but regional and linguistic institutions would need to reinforce a trend towards a new politicization of women. There should be a systematic attempt to increase the participation by women in these bodies. It may therefore be stipulated as a condition that representatives from, say, the World Community of Arabic-Speakers should be no more than two-thirds males. Ideally the proportion of men to women in the world bodies of decision-making should as far as possible be on the basis of parity. But for historical and other reasons complete parity should not be insisted upon, certainly not within this century. A safeguard to ensure that at least one third of each decision-making body consists of women would be an important contribution towards the partial demasculinization of decision-making in the world.

Any world that concedes to culture the status of a determining factor behind politics, commerce, and war is a world that must concede to women a much greater role in determining its direction than they have enjoyed. The role of women as agents of socialization among young people is only one fundamental idea. The disjunction between infant-socialization and adolescent-socialization, the move from a world of maternal transmission in the home to a wider world of masculine dominance, creates a disjunction in the socialization process that could be mitigated by making the future world less dominated by the male.

Issues of what is virtuous and what is vicious, what is honourable and what is dishonourable, and what is desirable and what is not could be modified to a significant extent if women help to shape the political and economic directions of whole societies.

We distinguish between the *enfranchisement of women,* which merely means acquiring the vote, and *the politicisation of women,* which means their readiness to enter the next level of political effectiveness—holding political office. It is one thing to be given the power to vote for somebody else; it is quite another to be a candidate for whom votes are cast.

One major way of politicising women is simply to insist on a minimum number of women in major institutions of decision-making, especially those concerned with security, war, and peace. It is because of this that our Model World Federation of Cultures has insisted on a ratio of at least one woman to two men.

Out of all these principles should emerge institutions that will seek to regulate the world in the direction of maximising cultural interplay, consolidating consensus, enhancing economic welfare, promoting wider agreement on social justice, and helping to diminish violence in all those senses held valid by the global institutions concerned.

Conclusion

We have sought to indicate in this study a perspective on world order that puts a special premium on cultural integration. Our preference for culture is partly derived from the conviction that a shared pool of values is what consensus is all about. The reform of the world in the direction of greater social justice, enhanced economic welfare, and diminishing prospects for violence requires human consensus behind core values. The world of tomorrow can be tamed either through outright force or through shared values. And shared values are the very basis of cultural convergence.

We began the study with the paradox of violence emerging precisely out of cultural integration. Case illustrations drawn from recent African political experience, in societies small enough to offer opportunities for discerning the dynamics of human relations, have in fact revealed the tension-generating defects of cultural integration.

But the viable world order we are pursuing includes not only reduced violence but also economic welfare and social justice. The cases of Zanzibar, Rwanda, and Burundi revealed the agonies of violence. But why did violence take place? Mainly because the stratification systems within those countries were no longer viable. Cultural integration was therefore helping to reveal more glaringly the injustice of a stratification system that was too unequal. The Arabized Waswahili of Zanzibar therefore rose up against their cultural kin, the Swahilized Waarabu. The rebellion was in part a rebellion against a system of inadequate social justice and asymmetrical economic welfare. It was a rebellion against dependency.

The successful Hutu rebellion against the Tutsi oligarchy in Rwanda and the unsuccessful Hutu rebellion against the Tutsi militariat in Burundi were again convulsions connected with the pursuit of social justice. But all three have been very expensive rebellions in terms of the violence that accompanied them, as compared with the modest returns of egalitarianism achieved in Zanzibar and Rwanda. Even these returns are very fragile, tending at times in the direction of a reversed hierarchical tyranny.

But cultural homogenization on a world scale has happier egalitarian prospects, mainly because of the scale of the unit of integration. It would be unlikely that consensus would be obtained on a world scale behind a system of gross inequalities between nations, states, races, and cultures. Cultural homogenization globally must therefore carry the seeds of human equalization. The emerging consensus would support a global stratification system that was not too glaringly unequal.

Two problems continue to be at the heart of it all: first, *uneven creativity* between races and nations, and second, *uneven dissemination* of what has been created. In some fields, especially in technology, the West in recent times has been disproportionately creative. Even particular groups in the Western world—like the Jewish people—have been staggeringly innovative in relation to their numbers.

But while the West has definitely been in the lead in technology, we cannot be quite as certain that it has also been in the lead in the arts and philosophy. All we know is that Western art and Western philosophy have been *disseminated* more efficiently and more widely than any other intellectual heritage in the modern world.

It may well be that the imbalance in both creativity and dissemination is in turn connected with an imbalance in *mobility*. The physical mobility of people and the intellectual mobility of ideas not only are agents of dissemination but may also be sources of creative stimulus.

We have already referred to the tremendous mobility of Americans intercontinentally and intranationally and of Europeans in terms of crossing each other's boundaries. By contrast, the great majority of people in Africa and Asia have not yet been one hundred miles from the village in which they were born. A world of more balanced mobility is clearly called for, if the imbalance in creativity and cultural dissemination is to be redressed. And only a redressing of that imbalance can ever stabilize the emergent compromise relationships in world integration that have so far been achieved.

Certainly much of the racism in the world rests on an assumption that certain cultural ways are inferior to others. The theory of *apartheid* in South Africa claims parity of esteem among different cultures and seeks to institutionalize their separateness. The reality of *apartheid* in South Africa rests in fact on an assumption that African cultures and African ways are inferior to the ways of the civilized white man. A lack of equilibrium in mutual conceptions at the cultural level have helped to deepen the tensions between the races of South Africa.

It seems probable that a really symmetrical world culture would be both a cause and an effect of growing egalitarianism in the world and help to consolidate balanced conceptions between peoples.

Out of this should grow consensus behind a form of stratification that does not entail gaps that are extreme. An egalitarian system of stratification is basically a contradiction in terms, but there can be no doubt that some stratification systems are further away from egalitarianism than others. As we indicated earlier, consensus could grow behind a very elaborate stratification system that has big gaps and inequalities. Consensus behind the Indian caste system is a case in point.

We are inclined to believe that consensus behind glaring inequalities can survive in very large states but can never indefinitely survive either in very small states or in the world community at large. Zanzibar was a small political community, and the convulsion that occurred was partly connected both with the size of the community and the tensions of cultural integration. Rwanda and Burundi are also compact states in Africa, having achieved a high degree of cultural integration partly because of that compactness, but vulnerable to violent eruption again because the society is small enough to have a large sector of face-to-face public relationships.

But India, the United States, and the Soviet Union are very large entities. Their largeness militates against rapid cultural integration, though given the centuries that India has had, a depth of integration has indeed been attained. But consensus behind special types of inequalities in the United States, in India, and in the Soviet Union is a little more tenable than could now be conceivable in a compact little community elsewhere.

But even more fundamental is that the inequalities in India, the United States, and the Soviet Union can more readily command acquiescence than the inequalities within an evolving world community. This is partly because the new post-imperial world was in any case born out of a special kind of egalitarian revolution in the first place. The revolt against Europe's domination of the world is now a *given*. Further cultural convergence on a global scale must therefore carry with it the seeds of counterassertion and the possibility that the underprivileged will not be acquiescent.

We have sought to indicate in this study that in fact the beginnings of world culture are already at hand, but for the time being it is a system of hierarchy in the cultural domain rather than a system of cultural federalism. Cultural hierarchy converts one culture into the dominant culture of the world, and yet the culture is drawn primarily from a specific subsection of the human species. The world community at the moment bears comparison with a multireligious state which nevertheless has a single established church. England is a multireligious state, which has chosen one of its denominations, the Anglican faith, as the dominant church of the polity.

The world is a multicultural entity but seems to have chosen for the time being overwhelmingly Western culture as the established cultural church of the human species. Again we are up against dominance and dependency.

The great change which needs to be made in the days ahead is to substitute the principle of an established church with a principle of cultural ecumenicalism. In our sense this would mean a World Federation of Cultures, with the constituent cultures coordinating their status and with the joint pool borrowing from a number of regionally and linguistically-based cultural contributions.

The principle of regionalism, combined with a creative utilization of the languages of the world, could gradually help to cope with the imbalance of contemporary arrangements and solve the problem of uneven creativity and uneven dissemination. Mobility in both the intellectual and physical domain could be critical in directing the human species towards that globalized community of cultures.

As we indicated, we may need to encourage the West to learn other languages. There even may be a case for requiring every school child, everywhere in the world, to learn three languages—a world language (e.g., English or French), a regional language (e.g., German or Swahili) and *either* a national language (e.g., Swedish or Persian) *or* a subnational language (e.g., Gujurati or Luganda).

Whatever the precise mechanisms used, the world does need a more equitable distribution both of creativity and its dissemination. It is because of these considerations that we see world order in terms of a federation of human cultural contributions, combining a global pool of shared achievement with local pools of distinctive innovation and tradition.

WORLD POLITICS AND WORLD ORDER: THE ISSUE OF AUTONOMY*

Rajni Kothari

As we enter the last quarter of the twentieth century, the proverbial burden of the past faces us in the form of an uncertain future. It is a future that is no longer remote and unfathomable, but it is not one that can be tackled by simple prognostication from the present. The ambivalence with which sensitive people round the world look upon the future underlines this ambiguity. They appear caught between the is and the ought, between the probable and the possible, between the empirical and the normative components in human endeavour. According to the *methodology of science,* strictly speaking, the future appears bleak. According to the *methodology of politics,* which consists in the exercise of will upon the available range of choices, however, the same future appears pregnant with possibilities for the better. It is because of this peculiar divergence between what will happen if men fail to intervene in the process of history and what can happen if they do so intervene, that the need to move from diagnosis to design (from determined probabilities to valued alternatives) becomes relevant. No doubt, the diagnostic and the predictive exercises are necessary for informing human intervention with an adequate sense of the range of possibilities and for working out the implications of alternative designs of action. The whole purpose of such exercises, however, is to make those choices, not to look upon projected developments as providing necessary outcomes according to some predetermined laws of history.

*This paper condenses my longer essay, *Footsteps into the Future,* which is being simultaneously published. For elaborations and supporting points, some documentation and a detailed philosophical rationale, the reader must turn to *Footsteps.* In writing this paper I have benefitted from close collaboration in earlier exercises in the project with B. S. Murty, Ramashray Roy, and the late Pitambar Pant and from the continuous critique and stimulation provided by Raojibhai Patel and my colleagues at the Centre for the Study of Developing Societies.

Diagnosis

To begin with, however, let us look at the trends at work. In most countries rates of economic growth will be ahead of rates of population growth, but the bulk of the benefits of such growth will accrue to small metropolitan elites who derive both their legitimacy and their political support from external linkages rather than by identification with their own people, who continue to constitute the vast and destitute periphery of the human species. The spatial distribution of land and other resources will continue to work against the poorer regions of the world. The widely accepted model of modernization along a preconceived course of change has already released forces that will accentuate ethnic and class cleavages, internal violence and armed conflicts between neighbours. The economic gap will continue to widen, minimum conditions will become increasingly hard to achieve except in a few fortunate or favoured nations, and patterns of dominance will continue with at least some of the big powers trying to exploit the existing misery with ready aid, distorting economic policies and mortgaging all future generations to mounting burdens of debt repayment. Poorer countries will continue to be told to engage in family planning to restrain their populations, to integrate their ethnic minorities and "motivate" their illiterate farmers, if necessary through coercive methods, and to leave the real problems of world power and its distribution to be tackled by the big powers through appropriate balances and spheres of influence.

The upshot of all this is a growing dualism in the world, in large part expressed along a North-South hiatus. As this hiatus cannot be resolved militarily—thanks to the oligopolistic control of the balance of terror—and as the institutional structure of international economic relationships will militate against a viable domestic economic solution, the poorer and dependent countries will continue to engage in militant anticolonial postures, exploited by local power-seekers and demagogues without any regard for the welfare of their people. The state of violence thus created will lead to increasingly authoritarian regimes and regional confrontations that will be mediated from a few world centres, producing a kind of "world order." Such a world order will undermine all the preferred values on which there seems to be almost universal agreement—freedom, justice, equality, and development.

Prevailing Doctrine

Such a pattern of dominance is already in operation. It has produced not simply a division of the world between dominant and dependent states but also deep cleavages within the latter. The spell of the doctrine of modernization has produced a basic schism between a tiny modernist elite and the people at large, between a few urban centres and a large rural periphery, and between the educated and the uneducated. Cumulatively it has produced a privileged class that concentrates local power and resources in its own hands and on that basis becomes part of an international establishment that in turn provides it with needed economic and military assistance. National power and economic success are increasingly measured by a race to amass large aggregate national products concentrated in either an oligarchy of leading industrial tycoons or a state bureaucracy, an increasing preference for strong central authority to mobilize the periphery for its own interests, and a growing reliance on the coercive potential of the state and the army for security against not only external threats but also internal discontent and upheavals. As those trends continue—and they will, unless the prevailing paradigm is disturbed—governments still committed to the values of freedom and justice may find it difficult to hold on to those values and yet survive.

Socio-Economic Trends

Meanwhile, world demographic and economic trends are likely to accentuate existing disparities and discord and further polarize the world. Although the bulk of population growth, increase in the proportion of youth in total populations, and consequent pressure on urban centres and educational systems will be concentrated in the poorer regions of the world, the parallel though smaller growth in numbers in the affluent societies and their enormous advances towards high technology for economic as well as defense needs will lead to a net flow of resources not from the rich to the poor areas but in the reverse direction. The result will be ominous for the outer half of the world: economic stagnation for want of resources, increasing pressure of numbers on limited opportunities leading to massive unemployment on the one hand and increasing malnutrition on the other, peasant revolts in the rural areas and youth revolts in the cities, and a growing pressure on governments to accept whatever solutions are imposed by the technologically and militarily advanced centres of the world, thus possibly heralding the beginning of a new colonial era without, however, any assurance of either political peace or territorial integrity for the colonized world.

These solutions are likely to be dictated by both the dominant world view and the interest structure of the colonial powers. They will be guided by a technoeconomic model whose increasing sophistication and speed threaten to reduce the importance of man in the civilization process. We do not intend to go into the details of the vast strides made by modern science and technology in altering the nature of biological evolution, in the revolutionary transformation of the chemical content of man's material culture and the manufacture of new life forms, in the use of mathematical language in reconstructing the basic elements of life, in the conquest of space enabling man to reach out to the mysterious heavens, and above all in organizational technology through the increasing scale of information processing and the growing capability for control and management of human systems. We are aware of these great exponential changes, most of which are irreversible components of human evolution that simultaneously afford man the capability to master the perennial threats to his survival—hunger, disease, natural calamities—and to undermine these very achievements through a Frankensteinian nemesis. But for the purpose of this paper our interest in technology as an aspect of human evolution is focussed more specifically on the manner in which it affects *man in society* and its impact on patterns of violence and nonviolence.

Technology and Man

Present trends suggest an increasingly inverse correlation between advances in technology and the value of man as a producer and a creative agent. For a time this took the form of simple mechanization, in part relieving man's drudgery and in part displacing him in productive operations. Up to a point both kinds proved beneficial to man, even the labour-saving kind, generating employment and incomes through a general process of economic expansion. More recent trends in technology, however, are in the form not so much of ordinary expansion of machine-based capacity but of processes that are replacing both man and machines that were an aid to man, turning stepwise operations and routines into "process systems" and continuous "flows." Automation of a whole series of manual and mental processes provides the key to this development. The resulting modernization and rationalization of industry has given rise to a productive system that relies more on equipment than on man, resulting in declining prospects for employment of human beings and a gradual redundancy of all but the highly skilled. Generation of surplus value will depend more on modernization of techniques and hence reduction of costs than on raising output or augmenting capacity or intensively utilizing existing capacity. Research and development expenditures will become concentrated on industries that are "science-based" and involve high inputs of technology and innovation rather than on those that are oriented to production and employment.

No wonder that unemployment is on the increase all over the world, even in some of the more affluent countries. As the basic character of this unemployment is structural, the main brunt of unemployment seems to fall on the less privileged strata everywhere—the semi-skilled and the unskilled, backward ethnic groups and underdeveloped regions, and above all the poorer countries. In their effort to modernize and catch up with the others, the poorer countries are becoming a breeding ground for millions of surplus men for whom society has no use. The growing penetration of these countries by the multinational corporation equipped with high technology and the resources needed for such technology that only they can provide, the far greater emphasis on export promotion than on expanding domestic markets by increasing the purchasing power of ordinary people, and the attraction of the Western model of technoeconomic growth as the only possible path to progress are all converging toward a rapid growth of gross national products and a still more rapid growth of unemployment and misery.

Marginality of Man

It appears, then, that both modern technology and modern population trends point to the same basic malaise. The chief characteristic of this malaise is the obsolescence of man himself. In fact it is worse than obsolescence. In the years and decades to come man will be looked upon as something undesirable, as a burden on both society and nature, straining the management capacities of the former and the life-sustaining resources of the latter. (Some of the present discussions on family planning, advocating harsh and coercive measures, already display such a view.) It is, of course, true that science and technology are man's own creation and that their only *raison d'être* is to enable man to deal with his problems. The fact remains, however, that anything that is able to concentrate power and energy in large doses, even if it be an inanimate quantity, acquires a life and momentum of its own. This is what has happened to technology in our time. The result is that instead of attending to the reality of a growing population, to the fact that a very large percentage of this population is born in poverty and misery, and to the further fact of a rapidly deteriorating nexus between man and nature, technology is generating forces that deny opportunities for a meaningful life to large numbers of human beings and condemn them to a state of dependence and indignity. It may be that

43

if there were not as many people on the planet as there are today, things might have been better. But it is even more true that if it were not for the present type of technology spreading all over the planet, things would have been better. Indeed, if there were not this technology, there would not have been this *surfeit* of human beings either. To continue to talk of population control without controlling this technology indicates how little serious thought has been given to this problem.

The principal solution on which national and international technocrats seem to be concentrating their efforts is to propagate the gospel of birth control to poorer countries without regard to the reasons for persisting attitudes towards family size and composition. That population control is part of a larger process of enlightenment and well-being, brought about through a massive spread of literacy and health among the people, seems to be overlooked in this approach. Meanwhile the unregulated and trendy spread of higher education in these countries, in their effort to emulate the "advanced" countries, is leading to the phenomenon of educated unemployment among the urbanized youth (including highly qualified persons), while the convergence of poverty and illiteracy among large sections of a fast-growing population is producing a class of subproletariat that flocks to the cities and adds to the numbers of slum and pavement dwellers, squatters, beggars, urchins, and mercenaries for militant causes. The result is a demographic picture that will soon become explosive both at the top and at the bottom of the social structure.

Given the present technological and economic trends and political-military structures in the world, the outlook for the future is alarming, unless imaginative countervailing strategies are adopted. There will be many more young people in the world than old or middle-aged, their proportions will be still larger in urban areas, they will be more formally educated and socialized in modern and cosmopolitan ways of thought and living than the others, they will be more mobile and restless, there will be much greater unemployment among them ten or twenty years from now than is the case today, and their generation will be less attached to their diverse traditions and thus more open to the trends and fashions set by the metropolitan centres of the world. The upshot of these various converging trends is likely to be seething discontent, a certain rootlessness, and a widespread feeling of futility and rejection among millions of men and women who are fondled and indulged as children and then thrown mercilessly on the streets. As this happens, the very carriers of a cosmopolitan culture may become susceptible to the appeals of national chauvinism and racial prejudice, play into the hands of mobilization regimes and army juntas, and sup-

44

port wars that escalate from localized conflicts for liberation and justice to much larger hostilities, the precise scope of which it is difficult to predict.

Thus in the way world power patterns and social and demographic trends are presently developing, one is faced by a scenario of growing fragmentation of political structures, a sharpening duality of the world in economic and technological terms and hence also in power positions, and a widespread sense of isolation and powerlessness among the more sensitives strata of the world. In the absence of a new assertion of values shared by the dispossessed of the world and the discontented intellectuals and scientists living in the metropoles of the world and a readiness to act in union against prevailing patterns of dominance and exploitation, these conditions are likely to further institutionalize those patterns and produce widespread misery and a growing combination of violent masses and coercive states.

Countervailing Trends

There are already a number of countervailing trends in the world that can, if systematically identified and strengthened, provide the basis of hope and reconstruction. Some of these may be briefly mentioned.

Regional Settlements

There is a growing perception of the dangers inherent in operating through a political structure based on the assumption of a world dominated by superpowers when in fact new centres of power are emerging. Nations are beginning to value regional autonomy and peace, often compromised in their previous search for external protection. This awareness is leading on the one hand to important modification of attitudes and strategies within the great power nexus and on the other hand to a realization by the medium and smaller powers that they must put an end to historic animosities that account for the dominance of the big powers. It was not a mere coincidence that just when Richard Nixon, Leonid Brezhnev, and Chou En-lai were laying the basis of a new balance of power, Willy Brandt and Indira Gandhi were striving to achieve durable peace in Europe and the Indian subcontinent respectively. Indeed, it is worth noting that in calling upon Indian and Pakistani opinion for a lasting solution to 25 years of national strife, Mrs. Gandhi pointedly referred to how the European countries were seeking to achieve peace and cohesion despite a long history of conflict and enmity. About the same time as the Indo-Pakistani summit agreement of Simla was made public came the news of the move for reunification of Korea. In both cases, the parties involved pledged to resolve outstanding issues bilaterally and to keep all others out. Although, in neither case, this resolve has been fully carried out, there have been important developments that hold out a promise of stable peace in the respective regions. Soon after these events came the dramatic developments in the Middle East where, after a long period of stalemate imposed by the big powers, the Arabs took initiative to force a settlement that was at once in keeping with their self-respect and sensitive to the realities of the region. The Middle Eastern situation is, of course, full of ambivalence, and the countries involved will not find it easy to shake off foreign interference; indeed, this may become more difficult given the *détente* between the two giants and the high politics of securing oil supplies. But a major step has been taken which is likely to have far-reaching consequences, with implications that go beyond the Middle East, shaking the complacency of the present framework of dominance, and through a dialectical process, enabling the world to be more truly interdependent. The same dialectic will strengthen the long-standing peace movement within Israel and the general desire among the Arab countries to work out an honourable way to end the state of siege in their regions, just as the war in Bangla Desh hastened the process of national and regional autonomy in South Asia. On the whole, there is evidence of growing prospects for peace in the strife-torn regions of the world based on efforts from within those regions, though it has not yet become decisive in shaping national policies.

Accent on Autonomy

A desire is growing also to end the state of dependence that the present world system entails and to secure autonomy and self-reliance for national political communities. The long and heroic struggle of the Vietnamese people in the face of the world's mightiest military machine and the mobilization of opinion round the world in support of that struggle, the establishment of an independent Bangla Desh despite the cynical support given by important world powers to one of history's worst genocides, the emergence of new centres of power in China, Japan, Western Europe, India, in the Middle East with its new found sense of power, and even parts of Eastern Europe and Latin America, which have long been regarded as backyards of the two superpowers, and the desire for regional integration among the countries of East and West Africa, Latin America, and Indo-China with a view to achieving political and economic self-sufficiency are all indications of the prefer-ence for autonomy and dignity among nations. This is in sharp con-trast to the earlier atmosphere of trading off national independence for a few crumbs of aid or promise of security against one's own neigh-bours and often against one's own people. There is a strong wind of creative nationalism blowing over the Third World as well as in parts of the other two worlds, including in such citadels of the erstwhile bipolar system as Canada in the West and Rumania in the East. In the mood that is spreading over these nations, progress towards world peace and a stable world order is closely linked with the struggle for national autonomy and equality among states.

Search for a New Model

In part reflecting the desire for national autonomy and in part re-sponding to the inequitable consequences of the modernization model, there is also emerging a new social perspective among some of the elites and intellectuals of the poor and underdeveloped countries. It is slowly dawning on them that the prevailing model of technology may prove to be more a curse than a boon for countries where a rapidly rising popu-lation and growing numbers of poor and unemployed call for a differ-ent technological package. Similarly, the kind of urbanization, higher education, and mass communications that have come in the wake of Western technology have resulted in a high degree of centralization and led to a wide chasm between the elite and the people. The need, in-stead, is to evolve new forms of differentiation that would promote a wide diffusion of capacities and greater measure of autonomy and self-sufficiency among human beings and human communities. These values and emphases are leading to a critical evaluation of policies and a vague realization of the need for institutional reforms.

Sense of Crisis

Providing strong support to such concerns and a reforming mood is a growing sense of world crisis among literally thousands of people living in the more prosperous parts of the world. Some of these occupy fairly influential positions in various societies and include outstanding sci-entists, intellectuals, administrators and men of affairs. These men and women are not just visionaries; they know that a crisis of major propor-tions is brewing in their midst and calls for concerted action at various levels. Such a sense of crisis is not simply a result of an objective under-standing of the dangers of war, overcrowding, and ecological breakdown that lie ahead; to a considerable extent it is due to the mood and behaviour of thousands of men and women belonging to the younger generation in the richer countries. Full of despair and a sense of futility, alienated from their own societies, and craving for new values and a sense of significance for themselves, these young men and women have raised a different kind of protest than we have been used to, in the process shaking Occidental civilization from its complacency and arrogance. By now many of these youth movements are on the decline in the West, thanks to the enormous staying power and both open repression and institutionalized coercion of the existing structures. Repelled by the "system" and its decadence, many among the young and the idealists have started working at a micro level, seeking to set up new kinds of communities and novel experiments in social and political engineering. But both the earlier movements of dissent and the more recent evidence of withdrawal from the dominant culture have sensitized the thinking strata of the world to the inadequacies of the present system and its underlying values. One can build on the trends just identified.

Alternative Perspective

If we take a broad look at the process of history over the last few centuries, we notice two major and divergent civilizational thrusts that characterize various societies: one that is positivist, manipulative, expansionist and man-centred whose essential aim is the creation of an ideal and perfect social order; and the other based on a view of life and its purpose which seeks to subdue the will to power, considers all life as sacrosanct, and has as its ideal the achievement of individual autonomy and self-realization rather than the perfection of a social order. The former derives its strength from the Hellenic-Judeo-Christian tradition (from which Islam also derived its credo) whereas the inspiration for the latter comes from the ancient civilizations of the East and the rich diversity of tribal cultures in Africa. The real failure of the second group over the centuries has been that those who held to such a worldview were not able to fulfill the necessary materialistic urges and needs of man; they failed, for example, to erect a political order that could withstand the massive external pressure that followed the Industrial Revolution and its colonial expansion. To these societies can now be added the large number of countries from Latin America that suffer from a serious identity problem arising in part from their religious affiliations but also from a growing realization that the game is lost if they continue to ape the West. The dilemma all these societies face is that not until they assert their political autonomy (their *power*), erect viable states, and handle the problems posed by modern science and technology in terms of their own needs can they give new life to the best in their own traditions. The autonomy and self-realization of the individual in those societies vitally depends on the autonomy of the state in which he lives, for only it can deal with forces of dominance that have been let loose during the past few centuries.

From this general diagnosis of contemporary reality follows our preferred model of a world order, a model informed by the values we seek to realize. To secure maximum autonomy and freedom for the individual, to enable political communities to reach minimum plateaus of economic welfare and social justice, and to minimize the degree of international violence, we have to admit three different levels of goal-fulfilment—the individual level, the national level, and the world level—into our scheme of things. To achieve both the autonomy of men and satisfactory states of community and fellow feeling among them, it is necessary to provide greater autonomy to individual states, a majority of which are at present not autonomous. At the same time there is need to find solutions to problems of production and distribution, choice of technology, prevention of both international and internal violence, and containment of the deleterious consequences of economic growth and consumption patterns that are increasingly becoming worldwide in scope and ought to be treated as such.

Thus the attitudes engendered by our guiding perspective are some-what different from those that move either the establishment intellectuals committed to modernizing the world in the image of Western technological civilization or the anti-establishment intellectuals from the same centres who are roaming the world after the fashion of new missionaries and preaching revolution. Both these sets of propagandists are moved by theories of predetermined change that provide little scope for alternative futures based on autonomous choices and diverse perspectives. We are motivated, on the contrary, to build autonomy, freedom, well-being, and justice *at a number of levels* so that ordinary men and women can realize these values. Neither the vision of an overriding world government in the image of some transcendental ideology nor the hope that a once-and-for-all smashing operation can do away with all encumbrances holds any attraction for us. Perhaps our approach comes from an ancient civilization seeking to reorder its elements on the basis of a new consciousness, seeking actively to realize preferred values through a series of challenges and encounters in the real world.

Model for the Future

Our preferred world is one in which the individual enjoys *autonomy* for his self-realization and creativity—what is generically known as freedom. This is our principal value. So we can move toward such a world, several other values have to be simultaneously pursued. First, the primary condition of freedom is sheer survival, a protection against violence—local, national and international violence, as well as violence tending toward either annihilation of the properties of life or toward a deadening uniformity of all forms of behaviour and social structure. Both the needs of survival and diversity may thus be subsumed under the value of *non-violence.* Second, all men ought to be able to liberate themselves from economic deprivation and misery, irrespective of their ethnic or national origin or their social status. For this to become possible, it will be necessary to achieve as much equality among human beings as is necessary for the realization of common goals. Operationally, this may be translated into the value of *justice* through which both the formulation and the implementation of common goals are to be evaluated. Third, the individual should be able (to the extent he wants) to *participate* in making decisions that affect his life; he must be a member of a functioning democracy in which he not only can exercise choices between given alternatives of policies and leadership at various levels but also can exercise initiative in making new decisions and persuading others of the desirability of certain community actions. The democracy in which he lives will be neither just an institutionalized scheme of competition between limited alternatives that are predecided by small elites (as is the case in most liberal democracies) nor some version of democratic centralism (as is found in most socialist regimes) but contain sufficient scope for personal initiative at different levels and in different sectors of life.

Alongside the values of autonomy, nonviolence, justice, and participation, there is need to ensure a larger ethic of behaviour that we may call the ethic of self-control. Our preferred world should not be a consumption society, aggressive in the cultivation of ever growing wants, destroying nature and ravaging land, plants, and the nonhuman species, and dehumanizing social relationships. In such a world there should not only be a *minimum* standard of material living for all but also a *maximum* beyond which resources must be transferred, first to those that have not yet achieved the minimum, and after everyone has achieved it or a tolerable multiple of it, to the production and consumption of nonmaterial goods. The notion of a constantly rising material condition that men and nations are aspiring to achieve everywhere is not a utopia but in reality a disutopia. A better standard of life in our preferred world will be measured in terms of not only material standards but also cultural and ethical standards. This involves limiting of wants, restraining artificial stimulation of needs, and making it possible for the individual to realize his potentiality through a combination of autonomy and self-control, an experience of unity with and obligation towards other beings and species, and a general disposition not to make excessive demands on either nature or organized society.

Changes from the Present

It can be seen that the principal stumbling block to achieving these conditions of life is not the absence of some centralized world authority but rather the present structures of dominance and inequality in the world that compromise the autonomy of individual states. Our preferred world would do away with this inequality and this dominance, or at least bring them within limits. Individual political units in the world ought to move towards a state of autonomy and a condition of equality. This involves two kinds of strategies, one to devise political instruments for a struggle against inequality and dependence in the world, and the other to develop and operate institutions at the world level to facilitate the same goals.

Regional Integration

As long as the less powerful and poorer nations of the world remain disunited and willing to be drawn into the vortex of big-power politics, there seems to be little chance of achieving real autonomy for them. There is need to join forces, declare collective goals, and confront the existing managers of world politics with a sound strategy of action for changing the terms on which relations between states are based. It is necessary to start organizing along regional lines and engage in a federalizing process in these regions, beginning with economic unions and gradually leading into a more comprehensive process of integration. There is need to make the number and diversity of nation states more rational and manageable and conducive to the values stated earlier. In our preferred world we would like a smaller number of nations (or "communities" of nations), and each large and efficient enough in carrying out economic and political functions to realize the twin conditions of autonomy and equality that we have postulated. As this would also make for near-equal representation at the world level, the various world-level institutions would operate in a truly participant manner, avoiding the present situation in which the existence of a plethora of diverse and atomized political units can be manipulated to serve the interests of a narrow oligarchy of power.

Instruments of Autonomy

The second aspect of the preferred world is the nature of the institutional system beyond the nation state. As we see it, there should be a complex of institutions geared to the promotion of autonomy and equality among both individual national units and individual residents of these units. These institutions are to be viewed not as parts of some monolithic world authority but, rather, as catering to diverse *functional* needs that transcend existing boundaries and call for larger, more united, efforts.

1. There should be a set of functional authorities of a multi-state kind dealing with technical and welfare needs of the world population that build upon the structures that have already emerged—e.g. in health, communications, transportation—but extending much further with a view to eliminating gross inequalities in access to technology, in means of production, and in the relationship between land and living beings. These institutions should, subject to the agreement of the states concerned, plan and undertake economic enterprises in the less developed regions and be backed by sufficient resources to balance and counter monopolistic corporations.

2. There should be regional and world political structures in which all the nations of the world are represented that will provide the technical and welfare bodies—which should be the core of the worldwide institutional drive—with sanctions and resources. Thus, in our preferred world model, while the institutions of a participant democracy will function mainly within national communities, they will also be significantly supplemented at higher levels.

3. There should be regional as well as world-level specialized agencies for dealing with functions whose scope extends beyond existing states, such as resource planning, development of new—as well as some old and wholesome—energy sources, ecology, and population and migration policies. These agencies should promote research on alternatives to the present technoeconomic model, communicate the results of this research widely, and bring authoritative pressures on national governments to carry out agreed-upon measures.

4. There should be a world security system that will at once restrain the growing militarization of the world and act as a catalyst for a

significant transfer of resources from the war industry located in the technologically advanced regions to both defence and development of the vulnerable regions so as to minimize conditions of violence in these regions. There should be at the disposal of the world body a world armed force, small in size on a continuous basis but expandable when the need arises, such as to curb genocidal acts of violence as occurred in Vietnam, Bangla Desh, and Mozambique, by calling upon countries who have demonstrated their commitment to the values of peace and justice to contribute their forces, as was done in the Congo crisis in 1960.

5. There should be a set of institutions designed to protect human rights and standards of justice wherever these are violated. This should include a high-powered World Court of Justice to which are organically linked an authoritative Council of World Jurists and an active Commission for Human Rights, both equipped with appropriate secretariats and regional field agencies.

Apart from these basic structures, there will, of course, be need to strengthen and develop various institutions at the regional and multiregional levels to perform functions whose logical locus is beyond the national unit—both preventive functions (such as against environmental destruction) and promotional functions (such as diffusion of information and sharing of scientific and technological research). The purpose of such institutions should be to neutralize economic and political structures that prevent the growth of genuine autonomy and self-reliance in political and economic spheres among the different states of the world. As argued above, there is need for the invention of new kinds of institutions on a continuous basis which respond to a fast changing—and endangered—world without undermining deeply laid loyalties and solidarities. Only thus can still wider loyalties, extending to the species as a whole, emerge and a just and nonviolent world be brought into being.

Autonomy and Integration

Thus, as we conceive of the world in the year 2000, we visualize a system in which the autonomy of the national political community is both retained and in the case of the large number of dependent nations considerably augmented. The impact of this autonomy will, however, be in part supplemented and in part countered by (1) a reduction in the number of sovereign units comprising the world community, enabling each of them to have a minimum size of population, territory and natural resources, as well as enough diversity of culture and of material and scientific skills, and (2) an authoritative complex of world institutions that will prevent exploitation and dominance. The world political system will thus, in its operating ethos as well as in its institutional structure, function at both global and national levels, with appropriate intermediate levels built into the system. Finally, while we place high value on the autonomy of each of the constituent political units, we hope that (thanks largely to the environment created by the spread of new values) there will be consensus among these units in at least one respect, namely, in the admission of individual survival, worth and autonomy as the final end of social organization and hence in the desirability of having participant structures at various levels of the world social reality. Justice and nonviolence, the other two values of such a world, will follow as behavioural components of this fundamental consensus on the value of autonomy.

The Domestic Level

For the kind of world we prefer, it is clear that appropriate processes and structures for the realization of our world order values will have to be evolved within domestic political systems as much as, and perhaps sooner than, within the international system. Few will deny that man's attempt to devise rational modes of government and justice has far to go even at micro-levels, let alone in evolving more inclusive structures of autonomy and justice in the world.

In the model we are proposing, national political communities will have to provide for the following essential conditions:

1. Institutions for optimum participation by people at different levels.

2. Commitment to principles of equality of all men and women, a minimum standard of welfare for all that includes the lowest deciles of the economic structure, and a maximum beyond which no one should be allowed to go, both for reasons of equity and for reasons of limiting the adverse effects of high incomes.

3. A balance between enlightened initiatives (based on a total perspective) of central authority and decentralized structures of decision-making, planning, and participation.

4. A fundamental obligation that the state and the various units within it should preserve human rights, violation of which should lead to legitimate intervention, certainly by the national central authority where it is enlightened enough to recognize its obligations, but failing that and in cases of mass violation of human

rights (to be decided by agreed upon information and intelligence agencies), by regional and world agencies as outlined above.

Economic Model

This brief statement of objectives to guide the national and subnational levels of the future world order needs to be spelled out in considerable detail, for which there is no space here. But two subjects may be commented upon a little more, for they have relevance to both domestic and world-level policies. The economic model entailed in our preferred world will need to move from the present *growth-based model* aimed at an aggregate production target to a *need-based model* defined by the principles of individual autonomy, social justice, and political community from which no one is excluded. This change will call for a revision of a whole lot of basic perspectives that have guided the model of industrialization that seems to have been accepted by intellectual and political elites in large parts of the world, for instance in respect to rural-urban ratios, economies of scale, and choice of technologies. It will give much more importance to small rural as against large metropolitan units, to minimum satisfaction levels as against constantly expanding consumption standards and the growth of a parasitic urban middle class, and to a policy of transfer of resources from developed to underdeveloped regions, classes, and ethnic groups within nations.

Size of Units

The second subject is the problem of the preferable size of units, an issue relevant to both domestic and world considerations. As we perceive it, national political units ought to be federal in character, combining the advantages of both large and small size. Our own preferred model is for somewhat large national communities composed of (1) small subnational units arranged along two or three levels vertically (states, districts, communes, or the like), each enjoying a measure of self-government, and (2) a large number of autonomous groups horizontally that are by definition self-governing. Within the national polity it is necessary to maximize participation, social justice, and economic development as a means of providing a fair deal to all, and a nonviolent mode of managing and absorbing conflicts and tensions. All this is best achieved if the constituent states or provinces of a nationstate are compact, single language units, characterized by ease of travel and communication and are dynamic enough to minimize elite-mass distance and facilitate a circulation of elites and counterelites.

On the other hand, the advantages of larger scale will be ensured by the total size of the national federal community being large.

Structure of World Order

In our preferred world we consider the structural issues of optimum size and diversity somewhat important. We prefer our model of 20 to 25 nation-states to the present more than 130 nation-states of highly unequal sizes and productive and power potentials or the alternative models of either five regional superstates or 500 mini-states. We prefer our model of size and number for a variety of reasons. First, as distinct from goals of participation and justice within nations, we would like to fulfill the goals of optimum distribution of power and minimal violence in the dealings between nations. Of course as already indicated, it is neither feasible nor desirable to have the various federalized units of equal size or uniform in any other respect (one is not building a system from the world level down but from the national level upward) but we would like them to be at least *comparable* in one or more of several ways—territorial size, population, productive potential, and cultural diversity—so as to ensure a measure of equality and respect for each other's integrity while still retaining considerable diversity in culture, politics, and social development.

Second, from the perspective of two or three decades from now— not a very distant future—the aim should be to minimize the dominance of a few powers, as is the case now, for this would militate against our operational values of justice and nonviolence. The model of a very large number of states would so weaken the national units that the world order would be kept going either through continued domination of the poor and weak countries by the rich and strong or by passing on substantial functions to some centralized world state. On the other hand, the model of just five or six states or regions can work only on the lines of the pre-First World War theory of a balance of power, in which periodic wars were an essential ingredient. We reject both these as undesirable. Twenty to twenty-five is a large enough number not to degenerate into a balance of power situation, but not so large a number as to permit domination of a colonial type. It should be remembered (from what has just been proposed) that whereas in our model we mean to develop world institutions performing substantial welfare, judicial, and security functions, we do not wish to underrate the reality of *power* in the world setting even of the year 2000.

What we are proposing is not entirely new. Various models of federation have already been proposed within Latin America, the Middle

East, East and West Africa, and South East Asia, in each case for the purpose of augmenting regional power equations (both political and economic). There are, of course, still many hurdles to face—psychological identity, the vested interests of existing elites, and the present system of alliances and balances engendered by the big powers. Considered, however, with other parts of the model proposed here, the proposal is not too fantastic to put into effect.

Like all other designs of a preferred world, these proposals are likely to be modified as different elements of the model are brought in touch with reality. We are convinced, however, that some restructuring of the present political map of the world is a necessary condition for realizing our values, though of course it will make sense only as part of a series of interrelated measures designed to promote the value of autonomy.

The model of a preferred world presented here is of a not-too-centralized system, with considerable autonomy for individual political units to pursue many functions, but balanced by an institutional complex on the world level whose principal function is to correct world imbalances in technology, resources, and political power and hence to enable national units to enjoy real autonomy and freedom. The model attempts on the one hand to prevent interactions whose outcomes are harmful—dominance, exploitation, violence—and on the other hand to respond to needs and demands of individuals and communities the world over. But it is still a limited institutional system, leaving a great deal to voluntary and community efforts at various levels and leaving the individual autonomous to pursue his own ends. The vision that inspires us in this whole exercise is not one of a perfected social and political order where everyone falls in line and efficiency is the principle criterion but rather of a state of creative anarchy in which there is scope for diversity and the pursuit of life as perceived by individuals and their place in nature and in the cosmos. If we have not dwelt at length on these wider issues, it is because we are constructing a model for the 1990s and not indulging in a free utopia without the constraints of time.

Transition to the Preferred World

There remains the question of how to move towards the preferred world as outlined here. The relevant strategies follow from our model, which is not just a statement of values but includes structural and institutional properties. In what follows, we shall spell out the essential steps that are needed.

Process of Consolidation

First, it seems clear that the next 20 to 25 years should see increasing independence and consolidation among the presently dependent or politically and economically weak states. As this happens, and the struggle over world resources—a sizeable proportion of which is located in these states—grows with the affluent nations trying to retain their lifestyles and the poor nations realizing how important these resources are for themselves, there is likely to be growing conflict between the former and the latter. This will happen despite the process of multipolarity based on the emergence of new world powers. We do not share the faith of several analysts of international affairs that multipolarity by itself will produce a better world. For this process is by and large limited to the great powers and potential great powers. While the movement from the neatness of bipolarity to the complicated cobweb of multipolarity may provide a good basis for restructuring world politics in favour of those outside the great-power nexus, it will not necessarily ensure either political autonomy or economic self-reliance for them. The need is to make the most of the changing context of world politics. While the major thrust of the last few decades has been an institutionalization of the process of dominance, the structure that was created to maintain it is no longer viable. The next few decades are likely to witness a new direction being given to nationalism within the Third World based on an urge towards achieving greater autonomy and a desire to provide strength to it through new economic policies.

Solidarity

Two broad strategies are called forth: transcontinental solidarity and regional cooperation within the various continents. There is need for the poorer nations to reaffirm their solidarity by finding a new and effective instrument than what was tried at Bandung and Belgrade. These earlier efforts had to be given up in part because of wide differences of approach among these countries and in part because of the permeation of great power rivalries into the regions of the Third World. Since then there has been greater appreciation of the need to prevent great-power infiltration, but there seems to be still little chance of evolving a full-fledged association of African, Asian, and Latin American states as an instrument of world change. There is, however, a greater chance of moving along the following directions.

1. There is need for closer consultations among the nonaligned countries in these continents with the aim of influencing world politics

more systematically than has been the case till now. The Algiers Conference and its follow-up through the efforts of President Tito, Mrs. Gandhi and some of the Arab leaders in the wake of the role of the big powers after the war in the Middle East are good beginnings in this direction. But the politics of the "oil crisis" also brought forth the inequitous consequences for the Third World countries—unless they acted in concert.

2. It follows that the socioeconomic solidarity among the Third World countries should be made more durable and more institutionalized, on the basis of the present (now expanding) Group of 77 within UNCTAD, the main aim being not political trade-unionism but an exertion of economic pressure in international forums.

3. There is need for a greater coordination of policies among the Third World states in the United Nations and various international agencies for influencing economic and social policies, fighting for human rights in the remaining vestiges of imperialism like South Africa, Rhodesia, the Portuguese colonies, and Indochina, pressing for internationalization of new resources such as the seabeds and outer space over which the great powers are seeking to extend their control, and mobilizing opinion for structural reforms of the United Nations and adequate representation of the populous but poor continents of the world in UN bodies.

Regionalism

Second, there is need for much greater regional cooperation among the various small and weak countries of the world, pooling their economic, political, and military resources, collectively redressing their individual isolation and weaknesses, entering the world power structure on that basis, and ultimately upsetting the system through which a handful of states are able to dominate the world. Such regional cooperation, on which many of the nationalist leaders in the Third World countries had pinned their faith at one time, has met with serious problems so far arising from the region based policies of the great powers, the mutual fears and conflicts of interest among states located in the different regions, and the fact that many of these countries have had stronger ties with imperial centres of the world than with other countries in their regions. But the most important impediment to regional consolidation has been the successful penetration of the great powers in the various regions through military alliances, economic aid, and political corruption. These states are gradually becoming aware that their cooptation into big-power politics in this way has only turned them into client states, pitched them into an unnecessary rivalry with neighbours with whom they have much in common, and exposed them to a state of perpetual tension with consequent neglect of real tasks at home. This awareness is likely to spread as the regimes propped up by outside powers are brought down and new elites closer to the people and in tune with the culture of their lands come to power. These new elites are likely to value regional cooperation as a means of consolidating their individual independence and promoting the autonomy of the region.

Federalization

There is need to galvanize this awareness into a series of institutional moves, starting with general regional political settlements that provide for mutual consultation and affirm the need to keep out other powers, moving towards comprehensive trade and cultural agreements, and then by stages towards economic unions, loose confederational forms in which certain functions like communications, defense, and international trade are delegated to a centre, and finally a genuinely federal state incorporating the various regional units into a single juridical entity that can still retain considerable internal dispersal of power.

We have already outlined our model of a smaller number of larger states as a means to span the present wide gaps in power and resources and counter the prevailing patterns of dominance and inequality in the world. We are convinced that without such a territorial restructuring of the world, the ability of human collectivities to attain autonomy and dignity for themselves and their citizens will be limited to a few large states—if that. The alternatives that face the large number of small states of the world are either to accept a neo-Hobbesian solution in which they surrender their autonomy to a great power or a concert of great powers that in turn would ensure security to all and provide resources for their development from a centralized system or to attain self-reliance and autonomy on the basis of political associations of adequate strength on the one hand and participation in world politics on the basis of such consolidated power on the other.

If the choice is the latter course, these states should strive their utmost to resolve internal differences and jealousies based on now wholly irrelevant historical animosities and move towards a political integration that, while respecting cultural plurality, derives strength from the need to forge a sense of regional nationalism and common destiny. At the present time only the stronger states in the world have shown initiative in forging such solidarities as found in the economic integration of Western European states and in the alliances represented by NATO and COMECON treaties, which have over time become more than mere military arrangements. The need for such integration is much greater among the states of Southeast Asia, South Asia, Latin America, the Middle East, Eastern and Western Africa, and the West Indies, if they are ever to acquire a sense of autonomy and undertake a concerted plan for the well-being of their peoples. Many of these regions include units with different levels of development, thus providing scope for a pooling of complementarities in economic, technological, administrative, and other spheres and for ending dependence on the aid and knowhow provided by the metropolitan centres, whose technological and institutional models are not really relevant to the poorer regions.

Decentralization

These steps will not be easy to take in many of the world's regions. One main reason for this will be the fear that the larger and more developed and cohesive units among these regions—India in South Asia, Indonesia in Southeast Asia, Egypt in the Middle East, Brazil and Argentina in Latin America, Nigeria in West Africa, Tanzania in East Africa—will dominate the regional federations. It will be necessary to deal with this fear in two ways, first by showing that even such dominance is to be preferred to dominance by a big power whose global considerations allow little regard for local aspirations and second by permitting in the regional federations considerable internal decentralization and diversity in socioeconomic and cultural policies. The alternative to this kind of an arrangement is a permanent state of economic and political dependence. The model of territorial reconstruction that we have therefore proposed provides a crucial component of the over-all model of a world order based on the values of autonomy, justice, and nonviolence.

Institutional Structure

Region-based federations also provide a step towards the ultimate emergence of world federal institutions to which certain functions can be devolved by the constituent political units. We are not interested in moving towards a centralized world system of government, as we are convinced that it would result in a violation of our basic values. We do, however, visualize a further development of institutional structures, beyond regional federations, that have the express objective of promoting justice and a fair distribution of resources, restraining powerful states and adventurist regimes from violating the freedom and rights of human beings, and ensuring the preservation of nature against undue encroachment by human agencies. The following institutional devices may be appropriate.

1. The Economic and Social Council (ECOSOC) appears to us to provide a good nucleus for the principal executive organ of the United Nations. Until the world territorial map is restructured into 20 to 25 states along the lines we have suggested, the present ECOSOC, which had until recently about that strength (27) but has lately been doubled (54), may be treated as the authoritative organ for decision-making at the world level. It should continue to be an organ of the General Assembly but should function with considerable autonomy because it is in the area of development that a truly global effort needs to be mounted. ECOSOC should be entrusted with substantial resources for carrying out its functions of social and economic development and reduction of world disparities. Apart from receiving contributions from member states in proportion to their GNPs, it should be entrusted with collecting taxes from users of international facilities like merchant ships and civilian aircraft calling at foreign ports and airports as well as commercial satellites and space vehicles, expatriated profits of foreign business corporations and incomes of multinational corporations, and royalties from new sources of wealth not under the domain of any state such as ocean beds and outer space.

As for taking on new functions, the ECOSOC should plan and undertake economic enterprises of a multinational kind in the developing regions, subject to the agreement of the states concerned, counter monopolistic tendencies let loose by the multinational corporations in that way, and take on substantial roles in resource planning, development of new energy sources, migration and ecological policies, and food conservation for assisting scarcity ridden areas anywhere in the world, all of these being functions whose scope extends beyond existing states.

2. The General Assembly may continue to be the world body that represents national governments (as distinct from national legislatures or the people) and to which ECOSOC reports its decisions, with the additional provision that any matter decided by a majority in both ECOSOC and the General Assembly should be considered obligatory on all other organs of the United Nations and on all member states.

3. As a step towards greater federalization of world political processes, a World Parliamentary Assembly (WPA) may be constituted. Its main function should be to act as a forum for discussing

various issues facing different regions as well as the world as a whole, articulating legitimate demands of different regional and cross-regional social groups, and generally promoting greater understanding of diverse points of view. The Parliamentary Assembly should consist of representatives from various national legislatures (or their equivalents). While we do not stipulate proportional representation for sending delegates to the WPA, a convention may be gradually promoted that each national delegation should include members belonging to opposition parties (or, in single-party states, other nongovernmental groups).

The Parliamentary Assembly can recommend measures to ECOSOC and the General Assembly for action. In the beginning we do not envisage any decision-making role for this body, whose main function is to sensitize representative political groups from different regions to each other's problems and viewpoints. We also do not stipulate that the General Assembly or any other executive organ of the United Nations should be accountable to the Assembly. We do not think such a jump in institutional restructuring is yet called for. As the world territorial system gets restructured into large units, greater equality in power and political status is achieved, and the present climate of fear and distrust gives place to greater confidence in world bodies, it should be possible to endow the Parliamentary Assembly with more substantial powers. In the absence of these conditions such a step is likely to prove abortive.

4. ECOSOC should be assisted by a number of agencies that can furnish requisite information, administrative expertise, and specialized action. We propose the establishment of technical commissions for such subjects as interregional planning and economic development, human rights, world population and immigration, science and technology, and human environment and ecology. Each commission should be provided with adequate staff and resources for undertaking studies, formulating targets, and recommending actions to ECOSOC and its subcommittees.

5. The various specialized agencies that are currently rendering considerable services should be continued and strengthened. Examples are ILO, PAO, ICAO, WHO, IMCO, ITU, UNESCO, and UNDP. Regionally based commissions should also be strengthened and their efforts gradually coordinated with the efforts of various governments at regional cooperation and federalization. Similarly, the present institutional structure for dispensation of justice may be strengthened by the setting up of a high-powered World Court of Justice, which should have the power to intervene in cases of genocide and gross violation of

63

human rights on recommendation of the Council of World Jurists and the Commission on Human Rights, which should both be institutionalized as regular parts of the organization of justice at the world level.

6. In the area of minimizing interstate violence and containing the arms race, we would suggest two steps. First, there should be at the disposal of the world body an armed force that is small in normal times but expandable when serious violence breaks out by calling upon countries that have a proven record of peace and neutrality to contribute to it. Second, there should be set up a high-powered Commission on Disarmament to initiate and supervise negotiations between states on various aspects of disarmament. The function of such a commission, which should consist of outstanding scientists and international civil servants, cannot be anything more than that of a catalyst. For we do not believe that much progress in disarmament is possible as long as the big powers continue to balance each other and themselves against the rest of the world. Indeed, the chances are that as long as wide gaps in political and strategic power exist the arms race will continue; there will also be greater proliferation of nuclear armaments, the nonproliferation treaty notwithstanding. Once the world territorial order is restructured on the lines suggested in our model, on the other hand, considerable progress towards disarmament will be possible. Until then one can only hope that the slow-moving negotiations on SALT will make some progress and that the emergence of new power centres and the possibility of nuclear proliferation will force the two superstates to come forward before world bodies with a satisfactory plan for disarmament.

7. The same argument holds for the Security Council whose present composition defies the principle of equality of states to which the UN is committed. We do not believe any reform in its composition is possible—the most "revolutionary" of all states is now part of the system—until the effective distribution of power in the world changes. This change depends on the success of the federalization process envisaged in our territorial model or of a workable alternative to it.

Political Process

Indeed, even the prospects of the transitional institutional arrangements here proposed will depend crucially on changes in the structure of world politics. The countries of the Third World—or rather those among them that value their autonomy—have to take initiative in this regard. It is for them to unsettle the existing world status quo affecting them. It is not only compromising their integrity as states through a highly institutionalized system of political stratification; it is doing so essentially by relegating them to a position of marginality in the techno-economy of the world; this in turn will concentrate poverty and social tension in their lands and subject them to continuous internal crises.

The international status quo, that is in a way the source of such a linkage pattern extending into domestic political systems, is once again becoming stabilized after a period of disturbance due to the emergence of China. The much-talked-of trend towards multipolarity is likely to turn out to be another coopting and balancing operation, with the development of a complex system of limited adversity among pairs of great powers and joint hegemony of the same powers over the rest of the world and the United States lording over the whole system, thanks to its tremendous technological and economic superiority. For a quarter century now the United States has been the core of the international *status quo*. What it has been trying to achieve now is a rehabilitation of this core which had been successfully challenged by a series of encroachments—starting with the Soviet challenge in the fifties and continuing ever since with some dramatic setbacks in recent years thanks to Vietnam, Bangla Desh and the Arab resurgence. Behind the formula of the five power concert is a clever move to restore the hegemony of the United States. While the other four powers —the Soviet Union, China, Japan, Western Europe—understand this, they have at least for the time being decided to cooperate with the United States. The prospects for the rest of the world appear bleak if other countries continue to play proxy to this elaborate "balancing" game. It is only by calling a halt to external penetration and interference and cooperating among themselves to acquire sufficient strength to withstand such pressures that those in the periphery have any chance to challenge the dominance of the centre powers.

Disturbing the Status Quo

Let us make it clear that we have no illusion that the entire Third World can stand solidly against the dominant establishment of the world. It is too mixed a group with many conflicting interests, and not a few among them would rather hang on to one of the great powers. Neither do we consider it necessary or desirable for the peace and sanity of the world to mount an all-out confrontation against anyone. What we have in mind is at once more modest and feasible and in the long run more effective for moving towards a world based on the principles of autonomy and equality of states. The need is, on the one hand, for several small and medium-sized states located in the same

65

region to close their ranks, cooperate economically, and gradually move towards federalized unions and, on the other hand, for them to evolve institutionalized means of consultation and cooperation across regions, in world bodies, and in multilateral agencies dealing with economic and social matters. It is within this latter framework of the need for cooperation among the myriad nations of the outer world, relying as far as possible on natural complementarities and world agencies, that regional consolidations and acquisition of self-reliance on that basis become meaningful. At the same time it is also clear that without the latter type of consolidation and self-reliance the more comprehensive framework of cooperation will become difficult to evolve: small and atomized states, each riven by internal problems, will find it difficult to assert themselves in any unified manner.

In working out such a strategy those in the outer world who care to assert their autonomy and keep big-power politics from intruding into their regions will also find that the inner world is not that homogeneous and has enough conflicts of interest and ideology to work on. It should be remembered that in the disturbance of the bipolar structure China played a crucial role. Even if China has for the moment agreed to act in concert with other big powers, it may still—given its own past and its assessment of the future—turn into a crucial link between the inner and the outer worlds and to make the balance in the former a precarious one. With all its recent tactical compromises China (which has been closely associated for long with the nonaligned world) is "different," and it is not too much to hope that it will see virtue in continuing to be so. The Soviet Union also, still working on the strategy of making bipolarity (which is not yet dead, at least in the sphere of military technology and strategic relationships) more advantageous to itself than to the United States and fearful of the future Chinese colossus, can be counted upon to provide entry points for disturbing the balance of the inner world. In some respects the Soviet Union is even more available to Third World regions seeking autonomy from Western domination than is China, in part because it is still wedded to an anti-imperialist position in world politics (so is China but it has had to make a number of tactical compromises because of its deep suspicion of the Soviet Union), and in part because the Soviet Union knows that its standing in the major regions of the world depends more on political than on economic linkages. Its role in the European détente and in the South Asian and Middle Eastern crises has established it as a highly flexible actor in world politics which is willing to subject the big-power system to pressures from other centres of power, while still continuing to play a major role in that system.

There are other important points in the industrialized world from which considerable cooperation and understanding can be expected—Yugoslavia, which is the only European country that has for long identified itself with the nonaligned world; Sweden, which has shown a remarkable record of cooperation with the developing nations; Norway, which had the courage to decline membership in the EEC; Australia, whose location and recent capacity to think for itself instead of continuing to be an outpost of the Anglo-Saxon world has made it revise its policies toward Asia; Canada, which is itself going through a deep sense of being dominated by its giant neighbour and is, on the other hand, beginning to play an important role in the Commonwealth; even France which itself symbolized, under Charles de Gaulle, the search for autonomy within the Atlantic world (just as Yugoslavia did within Eastern Europe) and which is willing to support similar aspirations in other parts of the world. It would be shortsighted to lump the whole of the "developed world" as if it belonged to one camp.

Finally, new powers are emerging which by the end of the century will be quite strong and whose very emergence is based on asserting their autonomy and bringing to an end big power intrusion in their regions by a policy of working out durable areas of peace in their regions. The most important among these is India, but there are others on the horizon—Indo-China, which should before long become a single state, Indonesia, Nigeria, perhaps a more united Arab community. But Japan too, as it asserts its independence vis-à-vis the United States and if it uses its economic might with imagination (this might is not based on very stable foundations), can provide a suitable link with the "inner" world, at least for the Asian nations. So can Iran which has lately shown a refreshing capacity to think for itself. The issue in the case of countries like India, Japan and Iran concerns the choice they will make: between joining the big-power club and the *status quo* and becoming catalysts of major structural changes in world political and economic relationships; between political opportunism and an enlightened use of political opportunity. Much will depend on what is done in the next decade or so in economic cooperation and political consolidation in different regions and their ability to start reconstructing the political structure of the world.

Internal Consolidation

To a significant degree the answer to these questions will depend on the ability of the Third World countries to attend to their internal problems, move rapidly towards economic policies that will raise levels

67

of satisfaction, develop durable political structures that can integrate the many fragments of language, tribe, and religion into which their populations are divided, and contain turbulent elements by evolving appropriate structures of participation. There is a close linkage between success on these fronts internally and success in achieving autonomy externally. In making this linkage work the leaders and intellectuals of these countries will have to think for themselves and evolve solutions on the basis of critical choices of both goals and instrumentalities that are likely to be quite different from those adopted by the industrialized countries when they were developing.

Intellectual Movement

Complementarily to these efforts, it will be necessary to launch movements of effective counterforce within the dominant metropolitan powers themselves. By their nature these should be movements of intellectuals and scientists, moved by a consciousness of the injustices of contemporary reality and based on a mobilization of sufficient strength to upset the institutionalized concentration of power and resources in these countries. A number of these countries are highly authoritarian in their internal make-up, where the legal constitution has been undermined by the growth of military power and its global engagement. It will be necessary for radicals of the New Left variety to meet the crisis in their own countries before undertaking worldwide missions. If they succeed in shaking the dominant value systems and institutional arrangements within these societies out of their present smugness, they will have simultaneously contributed quite significantly to the removal of patterns of dominance and injustice in the world as a whole.

The chief concern that has guided us in this paper is the realization of the dignity and autonomy of men, and hence of states. Other values —justice, nonviolence, participation—follow from this basic concern. Our commitment to these values has led us to suggest certain steps that appear necessary to us. These involve integrative efforts as well as a greater scope for diversity and individuality. We have no great attraction to grandiose schemes based on some overriding world authority that would assure peace and prosperity for all. We do not believe in the absolute and unchanging autonomy of existing nation-states either, as is clear from this paper. In fact, we have argued for substantial changes from the present atomistic state of the world structure. But the purpose of these changes is to enhance and not to control man's autonomy, as well as the autonomy of a variety of political structures and cultural identities that man has found useful and that evoke sentiments of pride and affiliation in him. Given our cultural predisposition, we are averse to undue concentration of power, however noble the motivations of those who conceive of such concentration as a way to resolve human problems. The world has already learned at great cost that all such designs become insufferable leviathans in disguise.

THE REVOLUTION OF BEING

Gustavo Lagos

The Roots of the Revolution of Being: the Failure
of the Revolution of Having

A stratified international system has always existed, but it revealed itself in full force only after the Second World War. The emergence of
the Soviet Union and the United States as superpowers—far ahead of
the rest of the world in economic, scientific, and technological capacity,
in military strength and prestige—has generated an international
process of dependence and inferiority and resulted in a deterioration of
the real status of the other nations, termed *atimia*.[1] Atimia, when it
affects such world powers as Britain, France and Germany, it is partial;
when it affects other nations, especially the countries still termed
underdeveloped or developing, it is generalized or complete.

An analysis that portrays the system of international relations as
being stratified need not be derived only from the construction of abstract indicators to measure the real status of a country in terms of
economic, scientific, and technological power and military strength,
with their repercussions on national prestige. My first real appreciation
of the stratified international system grew out of personal encounters as
a Latin American and a Chilean participating in international meetings
and negotiations. These personal experiences, which became the psychological basis of my theory of atimia, had shown me that by the mere
fact of my belonging to an underdeveloped country and region of the
world, the characteristics of the real status of that country and that
region—dependence, a sense of inferiority, generalized atimia—were
somehow, consciously or subconsciously, transmitted and ascribed to
me. In other words, through an indefinable process, involving a sort of
irrational fatalism, the characteristics of the national-regional group to
which I had belonged from birth became my own. Nor am I alone in
this; in one way or another, the same thing has been felt and ex-

[1]See Gustavo Lagos, *International Stratification and Underdeveloped Countries* (Chapel
Hill: The University of North Carolina Press, 1963), especially pp. 24-30.

perienced by all Latin Americans who move or have moved in international life, whether in financial, business, or academic circles, or in any of its other manifold spheres of action.

This same feeling of atimia, which I and many other Latin Americans have experienced in the real-life encounters of the international stratified system, exists for many more human beings within their own countries. Latin American *national* elites become second-class citizens in the *international* area. But these national elites are surrounded within their own states by masses of second-class and third-class citizens, human beings who do not have the economic power to travel outside their country, much less the political power to represent their country internationally.

At the beginning of the second half of the twentieth century, within the framework of the United Nations, the concepts of development and underdevelopment made their appearance as a theoretical attempt to account in scientific terms for an appalling situation that is still smiting the conscience of the world. At last our region was discovering a "rational" explanation for poverty, dependence, privation—death in life.

At that time Latin America believed that by conquering underdevelopment it would attain the promised land. Development came to constitute a value in itself. Thanks to the demonstration effect, Latin America aspired to become a developed continent, in the likeness of the developed models already existing: Western Europe, the United States, Japan, and the socialist countries. To this end it needed technical, financial, and educational assistance from 'the models'.

The international economic structure, however, continued to maintain the pattern of exploiting centre and exploited periphery, thus widening the gap between rich and poor countries.

The figures are not exactly encouraging for our continent. A population of 270 million human beings, which is increasing at the whirlwind annual rate of 2.9 percent, has an annual gross national product that in 1969 averaged $450 per capita for the region as a whole. For comparative purposes, it should be noted that GNP per capita in 1969 was $4200 in the U.S., $2460 in France, and $1200 in the Soviet Union.[2]

The Latin American's expectation of life is 55 years, against 70 years for an inhabitant of the U.S., Europe, or the Soviet Union.

---

[2]These figures are taken from International Bank for Reconstruction and Development (IBRD) *World Bank Atlas* (population, per capita product, and growth rates), 1971. The estimate of GNP has a wide margin of error, mainly because of the problems involved in deriving it at factor cost from net material product and in converting the estimate into U.S. dollars.

Similarly, illiteracy figures in our countries average nearly 32 percent, against a percentage very little above zero in the industrialized countries.

With regard to the quality of diet, suffice it to say that the intake of a Latin American averages 2500 calories a day, whereas the corresponding average in the industrialized world is approximately 3500 calories.

These figures, so disheartening for our region, cannot be analysed without brief reference to the influence exerted on the foregoing process by the U.S., which is at present Latin America's principal hegemonic centre. This influence must be viewed in a historical perspective, as the region's contemporary problems have their roots in its past history.

Latin America was drawn into international relations as a result of the incorporation of its peoples in the colonial systems set up by Spain, Portugal, and other powers in the region. This colonialization was the starting-point for a situation of absolute dependence for Latin America that took the form of economic, political, and cultural domination.

This absolute colonial relationship was abruptly metamorphosed when our nations won their political independence. Spanish restrictions on trade between the colonies and the countries of Europe and the rest of America, already weakened by contraband, were abolished altogether and replaced by free trade. Thus Latin America opened its gates to the industrial progress of Europe and the U.S.

At that time Britain was witnessing the apogee of the Industrial Revolution, which convulsed the entire structure of commerce and production. This industrial phenomenon demanded new markets for British products, and it was in newly independent Latin America that a good many such markets were found.

By the time the Industrial Revolution had been consolidated in Britain in the mid-nineteenth century, British commercial, financial, and industrial capitalism had already penetrated Latin America. During the second half of the century its influence increased: British vessels carried a major share of cargo to and from Latin American ports; British capital was invested in railways, public utilities, and government securities; British banks issued credit at half the rate of interest charged by their competitors. London was the financial clearinghouse for international payments to exporters in the European countries and the U.S. against sales to Latin America.

While the Industrial Revolution was being consolidated in Britain, on the other side of the Atlantic development processes were brewing which were to convert the U.S. into a new centre of industrial and financial capitalism that would supersede Britain, its former metropolis. Once this objective had been attained, the U.S. made its presence inexorably felt in Latin America.

The new hegemonic centre constituted by the U.S. grew into an exporter of capital. The policy of trade expansion in world markets had emerged as the accepted doctrine for contending with the frequent depressions experienced in the U.S. economy. This notion had a profound and calamitous effect on U.S. foreign policy, helped to lay stress on the ideology of "Manifest Destiny", and led to an aggressive search for new markets and new investment opportunities in Latin America. This was the origin of the "Big Stick" policy, which implied the unbridled use of force for imperialistic purposes, as was demonstrated by the process that culminated in building the Panama Canal. This expansionist policy too was the origin of dollar diplomacy, which meant that U.S. bankers were made the instruments of ousting European interests in Latin America, not excepting the use of force whenever it seemed necessary or expedient.

In the course of time, the violence-oriented policies pursued by Latin America's new hegemonic centre underwent a gradual change of tone, thanks to the action of certain progressive statesmen in the U.S., and also in some measure to a belated stirring of consciousness on Latin America's part.

The Latin American countries began to demand, separately rather than collectively, a change in their relations with the U.S., and this objective was apparently attained with the establishment of successive inter-American policies. But all these endeavours ended in crashing failure, an outstanding case in point being that of the defunct Alliance for Progress, the most recent of the U.S. attempts to rectify its policy on Latin America.

A few statistics may help to give a clearer idea of the magnitude of Latin America's situation of dependence, in which the U.S. plays a primary role. These data, in Tables 1, 2 and 3 are so telling that no explanation is needed.

These were the reasons that the Chilean Minister of Foreign affairs, Gabriel Valdes, together with the Latin American ambassadors to the U.S., personally delivered to President Nixon on June 11, 1969, the Consenso de Vina del Mar, which had been adopted by CECLA the preceding May. In his introductory speech at the delivery ceremony, Mr. Valdes made this comment: "It is a generalized belief that our continent is receiving real aid in the financial field. Figures demonstrate just the contrary. We can really say that Latin America is

TABLE 1.
Movements of foreign capital in Latin America and income from it, 1950–1967.

	(Millions of dollars)		
	Inflows	Outflows	Balance
Movements of foreign capital:			
Direct investment	9.601.2	947.2	8.654.0
Medium-term and long-term loans	20.360.4	13.102.2	7.258.2
Compensatory loans	11.418.7	8.753.0	2.665.7
Net movement of foreign capital			18.577.9
Returns on foreign capital:			
Profits and dividends		18.430.6	
Interests on loans		5.751.3	
Total income		24.181.9	− 24.181.9
Balance of movement of foreign capital and income			− 5.606.2

Source: Data from the Economic Commission for Latin America (ECLA) and the International Monetary Fund (IMF), tabulated by researchers working on the subject of dependence in the Centre for Socio-Economic Studies (Centro de Estudios Socio-Economicos—CESO) of the Universidad de Chile.

TABLE 2.
Sources and uses of direct private United States investment in Latin America, 1960–1964.

	(Millions of dollars)
Sources:	
Profits	4.782
Depreciation and depletion	2.899
Funds obtained in Latin America	1.361
Funds from the U.S.	404
Total	9.446
Uses:	
Plant and equipment	3.567
Inventories	562
Receivables	993
Other assets	601
Distributed Profits	3.723
Total	9.446

Source: U.S. Department of Commerce, *Survey of Current Business,* November 1965.

TABLE 3.

Latin America: Exports, imports, and trade balances, by principal regions and countries, 1958-1968.

	Exports (f.o.b.)		Imports (c.i.f.)		Balance	
	1958	1968	1958	1968	1958	1968
United States	3.831	4.186	4.312	4.770	−481	−584
European Economic Community (founder members)	1.297	2.277	1.518	2.229	−221	+ 48
European Free Trade Association	926	1.094	833	1.157	+ 93	− 63
Western Europe	161	729	105	1.072	+ 56	−343
Japan	169	617	138	515	+ 31	+102
Latin America	762	1.368	898	1.535	−136	−167
Total	8.396	11.799	8.589	12.405	−193	−606

Source: ECLA, on the basis of official statistics.

contributing to financing the development of the United States and other industrialized nations."

The figures given likewise shed light on the role played by transnational corporations in the region. In Latin America there are more than 2000 subsidiaries of some 200 U.S. companies. From 1954 to 1967, direct exports of U.S. private capital to our region amounted to 3361 million dollars, the total profit earned was 12,403 million, and the amount repatriated was 10,839 million. It may also be added that 17 percent of the financing came from the U.S.

But the harmful effects of the transnational corporations are not only economic and social. What the figures do not make clear is that these gigantic entities constitute a threat to the sovereignty of the countries in which they are installed. The danger becomes even more acute in view of the inordinate degree of protection some governments—notably that of the U.S.—accord these private enterprises, which is reflected in all sorts of international pressures exerted by the mother country on any nation that dares to defy the private interests in question. In this connection, Cuba, Peru, and Chile have faced or are facing obstructive action on the part of the U.S. Nevertheless, it would be a mistake to impute the generalized crisis Latin America is currently experiencing simply and solely to unfair and arbitrary international structures.

According to some partial data, in several of the less developed Asian countries the existing inequalities are not as great as in Latin America.

These inequalities in our region have been summed up as follows by

UN experts. In terms of income strata the distinctive features of distribution in Latin America are the following: The highest income group has a much larger share of total income than in the industrialized countries; a correspondingly smaller proportion falls to the bulk of the population in the wide middle ranks of income distribution. The poorest groups and those immediately below the highest group receive proportions similar to those of the same groups in the industrialized countries.

The reader may perhaps be surprised to learn that the poorest groups in Latin America and in the industrialized countries are in much the same position in this respect. But the apparent contradiction vanishes when the study goes on to point out that the poorest groups differ greatly from one type of country to the other. In Latin America they are made up of active members of the labour force, whose place in the lowest income strata is permanent; in the industrial countries, on the other hand, a very low income is not for the most part a permanent state, and most of the groups concerned consist of "special cases," many of whom are not active members of the labour force.[3] Nevertheless there is always a lower income group frozen proportionately. The ratios of rich to poor in the U.S. have hardly changed, at least in this century. The U.S. has always had a powerful class structure and is a stratified system, but there is mobility of individuals within the system, which itself remains almost completely unaltered with respect to wealth.

Table 4 shows the respective shares of the various income groups in Latin America and the U.S.[4]

If we now take into account the fact that the GNP of the U.S. is $861,623 million, with a population of 203 million inhabitants, and the GNP of Latin America is $119,842 million, with a population of 266 million,[5] the conclusion to be drawn is abysmally depressing. The 5 percent group in the highest income bracket in the U.S. receives more in monetary terms than all the groups in Latin America put together; in other words, 10 million privileged inhabitants of the U.S. receive more than the entire Latin American population. Consequently, those who live in the industrialized world must realize that the inequality of income distribution is not merely an internal problem deriving from the

[3]We have based our analysis on the ECLA study *Income Distribution in Latin America* (UN publications, Sales No.: E.71.II.G.6).

[4]ECLA, *op. cit.,* p. 33.

[5]Data taken from the *World Bank Atlas, op. cit.*

TABLE 4.

Percent of National Wealth Belonging to Each Income Class
in U.S. and in Latin America.

Income group	Latin America		United States
Lowest 20 percent	3.1		4.6
30 percent below the median	10.3	80% population 37.5% wealth	18.8
30 percent above the median	24.1		31.1
15 percent below the top 5 percent	29.2	20% population 62.6% wealth	25.5
Top 5 percent	33.4		20.0

exploitation and domination existing within national societies, but also, and primarily, a problem deriving from the unfair, arbitrary, and abusive structures of international relations in the political and economic spheres, which have opened this gulf between income levels in the industrial countries and in countries of the Third World. This at least is the opinion of many prominent Latin American political leaders and social scientists.

In view of these tragic disparities, economic development has taken on the status of a value in itself. Our societies, as we have already said, have aspired to become developed countries. Only now are some Latin American intellectuals and leaders beginning to grasp the fact that development in the countries ranking highest in the stratified international system does not necessarily imply true wellbeing. Latin America must never fail to bear in mind the need to forestall the emergence of development models calculated to turn its countries into sheer copies of the more developed countries, capitalist or socialist, as such modelling signifies the creation of veritable culture media to breed the same problems the advanced countries are facing at present. Our nations must learn from the developed countries to avoid stumbling into the same pitfalls as they. It is absolutely essential that our creative endeavour should be directed towards the formulation of genuinely Latin American solutions. Hence there is no point in persisting in a race for development that takes no account of the values inherent in a developed society.

The convergence of socialism and capitalism in the late twentieth century makes these pitfalls increasingly easy to identify: both go in for capital-intensive strategies of economic growth; for heavy industry using complex machinery; for massive and complex machine-driven economies of scale that threaten the world environment and local diversity. They do so in large part of course because of the dynamics of their chauvinist great-power rivalries. Capitalism as a global economic order has increased poverty gaps. Socialism has remained nationalistic and relatively indifferent to the plight of the developing countries. China and the Chinese economy so far constitute partial exceptions to these remarks, which are directed mainly at the other large industrialized countries.

The developing countries therefore need a profoundly new development strategy. It must be made quite clear that this is no new proposal. On the contrary, since the last century there has been a far-reaching movement on the part of authentically Latin American thinkers to lay systematic stress on the necessity of applying solutions of our own to problems of our own. A case in point is afforded by a great Uruguayan philosopher, José Enrique Rodó. Imbued with a profound romanticism, Rodó says in his *Ariel* (1900) that

> one imitates somebody in whose superiority or prestige one believes. Thus it is that the vision of an America delatinized of its own free will, without the coercion of conquest, and then regenerated in the image and likeness of the northern archetype, now hovers over the dreams of many who are concerned for our future, inspires the satisfaction with which at every step they draw the most suggestive parallels and finds expression in constant proposals for innovation and reform.

Lighting upon a response to the drama of Latin America far ahead of his time, Rodó wrote in *El Mirador de Próspero* (1913):

> The Hispano-American peoples are beginning to acquire a clear and steadfast consciousness of the unity of their destinies; of the indestructible solidarity which has its roots in the very essence of their past and stretches out into the infinity of their future. Auguste Comte expressed his profound faith in the future consciousness of human solidarity, when he said that humanity, as a collective being, does not yet exist, but that it will exist some day. Let us say that our America, the America of our race, is beginning to "be" as a collective person, conscious of its identity.

Rodó's prophetic vision extended to the U.S., and in *Ariel* he voiced what must have been one of the earliest criticisms of the consumer society:

> The life of the United States does in fact describe the vicious circle indicated by Pascal in the eager pursuit of material welfare, when this is made the be-all and the end-all in itself. Its prosperity is as great as its inability to satisfy even the most moderate conception of man's destiny. A titanic achievement, by virtue of the enormous willpower it represents and of its unprecedented triumphs in every sphere of material aggrandizement, that

civilization unquestionably produces a singular impression of inadequacy and emptiness. And the reason is that if we exercise a right conferred by the history of thirty centuries of evolution over which the dignity of the classical spirit and the dignity of the Christian spirit have presided, and venture to ask what is the guiding principle involved, what the motive underlying the immediate concern with those positive interests which set that formidable mass vibrating, all that will be found as the formula for the ultimate ideal is that same concern with material success.

The time has come when the visionary summons of Rodó can no longer be disregarded. It is incumbent upon us therefore to work out an original solution for our weighty problems. And it is precisely in this context that we formulate the proposition of the revolution of being, which we consider applicable to all countries alike, industrial or under-developed, affluent or poor, socialist or capitalist. But we would stipu-late that the revolution of being must take into account the situation of each region, respecting the idiosyncrasies, the customs, and the propen-sities of every people and of every nation.

The Nature of the Revolution of Being

What then are the values that ought to orientate and guide what we call "the revolution of being" that would lead to the integral development of man? Of course, if we are not to lapse into an idealistic position, these values must be embodied in socioeconomic and political struc-tures to make them operative. It would be illusory and hypocritical to talk of the integral development of man, to issue declarations in favour of democracy and human rights, unless at the same time socioeconomic and political structures are changed in such a way as to permit the implementation of the values in question.

Marxist thought has dismissed as unscientific the exaltation of values as the driving forces behind the historical process, formulating its famous thesis of the predominance of the economic base or infrastruc-ture over the superstructure, which includes the juridico-political struc-ture corresponding to the state and the law as well as ideologies. In this scheme of things the world of values would pertain to the super-structure, which would ultimately be determined by the economic base.

If we consider contemporary sociological thought, especially Anglo-Saxon thinking, and within that the ideas current in the U.S., we are frequently assured by these sociologists that a process of interaction does take place between the economic base and the juridico-political structure, which correspond to the state and the law, and the ideological structure. This idea of interaction between the two components seems to approximate very closely Engels' assertion that the infrastructure is related to the superstructure in a dialectical process of cause and effect, in an interplay of actions and reactions.[6] Thus "bourgeois" sociology would appear to coincide with this fundamental Marxist conception and in doing so to demonstrate that Marxism lacks a scientific basis, as it is impossible to prove that *ultimately*—which may mean in the course of ten, 20, 50, or a hundred years—either the infrastructure or the superstructure will be predominant. All that can be scientifically affirmed is that there does exist a process of interaction between the two, to which the Marxists apply the term *dialectic* and bourgeois sociology simply calls *interaction*.

Given these premises, let us see by what values the revolution of being should be guided. Its values would be those of peace, economic welfare, social justice, participation, harmony between man and nature, liberty, all of which in combination and embodied in socioeconomic and political structures should lead to the integral development of man, that is, to the revolution of being.

The antivalues are the values of the powerful capitalist and the socialist societies. The values of the revolution of being are those by which a humanistic society is guided in the pursuit of man's liberation, of his complete self-fulfilment as a human being.

These are the characteristics that give expression to the values that inform the essential dimensions of the revolution of being:

1. Multidimensional man (versus the unidimensional man of capitalist and socialist societies, the former being alienated mainly from the base, the latter mainly from the superstructure).

2. Community spirit guided by an ethic of solidarity (versus the rampant individualism of capitalist societies and the grim collectivism of socialist societies).

3. Work for the benefit of man (versus work for the benefit of the corporation or the state).

4. Tendency towards rationality in consumption oriented to being more rather than to having more (versus the tendencies towards unlimited production of goods in socialist societies and towards unlimited consumption in capitalist societies).

5. Liberating pedagogy oriented to the construction of the world:

---

[6]Letter from Engels to Franz Mehring, quoted by Marta Harnecker in *Los Conceptos Elementales del Materialismo Histórico* (Santiago, Chile: Siglo Veintiuno Editores S.A., May 1972).

teaching-learning society (versus pedagogy oriented to the installation of the socialist system and pedagogy designed to preserve the status quo or establishment of capitalist societies).

6. Dialogic society: dialogue between generations, social groups, ideologies, civilizations (versus the nondialogic societies of the socialist countries and the limited dialogue of capitalist societies).

7. Tendencies towards equalitarian income distribution (versus tendencies towards equal distribution limited by the emergence of a new class in socialist societies and wide disparities in income distribution in capitalist societies).

8. Participation of all sectors of society (versus marginality of sectors not belonging to the new class in socialist societies and existence of numerous marginal sectors in capitalist societies).

9. Rationality oriented towards the integral development of man, and subordination of economic growth to this goal (versus rationality oriented towards the attainment of economic growth that dominates both capitalist and socialist societies).

10. Rationality oriented towards integration with other national societies with a view to maximizing peace, economic welfare, and social justice at the world level (versus rationality enclosed within the framework of the national society in the capitalist countries and rationality oriented towards the ideological, political and economic conquest of other national societies in socialist countries).

11. Limitation of sovereignty by practical implementation of cooperation and solidarity at the world level (versus unlimited conception of sovereignty, except for satellite countries, prevailing in both capitalist and socialist societies).

The historical implementation of the values of the revolution of being entails the suppression of all kinds of violence, direct or structural. Direct violence in the international field may be perpetrated through war, preparation for war, trade in armaments, military alliances, and so on. By direct violence at the internal level, within a given nation, is meant all acts of direct repression deriving from the socioeconomic structure, from the juridico-political pattern followed by the organization of the state or from the prevailing ideologies or ideology: for example, action taken by the police or the army to repress street demonstrations of protest against the government in the exercise of a legitimate right to freedom of assembly and speech.

Structural violence, the kind of violence that is not direct, is exerted through innumerable channels not so immediately visible to all observers as for instance war is. These in contrast are disguised, more or less dissimulated forms of violence, occurring either at the external level, that is, within the international system, or at the internal level, within national societies. At the external level this structural violence comprises the domination-dependence systems in force between the in-dustrialized world and the so-called developing countries. It may take such forms as colonialism or neocolonialism and all the manifestations of imperialism in its various cultural, economic, political, scientific, technological, and other aspects. Internal or intranational structural violence consists of all those systems conducive to the economic exploitation of man by man; all systems that, operating at the social, economic, political and cultural levels in relation to the structure of production, produce alienation (estrangement from society or estrangement from self through society); and, lastly, all those structures of society whereby the individual human being may be prevented from participating in the various processes of social life that are the necessary and inevitable channels for his integral development.

Within this context peace is a synthesis value. Why is this so? Because, in a society pursuing the full liberation of man through the revolution of being, peace entails the implementation of a number of integrant values: it demands a measure of economic welfare, it requires social justice, it calls for participation, it necessitates the creation of a harmonious relationship between man and nature; in short, it involves all the values just pointed out as essential to the revolution of being.

Peace presupposes the suppression of both direct and structural violence at the internal level: within national societies it presupposes the maximization of the integrant values through the execution of the project of the revolution of being. At the external level, that is, in the international system, peace likewise presupposes the abolition of direct and structural violence as well as the maximization of the aforesaid values. The revolution of being implies a new conception of modernity, inspired neither in capitalism nor in socialism, both of which have meant in historical terms the revolution of having, the expression of the acquisitive spirit, the predominance of money, of trade, of business, that is, of economic motivation as the driving force of human activity, incarnated in the religion of GNP.

Being modern, in our view, is not living to have but living to be. This is the conception implicitly and explicitly embodied in the revolution of being.

The revolution of being implies the establishment of a biological and an educational structure for being. It implies what was said long ago by St. Thomas Aquinas, a modern man of the thirteenth century: a minimum of material welfare is necessary for the practice of virtue. That is, man must have at his disposal a minimum amount of material goods and services if he is to be able to develop as a human being. Hence our assertion that the revolution of being must be based on a biological and an educational structure for being. What is meant by a biological structure for being is a minimum of material welfare for each and all which will guarantee everyone human standards of diet, health, and housing, in other words an economic base of goods and services that will enable every man to enjoy the sound body the Greeks extolled as the prerequisite for the development of a sound mind. The biological structure for being accordingly implies a society in which the economic base and the juridico-political structure, that is, the state and the law, are organized to provide each and every man with this minimum of material welfare that will ensure integral development from the biological standpoint.

A structure for being further presupposes that the cultural system and the educational system of society are oriented to education for being, to training man for being more rather than for having more, because in such a society the economic base and the structure of the state and law will suffice in themselves to safeguard the biological structure. The biological structure for being, which permits the development of a healthy body, must be the precondition of education for being.

Education for being in its turn entails the establishment of a *teaching-learning* society. A teaching-learning society is one in which the classic educational systems are superseded, the systems under which it was assumed that an educated man was one who had passed through the primary, secondary, and university levels of education. In the teaching-learning society, the assumption is that education for being lasts throughout a man's life, and that within society all men learn and teach at the same time through a continuing process of dialogue. This dialogue stems from the common search for truth, which does not mean that everybody's truth is the same. On the contrary, it means that through dialogue the members of the teaching-learning society, starting from different ideologies and cultural orientations, pursue the truth and educate themselves and others. Society is organized as a great laboratory in which all men teach and learn concurrently through social communication. This basic concept of the teaching-learning society implies a revolution in the classic systems of education.

If we had to sum up the essential characteristics of such a society, we might say that over and above the aforesaid teleological element, it is a society that allows continuing self-criticism of its own defects and those imputable to the human being within it. It does not imply that truth is possessed by any one social group or man or class but by the concurrence of all its members in a joint quest for truth. Self-criticism is therefore one of its cornerstones. Self-criticism implies the capacity not only to critize oneself but to go on from there to criticize society and other people, not in defense of the possession of truth—for truth is beyond possession—but in pursuit of man's eternal search for truth, through words, which are his means of communication, and not through violence, the symbol of noncommunication. Accordingly the teaching-learning society is anti-Manichean. In it men are not divided into the possessors of good–the possessors of evil. Its basic promise is that society is made up of real human beings with defects and virtues, aiming at self-development through dialogue with their fellows. Dialogue implies that those taking part in it find themselves in the presence of a truth that transcends them. None of them possesses truth, but through dialogue each tries to discover it.

This quest for truth has been pursued by all religions, and different ideologies have claimed to have discovered the right path to it. All of them have failed. Mankind needs cultural revolutions, taking place in different national societies and international systems or subsystems (regions), to make the teaching-learning model of human communication and understanding operational on a world scale.

The teaching-learning society is only one aspect of a self-managed society in which a maximum of government is combined with a minimum of state. A self-managed society is one whose members participate in all the socio-economic and political structures, both in the economic base and at the level of the juridico-political structure of the state and the formulation of law. It stems from the grass-roots of the people themselves, of man himself, rising to its peak authorities by way of intermediate steps in the scale of government. It might be described as a community made up of other groups whose members participate in all the social structures with the conscious aim of enabling society to govern itself. This is why we said that in a self-managed society there must be a maximum of government through this range of communities, which extends from those of the lowest rank, with less decision-making power as units, by way of those at the intermediate levels up to the great national community.

Nor will there by any concentration of power at the national level. Here too it begins at the bottom and is represented by a state apparatus that incorporates a system of checks and balances, thereby making it impossible for power to concentrate in a single pair of hands or a single branch or a single structure. On the contrary, it is self-regulated by virtue of a new system, a reformulation of the theory of the balance of power that Montesquieu propounded long ago in his *De l'Esprit des Lois* and Hamilton, Madison, and Jay examined in their classic defense of the U.S. Constitution, the series of papers entitled *The Federalist*.

But a self-managed society presupposes a self-managed economy, given the constant interaction between the juridico-political structure of the state, the law, and the forms of social consciousness, or ideologies, on the one hand and the economic base on the other. The essence of the self-managed economy is that it must guarantee the biological structure and the educational structure for being we have described as the basis for the integral development of the human being in body and mind.

The economy of the new society must be based on a genuine and effective balance between man and nature. This new balance must be the product of a national decision that fully respects the relevant international agreements, to obviate the possibility that some countries will adopt measures for the conservation of the environment that might be prejudicial to the other members of the international community. It must end the irresponsible and indiscriminate abuse of natural resources and must make for a true return to nature: for example, a compulsory minimum should be fixed for the amount of green space per inhabitant in the great cities, which have nowadays become dreary concrete jungles; steps should be taken to prevent soil erosion, destruction of landscape, pollution of the air and of lakes, rivers, and oceans, and so forth.

Economic planning will have to determine the national economy's priorities and must faithfully reflect the decisions of the grassroots organizations of society. This implies decentralized planning, which obviously cannot be absolute, as it will have to be smoothly and efficiently fitted into an over-all plan agreed upon by the national community.

Resources for financing the development of national societies will have to be drawn from domestic savings and from foreign exchange earnings from exports, external financing being acceptable for specific projects and purchases of technology indispensable to the plan. Such external financing should be channelled through international agencies whose membership provides for effective representation of the recipient countries, to forestall the exertion of inadmissible pressure by the countries or institutions granting capital.

There can be no doubt that multinational integration is a genuinely positive solution for countries whose individual markets are too small to permit the installation of enterprises large enough to reap the benefits of economies of scale.

With regard to the ownership of the means of production, basic sources of wealth should be nationalized in the self-managed economy in accordance with the right every community can exercise under the principles recognized by the UN.

The general principle in respect of ownership in the new society must be that of workers' enterprises in which industrial employees and manual workers will take over the management of an industry and share in its profits within the framework established by law. Thus labour will replace capital in the management of enterprises. The ownership of capital will not be necessarily in the hands of the workers, although of course this possibility will not be excluded; in any case, capital will receive only a dividend fixed by law, with a ceiling. The state will however have to keep the ownership and management of monopolistic and strategic enterprises in its own hands, although still with the participation of the workers, as this is a human and economic *sine qua non* of the new society. In the case of small-scale industries or small farms or businesses that depend essentially on the personal work and capabilities of the entrepreneur, cooperatives afford an appropriate framework for their development.

An indispensable feature of the national community's over-all plan is the formulation of tax and social-security policies and of other similar measures conducive to effective income redistribution at the level both of individuals and of enterprises in order to prevent the accumulation of profits, which in practice leads to the emergence of privileged groups or classes. To that end, income distribution must guarantee every human being a minimum livelihood, while in addition a ceiling must be set above which the income of no member of the community must be allowed to rise. Work will be the main source of income for everyone of working age; it will not be permissible for dividends or rents from accumulated and inherited savings or goods plus income from labour to surpass the ceiling.

Thus in a self-managed economy work becomes a right and a duty for everyone, and policies of full employment and education for being, both based on true equality of opportunities, will ensure the effective exercise of that right and the effective performance of that duty.

A self-managed society, based on a self-managed economy and a teaching-learning society that guarantee the proper biological structure and appropriate cultural and educational structures for the revolution of being, culminates in a self-managed political system. Under such a system the political constitution gives expression to the idea of the self-managed society as the global concept by which all social institutions and processes are inspired. It reflects the power structure required to permit the operation of the teaching-learning society, the self-managed economy, and the self-managed political system itself.

We do not intend to make the mistake of over-precisely describing the pertinent institutions, as every self-managed society must grow out of the sociopolitical, economic, and cultural context of each individual country. It would therefore run diametrically counter to the very idea of the self-managed society to try to present a general model supposed to be valid for such societies of all types. Each national society must find its own way to the new world of self-management, the new world of participation, the new world in which all human beings play a part in order to achieve their integral development through interaction with others. The self-managed society is that of the socialization and the personalization of man.

The balance-of-power system is essential to the creation of a system of checks and balances, both within the central organs of the state, the juridico-political organization, and the law and within society itself, with the object of preventing the concentration of power in the hands of specific groups or parties.

In a self-managed society, alongside the three classic powers of the state—the executive, the legislative, and the judicial—there should in our view be other additional powers; but as we are not proposing a universally valid model, for the reasons given, these ideas are put forward as suggestions that should be studied in relation to the characteristics of each national society. These new powers we have in mind— purely, we repeat, as approximations or suggestions—would be:

1. An independent controlling power established in the political constitution to supervise the legal validity of the acts of the executive, as already current under the legal systems of certain countries.

2. A power responsible for the official defence of human rights. Here the idea would be to install, likewise under the terms of the constitution, an attorney-general of human rights, permanent in tenure, the system of appointment being designed to facilitate the choice of a person with the qualifications and the integrity needed for the discharge of his office. His function would essentially be to arraign before the court of justice any individual (even the head of state), any group, any institution that violated human rights in the self-managed society. His would be a monitorial power to see that human rights were not violated by any of the other powers existing in the self-managed society, the juridico-political apparatus, and the legal machinery of the state.

3. A constitutional tribunal to settle disputes between the executive and the legislature. The structure and membership of such a tribunal and the system of appointing its members would be of vital importance for its satisfactory operation. Just and upright men would have to be chosen to form it.

4. The people and the teaching-learning society as the ultimate source of control over possible deviations on the part of the powers established in the organs of the state or the powers established in the society through its various integrant communities and their expression and reflection in the state machinery. Our view in this connection is that the plebiscite or the referendum, as a properly regulated institution, might afford the people an opportunity of making pronouncements on certain issues of fundamental importance for the life of the self-managed society. It could be convened by any of the state powers (executive, legislative, or judicial) or by the attorney general of human rights, and also in certain cases by the constitutional tribunal, so that the people themselves might adopt decisions on basic problems or questions arising in the self-managed society in the event of differences of opinion between the institutions pertaining to the juridico-political machinery of the society and of the state.

To carry the idea of plebiscite somewhat further, a specific percentage of the electorate, or of youth or the female population, might also conceivably act as a controlling power if, in the circumstances indicated, they were given faculties to convene a plebiscite or referendum. To go farther still, it might be thought feasible for other social groups too—intellectuals, for example, or a given percentage of workers—to have recourse to a plebiscite. It is worth repeating that at bottom this would mean creating a system of checks and balances between the various powers, so that the people could adopt decisions as the ultimate controlling power if at any given moment the state institutions fail to meet the requirements of the process of change.

But a country cannot always resort to a plebiscite, and limits must therefore be set to the availability of this recourse lest it become an organ that paralyses state or societal action and government policy. In the future the progress of electronics might make it possible for the population to be periodically consulted on specific problems that might or might not be matters for a plebiscite. Such direct consultation of the people by the use of electronic techniques would be a way of achieving what in the Athenian democracy was done through the people's assembly, the number of whose members according to Plato's rule for his utopian republic should not exceed 5000. In self-managed societies this number might range from several millions to several tens of millions of persons. The refinements of modern electronics would be placed at the service of the self-managed society to obtain the direct opinion of the people, of the members of society as a whole, as often as possible on specific questions or on the actual running of the society.

Let us now analyse the international dimensions of the revolution of being. The following characteristics give expression to the values and antivalues that inform the essential dimensions of the revolution in the international arena:

1. Ecumenical and solidaristic conception of the international system, which consists of the interaction of national interests seeking their maximization through integration and participation in regional communities and in the world community (versus the nationalist conception of the system in the present-day world, which consists of the interaction of national interests seeking their own maximization in an antagonistic context).

2. Conception of sovereignty shared at the regional and world levels: the nation-states delegate part of their sovereign powers to supranational integration agencies in which they are represented. Thus sovereignty is shared by the state members of the system (versus the unlimited conception of national sovereignty existing at present).

3. Existence of an international society by virtue of values shared at the world and regional levels (in the present-day world no international society exists, for want of values shared at the world level).

4. Peace in the sense of a synthesis-value that implies the suppression of direct and structural violence at the level of the system and of its component units and the promotion of humanist values and therefore the overthrow of antivalues (whereas warfare, preparation for war, trade in armaments and military alliances form an essential part of the international system in the present-day world).

5. National autonomy and regional autonomy in the framework of world solidarity; these concepts relate to the sovereign decision-making capacity of the nation-states and of the economic and/or political communities.

Thus nations must pursue full participation in the structures, institutions, and processes of the regional communities and of the world community. This participation implies that the nation-states take an active part in the decision-making process of the communities in question (versus the existence of areas of influence and the domination-dependence systems at the economic, scientific-technological, cultural and military levels, existing in the present-day international system).

6. Dialogue between teaching-learning societies and civilizations:

cultural pluralism. This concept implies that nations develop their own cultures, not in isolation but through dialogue with other cultures and civilizations (versus the cultural domination by hegemonic nations existing in the present-day world).

7. International division of labour based on the harmonious and balanced development of the national economies (versus the international division of labour deriving from domination-dependence systems).

8. Fair distribution of the benefits resulting from the interaction and integration of the regional economies and of the world economy (versus the widening economic and technological gap deriving from the unfair structures of international trade and the other forms of interaction existing in the world economy).

9. International ownership of scientific and technological inventions, of the world system of satellite communications, of the moon and other celestial bodies, and of the resources of the seabed (versus the present-day system of private and national ownership of scientific and technological knowhow and of communications systems).

10. A world and regional levy for the purposes of solidaristic development (versus the present-day voluntary and insignificant contributions to the development of other nations).

11. A new type of international stratification in which the national and regional communities that have succeeded in affording their inhabitants a high quality of life will be those enjoying the greatest international prestige and constituting poles of humanist development to influence other systems as models of the new society (versus the existing international stratification based on military and economic power and on prestige deriving basically from these variables).

The international structures and processes of the revolution of being should emerge as the product of two types of interaction, interaction between societies that have adopted or are in the process of adopting the model of the self-managed society and others that have not yet done so, and interaction between the said societies and the power structure represented by the system of international stratification.

The idea underlying the revolution of being at the international level is that the nation-state is a feudal state, of which the most perfect example is to be found in the Marxist-Leninist socialist states that have nationalized the land and the means of production. The feudal state is nothing more nor less than the concentration of property and sovereignty in the hands of a single power. The Marxist socialist state is the owner of the land and all the means of production, besides possessing political sovereignty over its territory. Consequently, by a dramatic paradox, in a world on the brink of nuclear catastrophe, ecological disaster, and world revolution, the Marxist-Leninist state has reverted to feudalism holding both property and sovereignty in its hands.

The basic orientation of the revolution of being at the international level is towards the elimination of the feudal state created by socialism as well as the feudal patterns of capitalism, which through other media (military-industrial complexes, security agencies, transnational enterprises) has also set up a feudal state within a pseudodemocracy.

The only way to abolish the feudal state in both its socialist and its capitalist forms is to move towards socialization of the means of production, of the mass communication media, and of other areas of international activity through institutions forming part of or dependent on the UN. This entails establishing within the UN or its agencies a balance-of-power system similar to that described in connexion with the self-managed society; but in this instance, the checks-and-balances system would have to operate at the world level, and its object would be to forestall the concentration of power in a technocracy that might set up a world dictatorship. Should that happen, there would not even be a loophole for any citizen of any country to escape from the world power structure, precisely because of its global scope. But as the revolution of being will be brought about through a lengthy historical process, in the course of which societies of the new type will display varying degrees of development, steps must be taken to ensure that the mobility of persons from one country to another is guaranteed by the attorneys-general of human rights referred to in the context of the revolution of being at the national level. A further possibility worth studying would be to appoint as part of a restructuring of the UN, regional and world attorneys-general of human rights who would exercise functions similar to those of their counterparts in national societies, but at a multinational level.

The socialized areas of the world economy would be:

1. World agency for the seabed: The main objectives of this institution would be to exploit those seabed resources outside the limits of the jurisdiction of states and regional economic communities and to establish a system of research, investment and exploitation which would permit rapid development of the physical, chemical, geological and biological resources of the seabed.

2. World agency for science and technology: Its objective would be to administer the rights to the use of all scientific discoveries and/or technological innovations, taking special care to promote the develop-

ment of the relatively less-developed regional economic communities and nation-states. The agency would in due course acquire ownership of the rights to the peaceful use of scientific discoveries and technological innovations.

3. World agency for global mass-communications media: This strategic and outstandingly important agency would acquire ownership of the world system of mass communications and administer it in such a way as to guarantee the regional economic communities and states members access to the use of the system, to provide constant and factual information on world events, and to ensure real pluralism so that the agency's programmes would represent the various ideologies and political and cultural currents of the world's peoples.

4. World agency for outer space: This agency would establish norms for the exploration and utilization of outer space and the celestial bodies for the benefit of all countries and regions, whatever their degree of economic and scientific development. All areas of the celestial bodies would be freely accessible, and freedom of scientific research on them would be guaranteed under the principles of the UN.

5. World agency for ecological balance: This new world institution would seek an increasingly satisfactory balance between the life-sustaining systems of the earth and the demands—industrial, agricultural and technological—its inhabitants make upon them.[7] It would organize, share, and deploy knowledge and expertise, identify priority problems, and coordinate national measures within an effective global framework. The agency would be empowered to establish standard and compulsory world norms for the conservation of the environment and would be endowed with the appropriate means to police and enforce its decisions.

6. World agency for development planning and financing: This agency would establish an indicative plan for world development in close collaboration with the agencies for ecological balance, the seabed, science and technology, outerspace, and global mass communications media. The plan would contemplate an equitable international division of labour to secure the harmonious and balanced development of the national and regional economies and of the world economy and an equitable distribution of the benefits resulting from the integration of regional economies and the world economy.

---

[7] The ideas about the functions of this agency have been taken from the speech delivered by the Secretary-General of the UN U Thant at the University of Texas (Austin), on May 14, 1970, under the title "Human Environment and World Order."

This agency would also pursue the aim of establishing a monetary system to afford sufficient liquidity for international payments. Special drawing rights would be allowed mainly to economically less-developed regions and countries.

The new institution would have to be empowered to provide long-term credits at low rates of interest to finance specific projects or development programs; grants for the purposes specified; technical assistance of every kind (in close collaboration with the agency for science and technology).

7. World agency for the control of transnational corporations: It would lay down a code of good conduct for the operation of transnational corporations, backed by the appropriate means of policing and enforcing its decisions.

The creation of these world agencies would entail a drastic revision of the UN Charter. This organization would be replaced by a new one, the world community of peoples, whose members would be regional communities and nation-states.

The term regional community is used here in a broad sense. It may signify either a country, such as the U.S., Japan, or the Soviet Union, or a group of countries organized as an economic community, for example the European Economic Community of the future economic community that may emerge from Latin American integration.

The general assembly of this new organization would be formed by representatives of each regional community elected in proportion to the size of its population. For example, each region would have the right to two votes and to one or two additional votes for every hundred million inhabitants. Each state would have the right to one vote. All representatives from each regional community and from each member-state would be elected by popular vote. The assembly would elect the directors of the agencies by a majority of two thirds of its members, with no possibility of a veto for any region or state.

The secretary-general of the world community of peoples, together with the directors of the world agencies, would submit the programmes of the respective agencies to the general assembly, which would be required to pronounce on them within a given period after hearing the reports of the specialized commissions it would itself appoint. The plan would be implemented by each world agency in its sphere of competence. The agencies existing at present, such as UNESCO, ILO, FAO, WHO, and UNCTAD would be sweepingly reformed, and their work would be carried out in co-ordination with the new agencies to obviate duplication of effort.

What must be stressed as of unquestionably paramount importance is that the decisions of these agencies would be binding on all the regions and countries of the world. For example, if certain norms were adopted for world trade, IMF, UNCTAD, and other related agencies would be obliged to apply them. If certain programmes were formulated, in education, science, and culture, UNESCO would have to play a salient part in structuring the teaching-learning society at the world level by promoting a dialogue between civilizations through projects similar to the East-West intercourse currently in progress, reformulating it in a world dimension, allocating it resources appropriate to that scope, and gearing it to the basic ideas of the teaching-learning society just analysed.

ILO, for its part, would have to direct its whole effort towards the study, analysis, and implementation of workers' enterprises (self-management) on the basis of technical assistance.

FAO in turn would have to draw up a radically reformulated world food program designed to ensure the necessary biological basis for the revolution of being in the field of nutrition. A similar course of action would be incumbent upon WHO in respect of health.

Thus UNESCO, FAO, and WHO would have an important role to play in seeing that the biological and educational bases for the revolution of being were established; but in fact all the mechanisms and agencies of the world community of peoples would be oriented towards attaining, within their specific fields of competence, the objectives of that world metamorphosis that constitutes the revolution of being.

To give a final example, the world agency for the control of transnational corporations would not only formulate a code of good conduct laying down precise regulations covering the activities of these important enterprises (in respect of profits, salaries and wages, discrimination by nationalities, tax declarations) but also directly supervise the implementation of the code through the appointment of specialized official inspectors to audit the accounts and review the legality of the acts of such corporations. By this means the enterprises in question would be prevented from proceeding with impunity in some of the less-developed countries whose administrative and legal structures are not efficient enough to counteract the tremendous power of these transnational bodies.

The Transition to the Revolution of Being

We will now endeavor to identify some of the basic features of the historical process whereby the transition might be made from the world of today—particularly Latin America—to the world of the revolution of being.

The first point to be stressed is that the period of transition is *permanent.* This is apparently a paradox, for the existence of a transition towards something implies that a stage will be reached at which the process of transition ends. But as the French philosopher Renan put it, contradiction may sometimes be a sign of truth. What is maintained here is that the transitional period is permanent, that there are transitions within the transition, and that the goal is never reached. Why not? Because arrival at the goal would signify the final triumph of the revolution of being, the entry into the promised land. It would signify the integral development of the human being in a stateless and classless society such as Marx dreamed of, a society in which man would be perfect, in which he would be freed from every form of alienation, in which he would achieve full and limitless self-expression. If the period of transition were *temporary,* the goal would one day be attained. But that uttermost human perfection will never be reached. The revolution of being will never be fully consummated, for that would mean the ultimate triumph of the new man, the ultimate triumph of the liberation of man, a human paradise on earth.

The period of transition is permanent, and in this contradiction in terms lurks the profound truth that man cannot change his nature. But it is not a pessimistic assertion, for although it is true that human nature cannot change it is equally true that man is infinitely more than man, as Pascal maintained. In other words, man can strive for self-perfection, can discover within his own being unsuspected potentialities that enable him to rise above himself. History is full of amazing cases in which man's capacity to surpass himself is revealed.

There is no society in the world, whatever its degree of development and whatever the yardsticks by which that development is measured— the religion of the gross national product or the quality of human life —which has at its disposal all the means and instruments wherewith to attain the targets implicit in the revolution of being. The new man of whom St Paul spoke, as did Marxism-Leninism somewhat later in the day, cannot grow spontaneously out of the old Adam. In fact, the old Adam is continually laying ambushes for the new man, to confound him through selfishness and turn him back into what he was, or into something even more primitive. The transitional period will therefore advance under the banner of conflict—conflict between the new man and the old Adam, conflict between those who want man's liberation and those who want to perpetuate the exploitation of man by man.

This has been the eternal conflict throughout the course of history, the conflict that has engendered all social contradictions from time immemorial.

In a recent work entitled *Masse et Classe,* François Perroux goes deeply into the evidence that the Marxist theory of the conflict between labour and capital is no longer valid in the world of today. The struggle between two organized classes, he says, is not the only, nor can it be the chief, factor accounting for conflictive situations, whether in a developed country, in an underdeveloped country, or on a world scale. The coordinates of this struggle are to be found in conflicts of politically mobilized masses under the direction of power groups, which modify and expand the content and scope of the original Marxist conception. In the twentieth century the dependent wage-earner class no longer has a monopoly on the fighting spirit, suffering, and work.[8]

The object of Perroux's analysis is to establish a central fact through which he shows that the Marxist analysis is not inapplicable, at least to a large extent, to the realities of the twentieth century. His central contention is that the contradiction between capitalists—owners of private capital—and wage-earners is only a species of the genus. What does he mean by this? He means that beyond the contradiction diagnosed by Marx is the contradiction between the masters of the machines and the servants of the machines. The masters of the machines are those who hold the power within the socioeconomic, juridicopolitical and legal structure, and the servants of the machines are those who do not. Apart from this basic contradiction, which holds good whatever the existing system of ownership and social pattern and was quite unforeseen by Marx, there are yet others: the contradictions between the political state and the public administration, between innovation and routine, between creative types and cyclical types, between cultural poverty and genetic poverty, between elemental imperialism and the peoples' sense of solidarity.

Perroux ends his analysis with the observation that the simple opposition of two adversaries, sharply defined by their economic roles and doomed to destroy each other or to exchange their respective roles, turns into a singularly complicated matter in the multiple conflicts of masses organized by political élites.

Consequently the content of exploitation and domination in conflictive situations today has a meaning quite different from the original interpretations Marx put forward.

[8] François Perroux, *Masse et Classe* (Paris: Casterman, 1972), p. 44.

Owing to the diversity of these twentieth-century contradictions the historical process of transition to the revolution of being becomes not only a process of permanent transition but also one in which conflicts of all kinds are waged on a variety of strategic and tactical fronts in the society of masses, classes, and nations.

Accordingly our next step will be to identify those groups that might be able to do away with some of the highly complex contradictions described by the French economist. The question is, which human groups can put the revolution of being into effect? Which groups will be the bringers of the future, whose aim is the true liberation of man through the resolution of these conflicts? We shall call these groups *prospective actors*, with reference to the revolution of being at the world level.

Our hypothesis consists in the assertion that the worldwide crisis brought about by such conflicts generates the emergence of the prospective actors—that is, the agents of change—by its own dynamics, through three processes: (a) the marginalization and progressive alienation of social groups; (b) rebellion on the part of significant segments of these groups against the social structures and cultural objectives of society; (c) politicization of this rebellion through the quest, formulation and adoption of a new model of society to supersede the old. The dialectic of the contradictions in question does in fact place huge social groups—even entire nations—in a marginal position. When the marginalization process is intensified and the groups affected become *marginality-conscious*, the result is alienation from the existing order of things; and the marginal groups deny the objectives and the institutionalized media of a given national or international system.

We define the alienated marginal groups therefore as those that have not been socialized within the existing system and repudiate its objectives and institutional media, which they regard as arbitrary and illegitimate. The alienated marginal persons concerned are not necessarily members of the proletariat, although these may be in the majority; they may belong to the middle strata of the population, and even to the upper middle class. Their sole common feature is their denial and repudiation of the existing social order. Consequently it is precisely to such alienated marginal persons, who rebel against society as it stands and postulate a new society, that we give the name of prospective actors.

In Latin America a historical bloc of prospective actors formed by quite heterogeneous groups can be identified:

1. The various political parties whose prospective action will take

the precise form of the conquest of power. These parties are legion in Latin America, and it is impossible to discern a unitary political structure throughout the whole region, as every country's political parties are completely different from those of its neighbour. Nevertheless, no one can doubt the fundamental importance of the role these parties are called upon to play in the attainment of the objectives of the revolution of being.

2. The political, trade-union and social grassroots movements. This group of prospective actors includes the powerful federations of industrial workers' trade unions, the federations of agricultural workers, and the millions of shanty-town dwellers who form veritable hunger belts around the larger Latin American cities. The future role of these groups depends upon the degree of freedom of association that the Latin American governments are prepared to allow. All too often the governments of the region have been implacable in their persecution of the industrial trade unions and have sought—successfully, alas—to prevent the emergence of agricultural trade unions that could make a stand against the interests of the powerful owners of latifundia in many Latin American countries.

3. Youth and university movements. In speaking of the prospective actors it is indispensable to stress the essential part that youth must play. We are living in an age when the youth sectors are steadily gaining importance because they have not yet been absorbed into the traditional establishment groups. Moreover, in the specific case of Latin America the preponderance of these sectors is absolute: 43 percent of the population of the region is under 15 years of age against 25 percent in Europe, 30 percent in the U.S. and 32 percent in the Soviet Union. Consequently, no serious attempt at change can hope to prosper and become irreversible without the sponsorship, enthusiastic support, and mass collaboration of youth groups. These groups have a better right than any other to participate in the construction of their own future.

4. The progressive intellectuals. This group of prospective actors comprises intellectuals, social scientists, social philosophers, and scientists in general who are disposed to level sweeping and well-grounded criticisms at the development model in force and to seek and formulate appropriate ways and means of attaining the new societies' objectives. In this process of discovery and formulation, pluralistic dialogue between the various ideological schools of thought must be an essential part of the work.

5. The radicalized church. In speaking of the bringers of the revolution of being in Latin America an institution of paramount signifi-

cance for the region cannot be overlooked. The Catholic church has played an immensely important role in the historical development of Latin America. During the nineteenth century and a considerable part of the twentieth it was a mainstay of the ruling sectors, because it effectively supported the established order.

Today the Catholic church in Latin America is coming out more and more strongly in favour of change, and even in those countries where the conservative sector of the clergy is still predominant the church seems to be abandoning its former commitment to the ruling classes and seeking new paths and new attitudes.

A good example of this progressive trend on the part of the Catholic church is afforded by the open letter addressed by Cardinal Raúl Silva Henríquez to the Christians of the Netherlands in February 1972.[9] The Chilean cardinal quoted a passage from the prophet Isaiah: "To loose the bands of wickedness, to undo the heavy burdens, and to let the oppressed go free, to break every yoke, to deal thy bread to the hungry, is not this the fast that I have chosen, saith the Lord." The cardinal also spoke of the people who cannot fast of their own free will during Lent because they have fasted perforce throughout the whole year. The progressive, and in many cases revolutionary, tendencies of the church will become more marked as time goes by, and it will thus become a true protector of the oppressed classes and a factor of change in the region.

6. Another sector of transcendent importance for the region, both in the past and in the present, is the armed forces. In Latin America these forces had their origin in the national armies that fought against Spanish rule and won political independence for our countries, often using the tactics of guerilla warfare.

Once the independence movement was over the role of the armed forces necessarily underwent modification. Moreover, the Latin American armies began to absorb powerful influences, first from Europe and later from the U.S., completely forgetting how to make use of guerilla tactics, as has been pointed out in a brilliant article by a former president of Colombia, Alberto Lleras Camargo. In many countries the armies became veritable pretorian guards of the existing régimes, justifying by the use and abuse of force what could have been justified in no other way. Elsewhere, they filled the power vacuum created by anarchy and political *caudillismo.* In short, they played all sorts of roles.

[9]Published in the periodical *Mensaje,* Santiago, Chile, March–April 1972.

At present the armed forces are passing through a third phase, of which the training of the troops, warrant officers, and officers constitutes a salient feature. In various war academies interesting training programmes are being implemented through which members of the forces are attaining high standards of specialization in the most widely varying fields, including social science subjects such as sociology and economics.

Consequently, in many countries the armed forces are becoming an active and dynamic factor of social change. Happenings in Peru are a highly significant case in point.

Politically speaking, this trend is represented by the formation of joint civil and military governments within political systems, and an impressive degree of topical interest is beginning to attach to such coalitions in the region. These new patterns of government may be the result of freely concerted agreements between civil and military sectors or may simply be imposed by the armed forces.

7. We cannot conclude this enumeration of prospective actors without referring to a development which has characterized the social structure of certain Latin American countries, for example Argentina. In some countries the middle class already represents a substantial proportion of the total population. In all probability this development will spread through the other countries of the region, and sizeable intermediate strata will be formed in the national societies concerned, consisting of professionals, employees, government officials, small and medium entrepreneurs, shopkeepers, and skilled workers.

Members of these intermediate strata have frequently become the most dynamic factors in Latin American societies. But it would be a mistake to suppose that the middle class *en bloc* exhibits a uniform ideology or political role, for which reason this socioeconomic phenomenon may have widely different projections in the future. We cannot, therefore, include the middle strata as such among the prospective actors, but only some segments and members of them.

The time has now come to indicate some of the arduous tasks that will have to be initiated or continued by this comprehensive and heterogeneous group of prospective actors in Latin America. Fortunately many of these tasks can be identified with tendencies which are already discernible in our region. A word of warning: we make no claim to deal definitively and exhaustively with the subject. On the contrary, all we shall attempt is to establish a few salient landmarks that give some idea of the road on which our region is, and ought to be, setting out. For the purposes of this analysis we are not going to turn to the past, nor will we lapse into the unhealthy fatalism of some intellectuals who believe that our future is completely predetermined by our colonial inheritance or by existing circumstances.

The Grand Strategy of the Revolution of Being and Its Specific Strategies

The main distinction between grand and specific strategies needs to be made here: The implementation of the revolution of being is the grand strategy of prospective actors in Latin America as elsewhere in the world; specific strategies are only part of this grand strategy.

Among specific strategies we shall indicate those of the greatest importance:

1. The elimination of economic underdevelopment and external dependence. The new Latin American economy will necessarily imply an economic restructuring designed to satisfy the basic needs of the population and involving therefore the programming of economic activity at the national, subregional, and regional levels. One indispensable measure will be the application of drastic controls to limit all those forms of nonessential consumption now transmitted to the Latin American economy through the propaganda and sales systems of the great transnational corporations and through mass-communication media.

The introduction of radical changes also necessitates the regulation of foreign investment and technology. Clearly defined policies—such as those designed by the Andean group, the emergent subregional market—must be adopted with respect to the huge transnational corporations that are becoming the chief instrument of the region's economic domination by foreign interests.

Actually the nationalization of basic sources of wealth and means of production, in the hands of foreign capital is unquestionably the Latin American trend that has had the greatest impact on powerful and influential groupings of industrial countries, in particular the U.S. Argentina, Bolivia, Chile, Cuba, Mexico, Peru, and other countries have at some time in their history carried out nationalization. Although this process has taken radically different forms, it has invariably been vigorously resisted by the countries affected.

Because this trend towards nationalization will intensify as time goes by, there will certainly be a tightening of the tension between our countries and the U.S., whose government so far seems always to have made common cause with the great transnational corporations. The only way of relieving these possible tensions is for the U.S. and other governments concerned to adopt a new criterion that recognizes the distinction between the public interests of a nation and the private interests that control large enterprises and have been affected by nationalization.

It is not superfluous to recall that in resolutions of the UN General Assembly express and solemn recognition has been accorded to the permanent sovereignty of states over their sources of wealth and natural resources and to their faculty to nationalize these in accordance with their own norms.[10]

Another reaffirmation of the new independent trend of our countries is represented by the strenuous campaign to secure recognition of the Latin American stand on the 200-mile limit for patrimonial waters.

We should make it clear that this struggle against the dependence by which we have so long been oppressed does not seek to convert the region into an isolated unit, cut off from economic intercourse at the world level. Our sole aim is to reach a stage at which we can speak of an interdependent region that plays its part with perfect freedom in trade with all the world, unhindered by blackmail by the powers that have dominated us hitherto. Unfortunately there are countries that fail to understand the challenge this implies and believe that the best way to escape the shameful dependence into which they were plunged by one power is to fall directly into the sphere of economic dependence dominated by the rival hegemonic power, as has been the case with Cuba.

2. The reaffirmation of regional and national autonomy. Since the end of the 1950s there has been a noticeable trend towards depolarization of the international system, which from the Second World War up to that period had approximated a bipolar structure. Several indicators make this apparent: (a) the revolts in Cuba, Yugoslavia, Albania, and, up to a point, Romania, which have broken the monolithic character of the areas of influence of the two superpowers; (b) the reconstruction of Europe, its economic recovery and its high level of development, which in conjunction with the formation and strengthening of the European Common Market have set Western Europe on the road to becoming a new economic power on a world scale—a tendency strengthened by the accession of Britain, Ireland, and Denmark; (c) the emergence of China with the status of a nuclear power, its dramatic rupture with the Soviet Union, and its recent opening to the western world through trade with the U.S.; (d) the Anglo-Saxon loss of mo-

---

[10]Resolutions of the UN General Assembly, No. 1303 (XVII), December 14, 1962, and No. 2158 (XXI), November 25, 1966.

nopoly of the manufacture and supply of arms countries of the Third World; (e) Japan's access to the status of a world economic power; and (f) the successive crises that have undermined the dollar as a leading international currency.

It would be incumbent on the prospective actors to strengthen such trends in Latin America, because in the first place they imply a decentralization of the international systems and second they help create multinational regions that are viable from the standpoint of modern economic development. The decentralization of the international system would pave the way for an international system with a polycentric structure, in which our region should find its appropriate niche. Latin America should stress the obsolescence of the old system of military alliances that the cold war zones of influence organized in defensive and offensive blocks.

The Latin American countries are giving proof of a clear-cut and indisputable tendency towards autonomy. The time has gone when some of our governments seemed to follow the dictates of the U.S. State Department to avoid offending their powerful neighbour to the north.

Particularly since the end of the Second World War our countries have become conscious of their former submissiveness within a stratified international system and have started international action to improve their real status in the system. Some international economic organizations have helped on occasion to clarify our countries' situation in this respect and have been instrumental in the region's efforts to raise its status. Further, in some instances the creation of such organizations has constituted a political act whereby the Latin American countries have asserted their will to change the distribution of power within the international system with the object of making it more democratic.[11]

This determination was evidenced when the Latin American countries—acting on Chile's proposal—insisted that the Economic Commission for Latin America (ECLA) be established despite opposition from the industrial countries. Creation of the Inter-American Development Bank (IDB) at the regional level was likewise the product of lengthy negotiations between the Latin American countries and the U.S.

---

[11]Gustavo Lagos, "The Political Role of Regional Economic Organizations in Latin America" in *International Organisation: World Politics,* edited by Robert W. Cox (London, Macmillan and Co., Ltd., 1969), p. 43.

Our countries have also demonstrated their increasing autonomy at the various sessions of UNCTAD, where they have directly confronted the industrialized countries with demands for the adoption of specific measures to reduce the gap between rich and poor countries. A Latin American, Raúl Prebisch, strove with inexhaustible energy for the creation and effective operation of this conference.

Another manifestation of our countries' new struggle for independence is to be found in the establishment of the Special Committee on Latin American Coordination (CECLA), the aim of which is to unify criteria in respect of relations with the U.S., Europe, and the rest of the world. In this perspective CECLA appears as the first valid attempt to set up a Latin-American subsystem of nations to enable the region to formulate policies of its own with due regard to the interests of all the countries in it.

3. The integration of Latin America. This process, closely related to the preceding point, is one of the region's most noteworthy tasks and has incalculable implications for the future.

New models for the integration of national economies in the world economy should be designed to further the rapid progress of regional integrational movements and new economic policies at the national level closely linked to the integration process. It is therefore indispensable that the Latin American integration movement should be based on the programming of development and not exclusively on schemes for the liberalization of trade. The objective of the new policies should be the production of industrial goods at levels of efficiency comparable with international standards to enable Latin America's products to compete in world markets and augment intra-regional flows of manufactured goods.

In this context, it must be acknowledged that the line followed by the Latin American Free Trade Association (LAFTA) does not exactly coincide with these propositions. Many problems and contradictions have turned this important agency into a mere forum for negotiating the liberalization of trade in specific products, and even here major difficulties have arisen.

By way of reaction to this stagnation of the regional integration process a new integrationist trend has come into being, and is reflected in agreements at the subregional level. A case in point is the Andean pact, which represents one of the most ambitious subregional integration projects in the whole world.

The signatories to the pact (Bolivia, Chile, Colombia, Ecuador, Peru, and recently Venezuela) have adopted common measures with respect to foreign investment and transfers of technology, a question on which no integration project had dared touch before. Another salient feature is the adoption of a major sectoral development project for the metal-transforming industry covering the entire subregion.

Subregional integration will therefore presumably start booming in the next few years, provided a solution is found for various political and economic rivalries and problems that presently cast a shadow on integration processes.

4. The democratization and stabilization of political régimes that guarantee full popular participation. When we speak of democratization we are not referring to the abolition of repressive dictatorships and their replacement by democratic régimes in the style of the republican-liberal system prevailing in western countries. On the contrary, the appalling conditions of exploitation and poverty existing in so many Latin American countries will not end with the establishment and observance of a few formal liberties deriving their inspiration from liberal thought in the eighteenth and nineteenth centuries. It is useless to proclaim equality in the sight of the law when the great majority of people lives out of reach of the administration of justice and to introduce universal suffrage when there are vast areas where powerful political *caudillos* impose their own opnion on the masses, who have nothing to do with major political decisions affecting them. What is the good of freedom of speech when a few enterprises, nine times out of ten under foreign influence or management, play false with the people's right to be told the truth? What is the good of freedom of association when the oligarchies and their hangers-on refuse to countenance the formation of agricultural trade unions and workers' federations? These values, worthy in themselves of all respect, become truly meaningful only when accompanied by real and effective popular participation at all levels of society. Accordingly, everything that we have said of participation in the revolution of being is fully applicable to Latin America.

Another point to be clarified is the concept of stability. Many sectors in the international hegemonic centers have displayed great concern over Latin America's chronic political instability. What they are anxious about however is the uncertainty of the future outlook for foreign investment in the region. We, on the other hand, interpret stability as the only alternative that will allow a social process to mature and strike permanent root in a given nation. Otherwise changes would never be irreversible, and processes could never be consolidated.

In the context of democratization and increased popular participation, a pause to dwell on national integration is worthwhile. National integration is a task of vital importance for Latin America because there are millions of human beings in the region who are completely cut off from their national communities by an inextricably tangled thicket of geographical, political, cultural, and socioeconomic factors.

We therefore believe that measures should be taken to ensure that these huge marginal sectors formed by indigenous population groups, illiterates, shanty town dwellers and the like are integrated in their respective national societies. Only through radical structural changes in the political, social, educational, and economic spheres, to secure effective participation, will it be possible for this objective to be attained.

National integration also implies the adoption of formulas for participation through communitarian grassroots organizations at the level of neighbourhoods, trade unions, youth groups, women's institutes, sports clubs, and so on. In this connexion some of the measures carried out in Chile by the Christian-Democrat Government (1964–1970) may constitute an interesting precedent. More recently Peru too has been conducting noteworthy experiments in economic selfmanagement and popular participation through the creation of agricultural and industrial communities in which rural and urban workers play an essential role. This trend is in striking contrast to the ideas of traditional Marxism-Leninism, which aims at replacing the old employers by highly centralized bureaucratic bodies under which the workers are just as far removed from the decision-making process as they were under the capitalist and neocapitalist systems.

5. Land reform. Outstanding among the structural changes in progress and in need of acceleration is land reform. Various countries have embarked with greater or lesser degrees of success upon the difficult and controversial task of changing obsolete agrarian structures. It could hardly be otherwise, as the structure of agriculture in Latin America is in many cases a mere prolongation—sometimes lightly modified or "modernized"—of the old structures of colonial times. In many countries the scourges of the *latifundia* system, ignorance and poverty, still keep the broad rural masses under the yoke of an up-to-date version of slavery.

For some time now Chile, Cuba, and Peru have been putting interesting and much-debated land reform programmes into effect. Other countries such as Mexico and Bolivia have made experiments of this kind in the past.

The great majority of the countries of the region are conscious that agrarian reform is an inevitable phase in the battle for national welfare, and this consciousness will no doubt be reflected in political and social movements to introduce structural changes. Obviously such processes will not follow the same lines everywhere. Some countries may adopt the classic Marxist-Leninist model in the Cuban fashion, which will finally culminate in absolute socialization, with the state becoming the owner/manager of the land. Others will perhaps choose the path of communitarian socialism, leading to selfmanagement at the agricultural level; yet others will perhaps prefer to carry out a reform that will turn the agricultural workers into owners of individual farms in the framework of a neo-capitalist society; again, various combinations of these formulas may possibly be devised. In short all that is clearly foreseeable is that radical changes—widely differing and even opposite in their content—will be brought about in agrarian structures. As the agrarian problem has very different nuances in each country, it is impossible to make recommendations of generalized feasibility to bring about rapid and effective land reform in Latin America.

6. *Educational reforms.* Sooner or later our countries will find themselves compelled to change and intensify the aims of education at the primary, secondary, university, technical and other levels. These changes and aims will constitute important components of the process of creating teaching-learning societies in Latin America. Reforms seem likely that will take into account the necessity of formulating educational policies consistent with the realities in which they are applied and repudiating programmes imported from regions whose special characteristics have nothing to do with those of the recipient peoples. Thus the deep-rooted European and American influences in our education should begin to give way before educational systems created by Latin Americans and inspired by our own national values.

One important branch of activity will consist of intensive campaigns, aimed at wiping out the illiteracy that blights the lives of millions of Latin Americans.

To sum up: The different aspects of the Latin American reality just analysed show the unity and multiplicity, the variety and uniformity of this immense human and geographical world that is Latin America.

This reality, in which heterogeneity and homogeneity are mingled within and among the nations of the region, is full of contradictions that embrace socioeconomic, cultural, and political systems in the society of masses, classes, and nations.

Different groups, social and political movements, are emerging from the very heart of these contradictions, antagonisms, conflicts, and oppositions. Some of them are carriers of the future; they are the prospective actors mentioned at the beginning of this section.

If they can really interpret the deep aspirations all Latin Americans cherish in this continent—the continent where, if direct violence in the form of warfare does not exist, structural violence does, partly created from within but mainly fostered from outside—these prospective actors may come to be the builders of the revolution of being.

A SCEPTICAL CONTRIBUTION

Carl-Friedrich von Weizsäcker

Introduction

The World Order Models Project presents us with the task of developing relevant utopias and the image of a preferred world for the decade of the 1990's. By utopias are here understood models of a possible condition of the world in that decade and models for attaining that condition. The image of the preferred world should be a desirable condition, the pragmatic intention being to stimulate hope, and through hope, activity. Yet the utopias must be relevant. By this is meant that their architects see a real chance for their realisation. So the task set can also be termed a minimum-maximum task: of the conditions considered attainable the best one should be described, or of the most desirable conditions the most feasible. The choice of the decade between 1990 and 2000 itself serves to optimise the task. One can only dream about a more distant future; the relevance of such dreams cannot currently be assessed, nor would they stimulate sufficiently the required action. Conversely, the near future is too near to make realistic plans for genuine targets. The multitude of special political, social, economic, and intellectual constraints existing today is not—short of a catastrophe—susceptible to rapid change, and our task is not to determine what changes will of themselves come about but to consider with what goals in view we should work towards changing or retaining these constraints. The assessment of possible goals is made under the influence of certain senses of values. The public conciousness of our age—and the concrete project of the Institute for World Order, Inc., too—gives us a short list of leading values; I would name as the most important here peace, freedom, social justice, and prosperity. The mutual relationship among these values is one of the themes that must be considered.

But first I should like to ask from what kind of thinking such a project is derived. One of its strongest motives is indubitably concern. This project is not derived from naive optimism. It sees the dangers of the future and seeks to meet them by looking at positive aspects of the future and deriving from these a model showing how the dangers might be overcome. One might term the mood behind the project "concerned activism." The project follows the typically "modern" mode of thinking that mankind is capable of a radical change in its way of life. From the start it is necessary to point out that such a mode of thinking is by no means self-evident. In practically all previous cultures and epochs the question of the future would have been considered as a question not concerning a change of structure but rather concerning the ups and downs of personal, familial, national, and imperial destinies within a structure itself in principle immutable; a question not asking "Will there be kings?" but "Who will be king?" The modern mode of thinking by its very existence proves to a degree its rightness, representing in itself a structural change brought about by mankind. It opens a vista on past history and at the same time teaches us to regard the past as a chain of irreversible events. It is indeed not the intention of this paper to cast doubt upon the mutability of human life. The difficulty seems to lie in the opposite direction: the changes that actually occur go so deep always that man's imagination is insufficient even to imagine the possibility of such a change. I am convinced that the nineties will in many aspects—aspects we cannot today conceive of—differ from the picture any contemporary prognosticator has of them. At the same time many structures existing today will remain unchanged, even if their rating will be different. With what concepts are we equipped to think into the future, and with what right do we think towards it?

The project's answer to this question is intellectual activism, the style of which fits the mode of thinking of science and technology; in this respect too the project is modern. On the one hand developing tendencies are observed and extrapolated, using causal analysis as much as possible, to determine future developments. On the other hand one formulates goals and seeks ways of attaining them within this interplay of causes and effects. The interpretation of the Good by the concept of value serves this mode of thought. Values such as we have listed are goals to be attained by action. This mode of thought leads automatically to the triad: prognosis, utopia, and planning.

These notes begin by consciously accepting this methodology, but one must try to see within what limits it can hope to succeed. The planner generally does not see what he has at his back and what causes him to plan. From this fact is derived the currently widespread method of criticizing ideologies by observing that it is often my own material interests that, unknown to myself, lead me to accept this or that idea as true. I shall subsequently have cause to apply this method particularly to ourselves. But this method, as it is mostly used today, also lies within the framework of the undisputed premise that I have called intellectual activism. Intellectual activism stands behind all our planning. Its highest-ranking value is de facto not one of the concrete ones just listed, such as peace, freedom, justice, prosperity. The as it were abstract idea of the Good, by which values and successes are measured, is progress. But this criterion is in fact not clear but ambiguous; it creates an ambivalence of the modern world that is the root of the world's greatest dangers.

It seems that this last thesis calls for justification. The most transparent form of progress is that of science. The value to be achieved is given: knowledge or, as we also say, truth. To those who know science it is evident that here too the valuation of knowledge represents a serious problem; nevertheless science is nowadays generally taken as the model for progress. The problem is more evident in technology. If technology means the creation of means to achieve certain ends, progress can be seen and measured in the creation of these means. But two problems arise: side-effects and the questionableness of the ends. The side-effects (air and water pollution, diseases of civilisation, hunger derived from lower mortality) show that the ends cannot be separated; the system of meaningful ends represents a whole, but a whole not fully understood. Especially when the ends themselves become questionable and are therefore proposed without conviction, technical progress tends to become an end in itself. The creation of wants by private producers and the technical nimbus as a tool of foreign policy, targets attacked by social critics, would hardly be so successful but for the deep-rooted idea of the value of progress. This idea of value is symbolised today by flights to the moon; for a century in ancient Egypt, the building of pyramids may have represented a similar value.

Of course, mankind today is aware of these shortcomings. Men seek to determine the goals of technology according to specific values (such as those given), and there is no alternative for our study. But these values are implicitly understood in the sense of the prevalent mode of thought and thus remain unclear. *The more they indicate the absence of an evil, the clearer they become.* In wartime the desire for peace, in hunger the desire of satiation, under foreign domination the will to emancipation—all these are immediately comprehensible. But when after frightful periods of war a generation, with the help of technology, has achieved a situation that it conceives to be peaceful, prosperous, with freedom and some degree of justice, the next generation finds in it manipulation instead of freedom, injustice, hunger, and war. Battle is joined not over the verbally formulated values themselves, not really even over their order of priorities, but over their meaning and their content. In the ups and downs of victory and defeat of this battle all that ultimately survives is that which is a possible goal of intellectual activism, or the side-effect of such a goal, which often may be unexpected or even frightening.

The consequent answer of the intellectual activist to this problem is: enlightenment. Progress is indeed ambivalent, even dangerous, as long as it is only progress in means and not progress in consciousness of goals. Enlightenment is the leading value of a reasonable impulse for progress. But the word is in turn ambivalent. Taking two main meanings, it can signify enlightenment of the people or enlightenment of the self. The former implies the spreading to the multitude of a level of awareness already existing in the few. Mass education is indeed an essential ingredient of all preferred worlds, perhaps the most important of all. The almost insurmountable difficulties previously named stem, however, from a lack of self-enlightenment. The battles between religions, between capitalism and socialism, between technocrats and democrats, are all fought about different ideas as to the right major condition of consciousness.

On all these fronts it is easy for the ideological critics on both sides to see the mote in their brother's eye. It would be unworthy, in such a study as we intend, not to take these clashes seriously as a dispute about the self-enlightenment of leaders of mankind. The battle can only be understood as an attempt at self-enlightenment.

To attempt self-enlightenment is to search for the truth. But the way to the truth cannot be programmed, for were this so we should already for the most part possess it. It is not a relevant utopia to say, "In the nineties we shall have found insight into the nature and conditions required for peace, freedom, and justice, and we shall act according to this insight." Even if this were the case, such a hope represents no concrete model that could be designed today. It is no relevant utopia. What sort of utopias can we then plan in these circumstances? In my opinion there are two kinds: a modest one or a challenging one.

A modest utopia is based in the undisputed valley of the scale of values, where generally recognized evils can be fought with technical means which in principle are unproblematic. In view of the sheer quantity of crying need in the world, even a programme of modest utopias is highly ambitious and highly important. If, as a result of our study, a well-thought-out programme of modest utopias resulted, we should have fulfilled a great task.

A challenging utopia is of necessity contentious. The strife it may cause should be in the service of self-enlightenment. Just as important as the planning and execution of aims presented by modest utopias is the realisation that some great, vital questions cannot be solved in this way. I believe that this nowadays particularly applies to the problem of world peace. Here we should not only picture the immodest possibility of a solution, which because of its immodesty rightly appears as "utopian" to contemporary practitioners; we must also consider the negative utopia, elsewhere banned from the original framework of our study. We must picture the consequences if the problem of world peace remains unsolved.

Attempts at Prognosis

The Probability of an Atomic World War

With continuing technical progress and the current world-political constellation, it is highly probable that there will be an atomic world war before the end of this century. This statement is basic when it comes to assessing the problem of peace. It does not correspond to current public consciousness, at least not on its superficial levels. It must therefore be justified.

To justify this statement it is not necessary to assume acts of madness will occur. It suffices to assume that the governments of the world powers will continue to act according to the rationale of inherited power politics, as they do now. The reason an atomic war is not started today is that it would practically be suicide for the initiator. This in turn is due to a special technical situation, the existence of the second-strike capability of both the current world powers, which cannot be destroyed by the attacker's first blow. This technical situation is a characteristic of today's weapon systems. The dominant weapon system is in a state of flux: it can be said that each system is replaced by a new one about every seven years. Each new weapon system offers the possibility that it may not be able to be stabilised. With respect to the ABM and MIRV systems this theme has been much discussed by the public at large. But should a weapon system not stabilized in this sense of reciprocity come to dominate, it would again seem possible that an atomic war could be won. We will not then be able any more to rely on governments' caution, but only on their desire for peace. But this will be influenced by the possibility that one's own current arms lead may within a few years pass to the opponent or that the first side to strike will win. According to the classical rules of power politics, in such a situation war will break out sooner or later.

This very terse argumentation is illustrated by three negative utopias. None of them assumes extraordinary malevolence or acts of madness on either side.

1. Arms race. Both world powers today recognize that the preservation of peace is in their mutual interest. But each mistrusts the intention of the other, i.e., each believes the other would grasp the opportunity to achieve a decided lead in armaments. It is the intention of the SALT talks to alleviate the resulting military dangers and economic burdens. The arms-race negative utopia begins by assuming that these talks will fail for practical reasons (inadequate possibilities for inspection and the like). An unchecked arms race ensues, eventually—perhaps in the eighties—leading to the existence of a first-strike capability on one or both sides. The arms race prevents an otherwise possible thaw in political relations between the two sides. The reaction of world opinion and of intellectual youth at home creates such internal political difficulties for one or both governments that the classical way out is taken—war. The side starting the war wins it, but suffers more damage than anticipated. World casualties are initially a few hundred million deaths. There follow one or two decades of confusion during which world population falls by half as the result of hunger, wars, radioactivity, and disease. Finally, the interaction between a centre of power and the general consciousness of the necessity for peace leads to the formation of a world government.

It should be noted that in this relatively banal negative utopia we never assume any actor departs from the rules of rationality dominant in politics today, but nevertheless consequences arise that none of the players desire. Historically this has often been the case, as in the Thirty Years' War and World War I. We could say we have been warned. But while the public continues to regard atomic war as impossible, the greater technical rationality of the arms specialists is being developed to a point at which, unhindered by full public consciousness of the danger, they "must do the deed, since it was conceived."

2. Arms stop. Here the utopian assumption is that the ongoing series of SALT talks are virtually successful. ABM, MIRV, ULMS and a number of other specifically named weapon systems are not produced. Existing strategic weapon levels are frozen. Sample checks are agreed on and carried out, and no breaches of the agreement are found. It was rightly considered impossible to agree to stop research. World politics, freed from concern over atomic war, applies the means available to promote existing national, imperial, and ideological interests. Expenditure on science continues to grow. Research oriented to civilian technologies becomes one of the greatest means to power. Competition between the powers develops into a battle for world domination by civilian means. At infrequent intervals scientists offer their governments new secret weapons. The offers are repeatedly refused, but in a situation which has for other reasons become desperate, one of the governments accepts an offer. The result is as outlined in the scenario for the arms race dysutopia.

This negative utopia is banal too. The elimination of current technical threats certainly is beneficial. But as long as there is an interaction between technological progress and the power politics of divided powers, the problem will continue to present itself, each time being difficult to avoid in a new way, and ultimately perhaps insoluble.

3. Disarmament. Here it must be said in advance that voluntary disarmament of sovereign powers that fear each other is possible only if the balance of power is not substantially altered. This can at best be the case when two powers are involved, and even in such cases only when they feel safe from a third power. This is the reason why historically disarmament has hardly ever led to a relaxation of tension, but has rather followed it. A statesman does not need to be chauvinistic but only to think conservatively and responsibly to be still a very reluctant disarmer. Thus it is utopian in the colloquial sense of the word to assume that the major world powers would be prepared to disarm on any large scale.

But now we make this utopian assumption. A simultaneous radical internal political change in both the major powers brings governments to power who determine once and for all to eliminate the danger of an atomic world war. They manage to reach an agreement with China and Western Europe on the destruction of all atomic weapons, solemnly renounce research, development, and use of atomic, biological, and chemical weapons, and make drastic reductions in conventional armaments. They accept the principle of a nation's right to self-determination and abandon military dominance in their satellite systems. To settle international disputes they establish courts, and for communal economic problems create worldwide advisory and executive committees. The idea of a world police force is rejected as a relapse in the direction of outmoded power politics.

It can be left to the imagination of the reader to picture the failure of such a system. The following stages come to mind. The economic domination of capitalist firms and of state economies calling themselves socialist over former satellites and colonies will not cease and will lead to sharp political conflicts. In various countries "fascist" governments arise or retain power. The larger powers initially refrain from intervention until local wars develop, when they can no longer stand by and watch. This comes about because revolutionary movements ally themselves with segments of the population of the old imperial powers, threatening the major states by the decline of their internal unity. Systems of alliances develop which compel their leading states to rearm, within a qualitative framework of permitted weapon systems, beyond the quantitative limit permitted. The attempts of others to control this danger leads to world war. The never-forgotten knowledge of how to make atomic weapons makes nuclear rearmament possible during the course of the war. This scenario leads back to the first variant, with the order of some of the events reversed.

This negative utopia is less easy to see through than the previous examples because of its deliberately utopian premise. If one can assume that states are prepared to disarm totally, why should one not assume that they could then maintain peace? The answer is that although disarmament could ensue in a wave of emotion in one of those upsurges of hope that occur in history, peace requires a permanent change of structure. The sense of this dysutopia is not to question the possibility of a change of structure but to indicate the circumstances in the absence of which such a change could not come about. One cannot allow the material problems of world regions to continue largely unabated and maintain the classical form of political organisation of particular, sovereign states while simply eliminating the military means that previously held constant tensions in check. In the ensuing pages we must examine the question of whether and under which circumstances a change of structure is possible that will dam up the sources of war. Let us look first at the classical solution.

World Government

World government is the most conservative utopia for guaranteeing avoidance of future atomic world wars. I would venture three prognoses:

I consider it probable that in the next hundred years a way will be found for the long-term avoidance of major wars, for in a technological age this is a vital necessity, and mankind will have to solve the problem to survive.

I consider it probable that the creation of a world government will be a decisive step in this direction, disregarding the fact that it hardly solves any other problems of mankind.

I am terrified by having to admit that it is increasingly probable that this step will be taken only as the result of an atomic world war, for the reasons already given.

World government is the most conservative possible solution. It does not require the cessation of progress in military techniques, which would be impossible today, although such a cessation might be a consequence. It does not require a cessation of conflict, but only the cessation of a particular form of conflict. Again, it does not require any change in the structure of human society but simply extends the well-known pattern of abolition of feudal law by a territorial state to the abolition of war as such. To what extent it will be centrally or federally inclined, technocratic or democratic, strong or weak, enlightened or repressive, will depend on its genesis and the further development of political life under it. Its definitive task is the prevention of a major war, its inevitable structure therefore an arms monopoly. For most people today this thought is rather shocking. One hopes that only more minor changes would be necessary or believes that other changes are more urgent. World government is regarded as unattainable or, if attained, as frightful. All these objections must be considered.

But I have already indicated why minor changes will not be adequate. If these considerations apply, those other changes deemed more urgent would have to overcome the structure of power politics. I shall discuss this problem later, just saying here that I regard such major changes as not only necessary but also more fundamental, and thus more difficult and requiring more time than the establishment of world government. One should seek to attain them in addition to, not instead of, world government.

It is true that world government is unattainable today; I do not dare suggest it as a relevant utopia for the 1990's. The reason for its unattainability is not human nature, but just the political structure of mankind it is designed to overcome. But its unattainability does not belie its necessity, for not all political problems have a solution. The pessimist's answer is that only an atomic world war will teach the required lesson and result in the new distribution of power necessary for its creation. The optimist's answer would be that a continuous change in consciousness and in power structures would suffice. It is also clear that a world government offers every prospect of being terrifying. If it is a dictatorship, one cannot escape by emigration. If it is based on the manipulation of opinion, where is there room for truth? Which of mankind's great social problems will its existence solve? All the same,

I maintain that once it is formed, an irreversible step in world history will have been made. World civil wars may follow, but never the serious intention to do away with the world unity achieved.

What preferred world for the last decade of our century might one add as a corollary, if this idea is correct? Not the attainment of world government but, dominating public consciousness throughout the world, the necessity of attaining it; in addition, one sees the political forms and social conditions facilitating its attainment. What these forms and conditions would have to be can only be examined after discussing the other values. World war could be avoided if the priorities of politicians and of those on whom they depend for votes were determined by considerations such as those presented here. The danger of war lies in the fact that politics are carried on as if there were no danger of war.

Society and Economy

Our study is supposed to concern itself with five themes: the avoidance of violence, economic well-being, social justice, ecological balance, and overcoming the alienation of the individual. Preventing a world war, the first theme discussed herein, is related to all these values, as war would represent an almost mortal blow to all of them. What are the prospects for these values in a period in which world war is avoided? I shall illustrate the problem with the currently much-discussed theme of ecological balance.

Especially relevant to this theme is what one may term the definition of values by the negation of a negation. As long as there was no danger to ecological balance nobody thought of regarding it as a particular value. But today it is in danger. The task of saving or restoring it presents itself for analysis as a series of layers of causalities.

The first layer may be termed the technoscientific layer. We are confronted with certain phenomena such as smog or the heating of the Earth's atmosphere as if it were in a hothouse caused by changes in its chemical composition. Both examples are connected with the products of combustion from industry and traffic. There is no doubt that such phenomena result from the operation of natural laws, being unintentional side-effects of intentional technical processes. It is both possible and necessary to study the genesis and the (medical, social, psychological) effects of such phenomena on a broad scientific basis. The same science and the same technology that produce these dangers must concentrate ever-increasing attention on determining means of combating them. In this layer the problem does not appear insoluble, even if it requires us to make sacrifices.

The second layer covers the political, economic and pedagogic measures that must be taken to allow the necessary scientific and technological action. To some extent these measures are within the capacity of an individual state. In principle both the dominant political systems of today, parliamentary democracy and state socialism, possess a political apparatus designed to solve such problems; presumably it is necessary in both systems to create in the majority of the population an understanding of the dangers and of the necessity and possibilities for a solution. Other problems can only be tackled by the cooperation of several countries, sometimes on a worldwide basis. Here international law and the forms and institutions of international politics offer a suitable framework of action. It will be difficult to a degree, but nevertheless possible, to work out what steps must be taken here.

The third layer, which is really the problematic one, concerns sociopolitical structures within which measures relating to the second layer are to be carried out. Repeated experience, not only with ecological problems, shows that it is often known what measures must be taken, but that they do not come to fruition. Private business interests, cumbersome bureaucracy, and international struggles for power compete for the unhappy distinction of being the main cause of failure. In the battle of political opinion failure provides welcome ideological ammunition for opponents. Only too often is use made of the political syllogism which runs: "The actions of my political opponent lead to misfortune; ergo my actions lead to good fortune." In fact, the question may be raised whether any current political system is capable of solving these problems, whether it be a parliamentary democracy with capitalism, state socialism with one ruling party, or, overriding these, the continuous struggle for power between sovereign states. Help is offered by two systems of thought, both trying to establish themselves in each political system, and both seemingly diametrically opposed. One is technocracy, the solving of problems by delegating them to specialists with adequate political power. The other is participatory democracy, the solving of problems by those directly affected. There are major reservations against both. Experience teaches that specialists tend to succumb to the interests they serve, and the most important prerequisite of an acceptable technocracy, unbiased analysis of the problems viewed as a whole, simply does not exist to date. On the other hand, participatory democracy offers the best prospects where the problems are fairly obvious to those affected and thus small in scale. On a large or worldwide scale, cooperation between self-determination and expertise is still a pious wish that seems to offer no prospect of realisation. Although the value of ecological balance, of all those on the list, is the one that should be the clearest and easiest to realise in a scientifically and technically inclined world, I fear the forecasts of increasing disruption of our environment over the next two decades, taking the statistical average, will most probably prove correct.

Of course, such an undifferentiated analysis of social and political conditions is insufficient; in the ensuing pages I shall attempt to go deeper. My concern thus far has been to show that the actual problems do not derive from the insolubility of the technical tasks or from the lack of a suitable political apparatus. The analysis sees the problem in sociopolitical structures such as the domination of private interests, bureaucratic systems, or power politics. This is not a new thought. Political movements in the last and in the current century have, with changing fronts, repeatedly attacked the same evils, and the question really is what they saw as their goal and why they were not more successful.

The Ambivalence of Progress

The Concept of Ambivalence

We are looking for the reason for the inadequate rate of progress, for the growing danger to modern man. We must first take a close look at the phenomenon whose cause we seek, which we may call ambivalence. We may regard as its two aspects the ambivalence of technoscientific progress and the ambivalence of political progress.

Technoscientific progress today has a peculiarly irresistible force. Its consequences radicalize the problems of the society we live in. It does not simply improve or worsen the situation but gives us new instruments, and because the tendency exists to realize everything that is technically possible, it radicalises opportunities and dangers. It creates prosperity but can also increase social inequality. It protects man from the violence of nature and threatens man by destroying his natural environment. It creates the conditions necessary for freedom and stabilises conditions of domination. It increases the destructive force of war and thus creates a radical requirement to avoid war, and as a means thereto offers an order containing the danger of extreme tyranny.

The negative side of this ambivalence can be largely explained by realizing the falsity of the supposed neutrality of technoscientific values. What may be seen as neutral in relation to existing values can be employed in many ways and will be employed in practice in the way most conducive to its own growth. The ideology of value-neutrality creates an artificially preserved blindness to its own consequences.

Political powers and ideologies tend to think science and technology are good when they are employed for the right ends, namely their own. But political progress shows the same and even greater ambivalence, though not the ambivalence of neutrality but that of partisanship. I do not mean the truism that everything good has its bad side, but that frightening phenomenon that we have all seen and experienced in our own actions, namely that a position taken which then acquires a radical form destroys itself and produces its own negation. This result is nearly always associated with the initially unconscious lie (which is capable of leading men, if they are honest with themselves, to a conscious lie) that the resultant negation represents the intended position. It is this lie that actually hinders a cure, and most of all the unconscious lie that deceives the liar himself.

This ambivalence of political progress is examined in the next sections with respect to the three positions of absolutism, liberalism, and socialism. Students of Hegel and Marx will be reminded of the dialectic by this concept of ambivalence. I am however avoiding the dialectic scheme of concepts, which often encourages its adherents to an unjustified optimism when they come to the point where they themselves historically stand and makes them all too easily blind to their own ambivalence.

Absolute Rule

In continental European history the absolute monarchy of the seventeenth and eighteenth centuries was one of the most important steps towards modernisation, or what today we call progress. It was preceded by a highly differentiated form of society and the blossoming culture of feudalism and city states, a culture in which freedom was partly in the form of privileges and partly due to the inefficiency of the central powers. This pluralistic world, with its mixture of splendour and misery, inefficiency and violence, was confronted through absolutism with a new value, that of effective unity. In terms of power politics there was the successful campaign of the prince against the nobility and clerical factions, a victory from which the bourgeoisie on the whole profited. The princely state created territories administered in a uniform way, an effective civil service, reduction of privileges, equality of justice, safety in travel. Looking back, we may regard organised administration and equality before the law as the legacy of absolutism to the succeeding bourgeois society.

The monarch himself of course stood outside this framework of equality. This is a self-evident necessity in absolutism's interpretation of itself. The creation of the unit called the state to serve the common interest was a problem of power, and the Prince had the power to break the power of the nobility, the Church, and innumerable privileged persons and to place them at the service of the community. An outright functional justification of absolutism such as that of Hobbes was, however, exceptional. This practice of power, like any other, generally demanded some ritual justification. The formula "King by God's Grace" was itself a formula of humility: The king was neither God nor of divine origin; he was what he was only by the incomprehensible grace of God, who had set him upon his throne and could remove him from it. In practice, however, God's pleasure was the justification for the royal position and was referred to often enough to justify acts that would commonly be thought not pleasing to God. The fundamental lie of all struggles for power, "my power is justified, because it serves the Good; thus everything that strengthens and supports it is also justified," found a highly welcome formula in God's grace. This, however, was increasingly the feeling of the subjects. The unity of the body politic collapsed exactly at the point that represented the precondition for its existence, the relationship between ruler and subjects.

I pass over the variegated intermediate phases of enlightened absolutism and constitutional monarchy and turn to the fully developed liberal bourgeois society of the nineteenth and twentieth centuries.

Liberal Democracy

The basic value of liberal democracy must be termed freedom or, more closely defined, the freedom of the individual. Absolutism bought unity at the cost of the suppression of many old freedoms, and in its later phases the lack of liberty was a manifest evil. The evil was felt the more strongly as the gift of absolutism, the protective unity of state administration, came to be taken for granted and was no more thought of as an achievement. The freedom of liberal democracy is however not intended as a restoration of the form of freedom as it was before absolutism, that is, privileges, but is the equalising freedom of all individuals. On the other hand, it is feasible only because it takes over a legacy of absolutism, a smoothly functioning state apparatus. In its very opposition it is thus a continuation of what may be regarded as the element of progress in absolutism.

I regard the political theory of liberalism in one respect as representing a high and previously never-reached level of political consciousness. All political systems discussed here share the conviction that political order must ultimately be based on a truth. I shall return to the meaning of this statement in the following pages. For the present I shall merely explain it by a few examples. The antique-Christian social theory, in which the society preceding absolutism found its self-interpretation, is clearly based on the concept of truth. It defines the true role of every member of society. Each member is happy, as far as humanly possible, and the society thrives when every member plays his appointed part. The religious justification for the principality is a justification in the highest possible concept of truth, as God is truth. The functional understanding of absolutism is based on another quite modern understanding of truth: those who can see through the causal chains of struggles for power and expedient distribution of goods will recognise that power must be delegated to one person and must be used by him to secure rational administration. Liberalism, too, has its specific relation to truth, namely that truth must be freely accepted and not imposed, which implies free discussion and tolerance. This conception, however, also implies a fundamental criticism of all previous systems, which all have assumed that the ruler possesses the truth. He must possess it in order to rule by it: that has been the constantly restated argument for religious obedience, and it explains the political necessity for religious wars, especially religious civil wars. The collapse of this absolutism of religious truth, which proceeds by stages on the principle *cuius regio eius religio* and which separates the ordering function of religion from its claim to truth, leads to a confessionally neutral natural law and the idea of tolerance, and ultimately makes possible the intellectual world of liberalism. Liberalism knows that no ruler and no political group may claim the possession of truth as its basic right. Political problems of truth are discussed freely by the citizens and representatives and finally magistrates are elected.

As far as I defend the liberal doctrine out of conviction, it is this principle I defend. It can be expressed by the somewhat paradoxical formula that good politics depend on truth, and nobody may claim to be in possession of the truth. Each horn of this dilemma is significant only when related to the other. In itself truth is intolerant: if one knows that two times two equals four, one can remain silent but cannot honestly admit that it might be five; and if the well-being of the community depends on two times two equalling four being known or recognised, one must fight for this recognition. Tolerance neutral with respect to truth is self-destructive. But as truth can be accepted only in freedom and not under compulsion, tolerance is essential to create an area in which truth may be found and recognised. Strictly speaking there is no justification for the use of force on the grounds that the force-user is in possession of the truth, even if he is. In practice, however, such principles cannot always be put into successful execution. Bourgeois democracy, not wishing to fail, took over and made use of the framework of the absolute state, including the police.

It is interesting to look at the conservative criticism of what was the rising liberalism. Not without reason tolerance was criticised as indifference to truth, and the emancipation of private initiative as the emancipation of private interests. The rule of shopkeepers was condemned by civil servants brought up in the ethos of duty. The defeated predecessor often sees with a critical eye the ambivalence in the behaviour of his adversary, who in turn will come to play the leading role for a limited period in history. The success of liberalism is, to a large extent, due to the unleashing of the extraordinary dynamism to be found in the combination of unhampered private interests and the breakthrough of the belief in progress.

This dynamism is most clearly seen in the economic field. Here, classical national economics makes its great discovery that free competition, which must appear as chaos to the antique-Christian scheme of thought and to the paternalistic-causal scheme of absolutist thought, can in fact be the driving force behind general prosperity. At this point I must confess to subjectivity. My own experience with market and state economies has convinced me, I would say empirically, of the superiority of the former. I admit the necessity of some interplay between the market and the planner, and here the question as to which of the two principles is the more correct has as little sense as the question whether one should walk on one's left or one's right foot. But it all depends on the determination of the right mode of interplay. More important in the context of our present discussion is the ambivalence of the principle of unrestricted profit, the ambivalence of capitalism.

The market is endangered by monopolies in the same Darwinistic way that is responsible for the market's success. The market does not create equality of income; an analysis according to the theory of selection will show the most probable form both for biological populations and for economies is the coexistence of large and small units. De facto, the market creates some crass inequalities, sometimes ameliorated in that they represent stages on the way to growth, but always bringing the merciless cruelty associated with the destruction of fully grown forms of life (this is one of the conservative objections to the liberals). To the victims of this system its freedom often enough seems be the freedom of sharks. The market is ultimately well designed for situations of exponential growth, but when it comes to problems of saturation, it can cope either not at all or only at the cost of cruel side-effects.

The central question regarding the liberal approach to the economy is ultimately the ethical one heard from conservatives and socialists almost in unison: by what right is private interest put before public interest? To this question liberal theory has an admittedly incomplete but nevertheless important defense, namely, that it is more honest. Show us, its proponents can say, show us the system that has fulfilled its claim that it consciously serves the public interest. We on the other hand, are perhaps cynics, but at least we do not lie on this point. Our success is deserved, for in the end truthfulness is usually the secret of the smooth running of things ("lying is so complicated"). It is true, particularly in the economic field, that self-interest is the most effective motivation for purposeful action and that the obligation to fend for oneself creates productive men.

On the other hand, this defense is itself full of ambivalence when it calls for truth. Cannot man be educated to look towards goals set over-high? May we not attribute to him some understanding of the idea of public interest? Certainly this very idea is promoted in the full political doctrine of liberalism. But does not successful liberal economics, in fact, divert us from attending to the public interest? The answer to the reasonable question, "Why should someone who has earned a million want to earn another?" is "Only the sort of person who wants to earn a second million will earn the first." So-called economic self-interest is no longer a direct vital interest at the current stage of capitalist development. It belongs to those curious self-motivated purposes of the mental being, man, such as power, artistic creation, knowledge, fashion, and sexual rites. We cannot understand what capitalism is about if we have no anthropological understanding of these processes.

Socialism

I would term the prime value of socialism solidarity, or one could call it *unity in freedom*. Here again we see continuity within opposition. The freedom of the bourgeoisie is the freedom of only a part of society, and with the increasing functionalisation of the technocapitalist world this freedom grows ever more fictitious, limited to freedom in one's private life. Only solidary freedom, freedom in unity, is true freedom. Only so, if it is possible, may progress towards full equality be made.

Socialism, in the course of its history of nearly a century and a half, has developed a split in its relation to the liberal world. Social democracy has taken its place as a reforming force in the liberal world. It has fully accepted the central political values of liberalism and has partly and in stages accepted its economic values. At the same time, classical liberalism has taken steps towards socialist ideals in Europe. The U.S. has moved more slowly in this respect. But perhaps Roosevelt would have been called a social democrat in Europe, even though Bismarck in many respects had already gone further than the New Deal in his social legislation.

Can social democracy, with its willingness to compromise, overcome the failings of capitalism? Revolutionary socialism in all its modern varieties believes not, but does it overcome the ambivalence of progress? Here, as before, we must compare ideals with practical accomplishments.

Practically speaking, communist parties and national revolutionary socialists have succeeded only in underdeveloped countries that have experienced no liberal phase worth mentioning. In such countries it seems obvious to measure success by the criterion of economic growth, and this is fully accepted by the socialists there. Measured by this yardstick socialism seems on the whole successful. But if one inquires as to the causes of success, I think they are due not to a built-in superiority of the chosen economic system—state economies tend to function miserably—but to the fact that the export of capital from the country can be stopped, inefficient latifundia abolished, and the population compelled to restrict consumption for the benefit of investment. In the early phase of great capitalistic development, outside barriers were not necessary in the most developed countries, and in others mercantile measures sufficed. In the early days of capitalism restraint on consumption could be achieved through the power of the entrepreneurs and the firmness of the apparatus of state supporting them. But as a rule, neither of these are achieved by the "soft" nonsocialist state in developing countries today. Another alternative to the soft state is of course military dictatorships, but these can often enough be given a socialist interpretation.

Thus far, the achievement of socialism, to put it somewhat pointedly, may be said that it brings the advantages of absolutism to a still-feudal society. This judgment admittedly overlooks the important role of the formation of social consciousness, the orientation of national thought in the direction of solidarity. Here, there is no king by God's grace who will at most change existing economic conditions in a reforming way, but usually a charismatic leader who, true to his egalitarian beliefs, must remove all power from the old ruling class. The relationship among the four components, which I would name charisma, terror, bureaucracy, and self-determination, is the problem confronting all important socialist systems. Used positively, socialist doctrine serves to anchor the will towards solidarity, without which this confrontation would be self-destructive; expressed negatively it serves to veil the radical contradiction between claims and reality. If cynicism is the danger inherent in capitalism, a compulsion and proclivity to lie is the danger of socialist rule.

Regarded in the light of Marxist expectations of history, this development seems initially paradoxical, and bourgeois critics of Marxism have often referred to this contradiction between expectation and actual history. According to classical Marxist theory, the present socialist countries should be just on the way towards a bourgeois society. I should like to apply my own concepts to this expectation. I think it probable, judging by their social development, that these countries have some sort of need for absolutism. On the other hand, they are part of a modern world that is no longer absolutist but liberal or socialist. They must therefore, while recognising such modern values, add a dash of absolutist practice. It is clear to what ambivalence that must lead. The cult of persons and bureaucracy are two faces of an absolutism that may not admit to its name. An optimistic forecast is that these countries still have the liberal phase before them. It is to be hoped for their sake that they will not also inherit all the problems of the western world.

This is the place to discuss the widely-held opinion that the real reason why there is a danger of war is the conflict of ideologies. This opinion is usually combined with the thesis that if only the other side would abandon its system so the whole world could become liberal capitalist or, alternatively, socialist, the problem of world peace would be solved. I regard this opinion as wrong. I suggest that the conflict of empires for world hegemony is misinterpreted rather than clarified by ideological differences. The battle for world hegemony (whatever the "world" was at that time) has been going on for thousands of years and, subjectively honest, the competitors have always seized on ideological means to brand the opponent as wicked, as barbarous, as representing a false system. It is true that the current conflict between capitalist liberalism and absolutist socialism represents a genuine conflict of structures as well as ideals. But it only overlays the age-old theme of the mighty power conflict. Even if Russia were liberal-capitalistic or the U.S. communist, they would still have to fight for world domination, and should the U.S. drop out, communist Russia would have to fight communist China for the same goal (all this assuming that the sociopolitical system in question fails to dismantle the structure of world power politics). Overcoming world-power politics is the theme treated at the outset of these deliberations, and I would be contradicting myself if I assumed a priori that this overcoming was impossible. But at this point I am discussing under the title of the ambivalence of progress why it is so difficult. Here we are confronted by the paradox that both the major competitors for world hegemony, the United States and the Soviet Union, owe their current political form to revolutions, which in each case included in its goal the overcoming of world-power politics. No world power has so unwillingly let itself be pushed into the role of world imperialist as the U.S. (although it has always practised economic imperialism in Latin America). The fathers of the American constitution wanted to provide an example for the rejection of power politics as practised by European princes; this was related closely to their acceptance of the freedom of the citizen and to the notion of the minimal state. By a worldwide revolution the Russian revolutionaries hoped to achieve the end of warring economic powers and ultimately the disappearance of the state; both ideas radicalise themes of the American revolution. Woodrow Wilson's war to end wars and Stalin's socialism in one country were, however, compromises with reality, and the power of this reality is our theme here.

The liberal democracies of the West can learn little from the practice of revolutionary socialism to date that would help them with their own problems. Currently their own socialist theme is participation. This demand takes up an idea of classical democracy and applies it to technoeconomic areas in which more important political decisions are made today than in so-called politics. The future will show to what extent genuine self-determining participation is possible in a complicated technical world, and to what extent this demand is simply a form of romantic compensation. Experiments in this direction must be wished every success.

Looking back at absolutism, liberalism, and socialism, each appears to me as a principle to represent some advance on its predecessor, which in practice, though, is made very questionable by the ambivalence of progress. I would not venture in this situation to accept any of these principles without reservation, but I ask what is the reason for this ambivalence, this human self-contradiction.

The Nature of Man

Factors

Can we track down the reason for ambivalence in the nature of man?

Human self-knowledge, a theme thousands of years old, is not very far advanced, at least not in the consciousness of modern intellectuals. Perhaps it will become the most important theme in human history when the current phase of scientifically overcoming external nature has ended. But such vital insights are necessary today. I shall pick out from the tradition of our knowledge a few ideas concerning man and shall refer to animal ethology, psychology, sociology, history, religious knowledge, and philosophic thought.

If we put the direct question as to whether the reason for the phenomena here termed ambivalences lies in human nature we come upon an old, conservative, and realistic theory, the theory of human egoism. It teaches that man is an egoist and that all schemes for an ideal society must fail where they seek to reform egoists, because they simply compel him to lies of expedience. A viable order of society must not try idealistically to change human nature but realistically to take it into account. This wise counsel does not go far enough. Is human egoism truly incapable of recognising its true interest? Do not these ambivalences harm our true interest? What factors decide what we regard as our interest?

The weakness of all traditional theses concerning human nature is that they underestimate the significance of history. It is the nature of the bee to gather honey; that is inborn. Is there a human nature in the same sense? Purely biologically man's coming to be can be described as a transition from largely inborn modes of behaviour into an enormously increased capacity for learning, learning both in the sense of social tradition and in the sense of individual insight. Man is the animal whose nature is to have history. Language is an example. Man is born with the ability of learning to speak; the language he learns depends on his environment. Is the ambivalence purely a result of the wrong social conditions, and would it disappear if they were changed? That was the hope of optimistic liberal and socialist theories. The failure of these theories to date gives occasion for the current question: What constant factors have determined the constant human failure in the changing forms of society?

In many religions the concept of the radically evil is found. Psychoanalysis uses a structurally similar concept, that of neurotic compulsion. Ambivalence is familiar in neurotic behaviour. On a conscious level, a neurotic can perfectly well set some value on an exaggerated pedestal and at the same time on an unconscious level be hostile to this value and unknown to himself hinder its realisation with all the means at his disposal. Is the ambivalence of history a neurosis of mankind? But how shall we judge if this is so? What factors could result in such neurotic behaviour? I shall here discuss five constantly recurring factors in human behaviour: possession, ranking, power, love, and partnership. All of these except power are found in animals, and it is worthwhile comparing these factors in man with their animal equivalents.

Every living being requires a place not just as an abode but also for the carrying out of its actions. The higher animals mostly live in societies. For man society is constitutive, as he owes to it his behavioural store of speech and custom, without which he could not live. In turn, for life in a society, there is a constitutive store of behaviour towards one's kind. Only this gives the individual a "place" in society, a framework for his action.

Elementary *possession,* which exists also in animal societies, is itself a place, what the economist would call possession of land. Behavioural researchers can show us how bravely even a fish will defend its territory, and they discern that the male nightingale sings to inform his nightingale neighbour which territory he may not penetrate. In judging human striving for possession of territory it seems to me fundamental that this factor has such a long animal prehistory. An animal's territory is its home. Of course it is the strong animal that will hold its ground, or at any rate the stronger will have a larger territory than the weaker. But it is an illusion when theories of society maintain that at some former time the strong divided up the common territory into private possessions contrary to nature. The historical process was probably the reverse. The recognition of communal property is the achievement of a society that demands a high degree of asceticism from its members. I believe that men can be persuaded to renounce private territory only when they have another home, an unquestioned place in society or a spiritual existence. The transitions between the cultural forms of gleaners, hunters, nomads, farmers, and town dwellers represent just different aspects of the disposition over land. The same is the case as regards the changing size of the group participating in possession (just as with animals).

Social *ranking* of members of the species is among the higher animals just as prevalent as possession. One can say that these conditions of higher and lower social ranks are constitutive for animal societies where there are any individual relationships between their members. As far as man is moulded by his animal inheritance, this will also apply to him. Again it is an illusion when certain theories of society maintain that rule and ranking are the unnatural fruits of power. Both by nature and custom, man is conditioned to hold on to his social position, to know who are his superiors and who are his inferiors. It requires an

extraordinary historical effort—and if successful is an achievement—
when men actually recognise each other as equal, and we must subsequently ask how such an achievement can be possible at all.

I define all animal societies as simple or topical societies, as well as
human societies in which similar characteristics, retained or restored,
may be regarded as dominant. Let us invent someone knowing only
such societies who is suddenly confronted with the sphere of *power:* this
would be to him a completely strange phenomenon, not derivable from
his previous knowledge. Being and having, aspects of the ever-recur-
ring struggles for rank and possession and limited by the exigencies of
the moment, are now faced by the essentially unlimited field of ability.
Power, as I use the word here, is discovered possibility. A possibility
is never fully and finally realised: it ceases to be a possibility when it
is fully realised. In principle, power can be understood as the ability
to do what one wants and as not having to do all one can. That such an
area of possibility exists at all is a discovery of man, a special ac-
complishment of insight. The types of human insight corresponding to
power I give the double term, will and understanding.

Power is firstly power over nature, via tools, hunting weapons, and
housing. I am now describing not the history of man's seizing power
over the earth but its effects on human behavior.

At an early stage of his history man must have been radically
changed and affected by the discovery of power. The fascination and
horror of this transformation are still reflected in the dreams of power
through magic, and religious atonement to the powers of nature attempts to restore a balance. From highly developed classical cultures I
quote just three examples: the calm order of God in the Pentateuch
(Gen. 1) "replenish the earth, and subdue it," the agitated choir in
Sophocles' Antigone "πολλὰ ιὰ δεινά" and Chuang Tzu's anecdote of
the peasant sage who would not use a well-wheel because "he who uses
machines acquires the soul of a machine."

Power reaches its most explosive form, however, as power over men,
by means of weapons, superior knowledge, and the framework of functions in a highly developed culture. Only through this force does traditional social ranking become the specific phenomenon of dominion so
debated today; only through this force do naturally occurring conflicts
between and within groups become transformed into the art of war and
the art of politics. Here we are a step nearer to the cause of the
ambivalence of progress. Power over men also has, when its potentiality is discovered, no immanent limit; when much is possible, then
more is possible. "Only the sort of person who wants to earn a second

million will earn the first." Here possession means no longer just the security of the home, the satisfaction of wants or the way to luxury, it means unlimited room to act in, that is, power. Thus the demand to measure profit by the need completely misses the point of the principle of maximising profit. The same applies to accumulating power by accumulating offices. And it is in the face of this structure of power that I am here arguing when I regard a third world war as probable and see world government as the most conservative solution: at least this solution does not attempt the stupendous task of breaking the power of power.

I am inclined to say that power is ultimately tragic, even when it is combined with goodwill and a sense of responsibility. It must make the opponent powerless, "harmless," or it will not last, and it is inherent in power that it produces opponents. But the victor, the successful wearer of power, discovers his deep powerlessness, his inability to change the basic structure of power by means of power. Blindness is part of the tragedy: to him, fighting for power, its powerlessness will hardly be visible.

But this tragedy is not all. I have considered power here in isolation. We must remove this isolation.

Let us now invent someone who knows only possession, dominion and power, and is now confronted with *love*: this would again be to him a completely strange phenomenon, not derivable from his previous knowledge.

Possession, dominion, and power are areas of the ego. Group behaviour in these areas can fittingly be named group egoism. Expedient rationality serves the expedients known to the ego. The tragedy of power is the impossibility of self-fulfilment. In love we find self-fulfilment in the overcoming of the self, a transformation of all values —completely incomprehensible in terms of expedient rationality. Instrumentally thinking, science can well describe possession and dominion, for its concepts are themselves designed to serve such finalistic rationality; the limitlessness of power finds its partner in the limitlessness of knowledge. To spell out love in scientific terms is almost impossible, because it transcends the concept itself. To understand man an understanding of love is vitally important. Nevertheless I shall pass it over in this politically oriented essay. But I had to refer to it to make us remember that there are forces in man that can invalidate seemingly rational scales of values.

There is yet another quite different tie between individuals, namely nonsexual personal *partnership*. As it is found in all aspects of communal life we have come across it often already, without its being a theme itself. Its quality must again seem nonderivable from possession, ranking, power, and sexual love. Every reductionism of theories of sexuality and theories of expedient behaviour breaks down when trying to explain it. The most interesting account concerning its animal prehistory is to be found, I think, in Lorenz' book *On Aggression* in the chapter "The Bond," which incidentally seems to me far more interesting than all the other more popular ideas in this book. Lorenz ascribes the personal bond genetically to aggression modified by ritualisation, in which he sees the possibility of individualised relationships in a group, which go far beyond the first stage of ritualised aggression, social ranking. Here, too, the ritual does not realise self-evident values but creates or makes possible values that are not self-evident. If Lorenz is right, he has succeeded in making comprehensible the structural relationship of the various types of personal bonds, even if these range over a wide field from indissoluble friendship or community effort to companionship and as far as lifelong hostility. This seems to me one of the important contributions towards understanding ambivalence. In particular, it contributes to the understanding of all institutions not reducible to rational-expedient or sexual terms, such as marriage.

Of course, man's personal ties, just as much and even more than all other relationships, are understandable only in their connection with insight. We finally have been led to this theme.

Insight

Insight is not self-training by trial and error but the ability to imagine the results of such processes in advance, being insight into the reason for such results. It may be just a partial insight or a broad consciousness, but it always relates to that which I can only call truth. Naturally, truth is not infallibility. Conversely, words like fallibility, error, and lie are meaningful only where there is understanding, even if not based on reflection, of what is meant by truth. Insight is a man's certainty by reason of some truth which has revealed itself to him. A consciously manufactured and utilised machine, for instance, is unthinkable without insight. In the social sphere customs may be passed on and followed without insight, but I doubt whether they arise without it. There is no personal relationship without insight. How far insight can take us we cannot say in advance because every special insight admits the question of the reason for its possibility, and if the question can be answered this opens up insight on another level.

Insight cuts across all compulsions of instinct, habit, custom, and "insightless" interests. This crossing is connected with its combining the three interrelated fields of facts, possibility, and freedom. I can only be free of a compulsion when I can envisage what it is that compels me. That is the meaning of "what wonderful things are facts." The fact is *as* a fact, as something that has happened, immutable. Not to see facts, "wishful thinking," is to lack a certain freedom, for which oneself is to blame. In this sense inborn behaviour, individual habit-forming behaviour, and behaviour moulded by social usage, however appropriate to circumstances, are not free. Insight into facts makes us free by opening up possibilities. The known and recognised fact is thus no longer compelling; perhaps it is a state that can be changed. Insight is insight into possibilities. The fact is only understood as such by being thought of as a possible fact or recognised as a fact that has occurred. This, however, supposes other possible facts as possibilities. Again, these possibilities are not dreams but are in fact possible insofar as they are based on established other facts. But to have factual possibilities implies freedom.

Insight not only opens up freedom; it requires freedom, even on the psychological level. If I examine the psychological motivation for the state of a man's mind, to him an insight, I am basically assuming insight into his character. This is a figure of ideological criticism. If my insight is determined by my economic interest (or my libido, my neurosis, my tradition, or my spirit of contradiction) my causal deduction is revealed as no insight. This revelation applies even if the "insight" in question coincides with the actual facts and thus formally fulfills the classical criterion of truth. For this agreement is then a chance one and needs to be reexamined with insight.

If human life is not possible without insight, neither is communal human life possible without communal insight. In this sense I would call a peace the body of a truth, and truth the soul of peace. By peace I mean here the possibility of living together. I speak of "a" peace because, as we all know, there have been and still are many ways of living together. Of course, in using the word "peace" an ethical claim is implicit. There is living together, in a way, even in conditions of conflict: a man who beats his wife or two great powers at war live in a certain state of coexistence. In such coexistence there are usually also the rudiments of a peace: the fact that the married couple still live together, the framework of martial law and the policy of having aims in war that envisage a future armistice. But here peace means above all a value that is striven for and whose absence is marked by the dreadful distress of the present. The peace so sought after is not mere coexistence but what, using the word "possibility" in a pregnant sense, I have termed the possibility of living together. It is for all men the communal possibility of living, opening the way to communal freedom. This freedom requires a communal insight, and hence a communal truth.

Now truth is, so to speak, by nature communal. Two men knowing the same thing are involuntarily linked in this insight; they cannot deny this community even if they want to. They have communal facts and consequently communal possibilities. That is why I have said that truth is in itself intolerant. Recognised truth eliminates the possibility of honest assent to the opposing untruth. In another sense orientation to truth is implicitly tolerant. Community in a given truth that I seek with my neighbour assumes that he recognises this truth, that it is truth for him. But the repetition of a sentence that to me is true is by no means true for him, even if he thinks he believes what is said. If I want to live in community with my neighbour through truth, I must permit him the freedom to assent to the truth, that is, I must grant him peace. In this sense peace is not just a consequence of insight but at the same time a prerequisite for truth in practice. In this double sense I term it the body of truth.

In the name of truth, in the light of a recognised truth, all purely factitious authorities are dissolved. What permits the achievement of equality between men is always a communal truth. An authority, on the other hand, is always inherent in peace grounded on truth, namely, the authority of him who has the insight. For him who does not have this insight the most important insight accessible to him is that he does not possess the insight in question; an egalitarianism that obstructs his knowledge of his lack of knowledge does not take him seriously in human terms as a virtually knowing man, and despises him by pretending to respect him. I have never found men so free as where the authority of insight was self-evidently recognised.

There is a pluralism of truths and forms of peace. Traditional societies lived by a religious truth and by the peace it made possible. The modern world lives by the truth of science and the technocratic peace it makes possible. But in the face of this pluralism what does truth mean? I am considerably compressing the philosophic problem. One can interpret error as false truth. If one understands by truth that something shows itself as it is, then error does not show nothing, but something as it is not. Nevertheless, something is shown and perhaps one can live with it for a little while or in some ecological niche. Insofar as this is the case, error that makes peace possible is an imperfect truth. Only when it makes the claim to be simply true does it become false. Now, we do not know the whole truth of anything. The insight we can express is always "a sort of error." Thus "truths" must compete. Precisely the legitimate claim of errors that they are truths joins them in battle. This battle impels the process of history, which can be seen as a chain of truths overcoming each other. This is stylised by dialectic. To us today the process of history can be seen only as opening towards the unknown. We cannot specifically think of world peace as the body of ultimate truth; wherever this hope takes a concrete form it becomes clearly unrealistic or tyrannical. We must seek to understand truth as a succession of truths, the truth of the process itself.

A parallel from individual psychology: a man can be at war or at peace with himself. Here, too, peace is the body of a truth. Here the limited value of every limited peace can clearly be seen. Man learns and matures; certain insights come at a certain age. The transition from one insight to another seldom leaves a man at peace with himself. Crises are the usual symptoms of a battle of truths within an individual. Inner peace can reflect either the happiness of an achieved insight or the suppression of a disturbing insight. One will be inclined to call the one a true peace, the other false. Are there criteria for assessment?

Values and Happiness

Is there insight into values? Or only into facts that we then assess irrationally? Is agreement over values only a community of irrationality? If not, what is the rationality of values?

I do not deal with this question with the philosophical rigour it demands. Our study was to be based on certain given values. In the first two sections of this essay I have accepted these values uncritically, for what thinking man of today would not freely agree to them? But insight into ambivalence simultaneously shakes the naiveté of our set of values. What does a look at human nature teach us?

I have several times emphasised that it is easy to be certain (and consequently in agreement) as to values when their absence is experienced as a manifest lack, manifest suffering. In this respect we can now say our situation is the same as that of our animal cousins. Animals do not need to ask themselves if preservation of the self and of the species are values. Hunger, fear, sexual love, and mother-love (if I may use anthropomorphic terms) impel them to do what these values require, and if they were not in nature of the animals, they would exist no longer. Man can ask if all these represent a value, or even the ultimate value, but in elemental situations the question does not usually arise, or is silenced if it does. It does not have to be silenced, however, for man can question the sense of his survival; such scepsis or doubt is even a natural side-effect of certain crises on the way to maturity. Furthermore, we regard human life (and, if we examine it closely, animal life, too) as not being such that it should be limited to the overcoming of elemental needs. We hope to make life secure, in order to make possible a good life. But what does good mean here?

Is happiness a criterion of values? According to the American Declaration of Independence the "pursuit of happiness" is a human right. But what is happiness actually? One can find the whole ambivalence in the concept of happiness. Shall we examine it step by step from biology to culture?

Pleasure and pain, biologically speaking, are indicators, warnings of what is beneficial and what is not. If we judge—as animals themselves do not reflect in this way—animal behaviour by the simplest of criteria, survival, there is a clear ranking by Darwinistic values. Today there are still individuals of those types which have been able to develop quickly enough. Progress (seen biologically) is a higher (i.e., more successful) value than just preserving the species, preserving the species is a higher value than preserving the individual, preserving the individual is a higher value than pleasure and freedom from pain. In each case the lower value only formulates a condition that usually serves the next higher values but is sacrificed (or succumbs in the fight for existence) if it does not serve it. Here, admittedly, pleasure and pain differ from the values of preservation and progress. On the one hand, they can be understood as purely functional, and where something functions by itself it does not need to be accompanied by these indicators. On the other hand pleasure and pain serve all values, not just the lowest; sexual pleasure, for instance, certainly does not serve the preservation of the individual experiencing it.

Now, to judge organic life purely by its power of survival is surely inadequate (did the saurians find no fulfilment just because some other species won the race of evolution?). For man, pleasure and pain are to be seen in a completely new light.

On the one hand man's mastery over himself involves the decay of instinctive compulsions, which considerably devalues the indicator function of pleasure. Civilised society has to a large extent divorced its basic instincts from their biological purposes. The fight against this divorce is itself age-old. What our tradition calls animal lusts (greed, drinking, whoring; murder too logically belongs here) are in reality purely human inventions. In them all a pleasure no longer serving as an indicator shares the limitlessness of ability with power. The same applies to the avoidance of pain via drugs. It applies especially to the higher, more abstract forms of pleasure that secure possession and dominion. Pleasure is in each of these cases a principle without insight, working in animals as a substitute for insight.

In organic development, and especially in human history, old material is frequently used for completely new purposes (as the swimbladder becomes the basis for the lung and aggression the basis of communication). And so the mental—often esthetic—stylised satisfactions of our basic drives represent the body of culture: eating as a communal meal under the aegis of *haute cuisine;* drinking as a symposium; dwelling in terms of landscape and town; society in terms of articulate social roles; love as a game; violent emotion, partnership. In respect to many of these forms, one may speak of happiness with insight rather than of simple pleasure. To the highest forms of happiness belongs the experience of progress, one's own productiveness.

In these examples happiness is again an indicator. That which it indicates I should like to call self-realisation. In this essay I shall not go beyond self-realisation as a measure of values. But what is self-realisation, and what makes it possible?

Self-realisation

It should first be pointed out that self-realisation as a principle of value includes the unity of the good as well as the multiplicity of values, includes what is good for the individual and what is good for society, includes conservation and progress. The multiplicity belongs to the realisation. Let us once more speak of happiness as an indicator: in general man is happier when he is not always doing the same thing; men are happier together when they are not all similar. Equality is equality in freedom, freedom is the freedom to be different. But realisation requires solidarity in recognised differences, unity in freedom.

But self-realisation is a difficult achievement. If we understand happiness and suffering as indicators of success and failure in the process of self-realisation, suffering is the more reliable indicator and at the same time an essential teacher and driving force. The experience of pleasure contains a natural tendency to superficiality. If one believes that progress is a leading value—and the limitlessness of possible insights and the very concept of creativity suggest this—such superficiality is to be expected, because the indicator of happiness invites us to tarry. The battle of truths is accompanied by suffering. The positive aspect of the ambivalence of progress lies in the insight-stimulating suffering that it produces; its danger lies in its acceptance without insight of. a partial happiness. Happiness as experienced by the individual cannot be the value at this stage either. The idea that suffering is only a consequence of faulty social development is naive (or a projection); why do we have the capacity to experience physical and psychic pain if we do not need this indicator?

Self-realisation represents, among other things, the gaining of the insights of which one is capable. In the first section I interpreted enlightenment as self-enlightenment. Kant calls enlightenment man's coming-of-age after a minority for which he is himself to blame. Kant himself explains this minority as the inability to make use of one's reason without the help of another. According to Kant this minority is blameworthy when the reason for it is not lack of understanding but lack of determination and courage to get on without the help of another. *Sapere aude!* To have courage to use your *own* understanding is thus the motto of enlightenment.

What has this to do with the historical process of enlightenment? The intention here is that a whole society should come of age. And so the parable of the development of the individual becomes pregnant with meaning. Every man is at first a minor, incapable of using his own reason; he must mature in order to achieve certain insights, then have the courage to seize on them, to shake off authority, and so become of age. But if we clarify the concept of minority in this way it seems that the concept of being to blame oneself disappears. Can I help it that I am born as a helpless child? And, seen somewhat differently, am I to blame for what my parents and teachers taught me? Am I to blame for the society I grew up in? Was not enlightenment to be understood as the escape from a minority not blamable, as emancipation from a foreign yoke?

Kant's idea goes much deeper than this thesis of rebellion. He touches on a theme found also in psychoanalysis in the curing of neuroses but also in every responsible person's attempt to come to terms with himself. If I recognise an error that has ensnared me, there is no cure, no becoming free of the causes of this error as long as I seek the causes outside myself, in what has been imposed on me by parents, society, or the emotional pressure affecting me, my unconscious, my instincts. All these observations may be completely correct. But the ability to overcome *my* error and not *mutatis mutandis* to succumb subsequently to the same dependencies rests in my being able to recognise it as my own error. *Mea culpa, mea maxima culpa* is not a formula of false remorse, but the recognition reporting I am of age, capable of being responsible to myself. Rebellion, when it attacks actual errors of others, contains the chance of enlightenment, but it is in itself not yet enlightenment, for recognising the errors of others serves to hide one's own errors in their projection beyond the self.

What, however, is the content of the insights with which we come of age? For the individual as well as for mankind there is a phase in which we must learn the facts and laws of our environment. But these insights must ultimately serve self-realisation. We return to the question of what self-realisation is. This question has been posed and answered in depth only in the great traditions of religious thought. The battle of the progressive against systems of dominion supported by religion has mistakenly given rise to the idea that enlightenment and religion are opposed. One may assume that intellectuals today are emancipated from dependency on religious guardianship and can pose questions about truth in religion without being biased.

I limit myself to the moral and meditative aspects of religion. I portray the moral aspect only in the form of that religious tradition to which European culture belongs, the Judeo-Christian. Religious ethics show a double tendency to that which is simultaneously unconditional and justified. The Ten Commandments, the commandment "Love thy neighbor," and the demands of the Sermon on the Mount are unconditional. Certainly it is observed that what is demanded is simultaneously what is sensible, what is reasonable for man and society. But the commandment is not derived from this reasonableness. Thus it is saved from being judged with the relativity each of us applies in our own interest when something is so derived. Keeping the commandments may bring happiness, but happiness is no criterion for the justification of the commandment. But the commandment is not unjustified. Formally its justification is the will of God. But at the same time God is the Creator. Man is therefore at one with the origin of his existence when he keeps the commandment. In the Sermon on the Mount those who keep the commandment at the seeming cost of happiness are promised blessedness. What does blessedness mean here?

We can help ourselves here with anthropological ideas. Take for example the problem of violence. Society cannot permit violence. The inner peace of society is disrupted by acts of violence. "Thou shalt not kill" is a sensible commandment. It is also sensible, accepted entirely in the Old Testament and predominantly by the Christian church, that society may use violence against the violator. But this does not solve the basic problem of the reason for the violence. Why do men kill? The idea of a society in which violence-producing violence is no longer practised is introduced in the late Prophets and in the New Testament as a historical hope. But it is not named as something that men can bring about, but as something that God will bring. We can only understand this ethic when we comprehend the difference between what is achievable and what is not achievable. The actual overcoming of violence can occur only where its roots are, in the human soul. Society will always give cause enough for acts of violence; I can overcome the violence in myself only when I can renounce the unquestionable right I have to hit back, can "turn the other cheek!" The overcoming of violence must always originate in myself. Here the ethic of nonviolence has its basis in truth. Only he who finds peace with himself, and that means peace with God, can radiate peace. But the peace that arises from a group of such men is no possible target of a plan any longer, no "preferred world" for intellectual activists. But it is impossible that a genuine, everlasting world peace will be secured without this force. Scientifically speaking this is no political programme, but psychology, in exact form.

But can that which we cannot achieve still be possible? The answer of the religious ethic is that the seemingly impossible must be attempted and that an inner force, which religion calls divine, will come to our aid. A common possession of the great religions becoming evident today to intellectuals is meditation. This inner activity in re-forming the self is at the same time passive, receptive; perhaps one can say it is a self-forming for receptivity. This indissoluble combination of active and passive aspects is not peculiar to religion. Far more, it characterises everything in human life that transcends the sphere of expedient rationality. Expedient rationality's world of will and understanding defines only what we (particularly modern occidentals) call activity. The experience of that which is received, that which the will cannot produce to order, is as peculiar to love as it is in another way to sensual and intellectual perception, that is, insight. Truth is not made, it is revealed, but almost always only to him who seeks it, and the manner of his activity defines the form of that which he can receive. This happens, too, in religious self-forming. The rite, as the external form, usually follows quite specific historical traditions; prayer applies itself actively and personally to the root of this tradition; meditation, often called internal prayer, is an opening up and training of an inner capacity for perception. All three, especially prayer and meditation, relate directly to the moral experience that the only thing that helps cannot be constructed, cannot be brought forth by mere exercise of the will. The purpose of meditation is to clear the way to man's true self, the way being blocked by the ego's desires. It is therefore something that does not supplant moral striving but rather presumes it. If we have understood ambivalence correctly, it is concerned with the removal of ambivalence. This, too, is taking place today in an unfinished historical process in which traditional and new experience meet.

These elevated forms of self-realisation have been achieved so far by few men and women in history. But their realisation was always also for the benefit of others who could not achieve it themselves. They showed these others that the way upwards to self-realisation is open. Although this experience is very old, self-realisation can presumably be described as a historical process. The breakthrough of the religious ethic and meditation that I have outlined occured in the great cultural blossoming forth in the first millennium B.C. which was also responsible for the rise of science and philosophy among the Greeks.

In more recent times the West has developed other characteristics of human existence. Most important for our theme is the pair of mental powers one may name will and understanding. I understand here by will the ability to aim at something specific and to take action to achieve it. Understanding is the ability then to think of objects for the will, or will is the ability to manipulate objects of the understanding. I distinguish between understanding (*Verstand* being the term in German philosophic terminology) and reason (*Vernunft*). Understanding is conceptual and thus isolating and discursive, not intuitive. Reason is is a form of intellectual intuition. The modern world is becoming to an increasing degree a world of will and understanding. To it belongs expedient rationality (an idea expressing both abilities) and power, although the will to power has no basis in the real content of the understanding or the will but only in the determination of both via available possibilities.

However, understanding and will are evidently not the only capabilities relevant for man. A society dominated by them is "one-dimensional." It is in a state of self-contradiction, for because of their finite nature understanding and will simply cannot suffice to determine their own goals. The emptiness of bare power is the consequence of this.

If this analysis is correct, simply exerting will and understanding cannot solve the problems of our future. Reason is the least of the remaining factors that must be brought into play. Self-realisation, where the reason is trained too, is then not only the leading value but the focus of the therapy. But all these considerations would be misunderstood if they were interpreted as advice to be passive. On the contrary, our sphere of action will be large enough only when we recognise the reasons for our failure. Reason should guide will and understanding, not supplant them.

Conclusions and Summary

What May We Expect?

I shall now attempt to summarise my expectations for the future, as derived from the considerations outlined.

The currently visible trends in development are dominated by what I called in the previous section the world of the will and understanding. This domination is both direct and indirect: the ideas of this world dominate the thought of most men who today consciously plan and act according to their plans; they dominate, too, the worldwide communal area of the thoughts of men who do not know what they want. It is also indirect: trends in another direction are mostly formulated as a negative attitude to the world of the will and understanding, as an opposite pole. Practically, the only men who are not closely touched by it are those whom it has not yet reached; one can forecast that it will reach them some day.

As long as direct dominance of the world by the will and understanding lasts, a technocratic structure of society will grow and become stabilised. Although it will solve a considerable number of material problems, we can already clearly see how many material problems it will create in turn. I think, however, that one should not underestimate its flexibility in solving those problems whose causes it can formulate in its own terms. Self-correction by trial and error is a feature of understanding subject to the will. Waves of fear such as those current about the environment can act as a corrective to planless, naive optimism and lead to constructive action. What this world cannot master are the realities in man that are not present in his expressed ideas. These show themselves in the phenomena I have described under the name ambivalence. The unconditional character of the growth of the world of the will and understanding heightens the ambivalence. I cannot help but expect growing crises culminating in catastrophe.

On the other hand, the sphere of the will and understanding has the character of the empty boundlessness of power only when the other realities in man are not developed, realities that set limits to this sphere and give it content. Of these, we have met in this essay—though not listed systematically—personal love, cultural creativity, meditative receptiveness, and perceptive reason. We can sense, but we do not know, how they interrelate. In the modern resistance to the penetration of the world by will and understanding, other quite different forces are also to be found: conservative obstinacy, blind or critical aggression, an inarticulate desire for happiness. I regard this resistance as one of the most important and in the long term one of the most helpful features of our time. But its immediate effect is chaotic and it can in the short term lead to catastrophe just as it may perhaps in the long term lead to the avoidance of catastrophe.

I shall now apply these general considerations to the three themes of the first part of this essay, taking them, however, in reverse order. Here, I distinguish between forecasts, those for the next ten years being short term, those to about the end of the century being medium term and those over a longer period, if one may dare to make them at all, as long term. My forecast for the developing countries is sceptical in the short term and moderately optimistic for the medium term, being more optimistic concerning economic development than concerning domestic political freedom. As regards their long-term development, a lot depends on how the dominant industrial nations of today fare. I think it quite possible that in the long term Asiatic countries will achieve a position of world hegemony.

Concerning the internal structure of the industrial nations I expect in the short term a predominantly technocratic phase and in the medium term a change almost impossible to forecast today. In the short term, however, no radical changes are in sight. I should like to regard the American crisis as deep and necessary, but at least partly capable of solution. As regards the relationship of the economic and social structures of capitalist and socialist countries I am inclined to accept that despite all retarding factors, there will be a slow convergence, though not even in the long term should identity between the structures be expected. Technical development will for a while continue to be rapid. Most of the problems of environment I regard as superficially soluble. But such progress and stabilisation will do nothing to solve the fundamental problems. The transition to a pleasure-oriented, post-industrial society will tend to displace what are actually burning questions, and even where solutions are technically possible they will be neglected. The idea that we can switch from being productivity-oriented to being pleasure-oriented and simultaneously maintain (not only in the short term) our standard of living seems a dubious idea to me. It underestimates the complexity of the effort required and the irreplaceableness of the motivation of productive competition. Unsolved tensions present genuine problems, but the superficial appearance of relaxation hinders their solution. On the other hand I am sure that men will not accept this state of relaxation or lack of tension as the ultimate state. I do not dare to prophesy the sources of change in the medium term.

Perhaps the area of world peace or world-power politics will continue to be, as so often in the past, one in which external, far-reaching decisions will come about. All I have said should have clarified the reason for my concern that there will be war (though I cannot prove it). The securing of world peace sets mankind today a clearly-defined task, a task just as clearly beyond the capacity of its current political, social and mental system. The truth this peace must incorporate is today sensed everywhere, but perhaps perceived nowhere. In the short term I regard a world war as very improbable, but in the medium term as quite possible.

What Should Happen?

I avoid the formulation "What shall we do?" It has the weakness that it gives the impression that we only need to say what is to be done and then do it. But from all that has been said we see that this would be inadequate in two respects. Firstly, expressed thus simply, it becomes a formulation of the world of the will and understanding. The attempt to give a simple answer to this question all too easily encourages the behavior that creates and perpetuates the need. Hardly anyone reaches a situation where he can act to some real effect without having despaired of the efficacy of direct action. Second, efficacious action presupposes that all questions have been carefully considered. In many situations requiring such action I have, to my bitter regret, simply not thought far enough to know what action I should suggest or myself undertake. One of the answers I would give to the question "What shall we do?" would be "Think hard." For this reason, among others, I have founded an institute instead of going into politics.

The question "What should happen?" formulates in particular a mental exercise. Action unsupported by theory will continue anyway; we do not need to promote it further. But what must the guiding principle of considered action look like? Here I seek to sketch an outline, allowing that it is a provisional attempt at an experiment one is hardly permitted to undertake. In doing so I restrict myself to the argument of this essay and seek only to draw conclusions from it.

In my opinion the guiding principle in politics must be world peace. It is the only idea that can integrate political action on a worldwide basis. It is just as essential for the avoidance of the catastrophe of world war as it would be for the avoidance of its repetition, should one war be inevitable. It is thus not invalidated even if it initially fails. On the other hand it is very demanding; it is a hard criterion by which to measure all other political ideas. Finally, it is comprehensible to all, even if its consequences cannot easily be seen by all. This peace should be no tyranny. It must be the body of a truth, and to think this truth is the sense of our political theory.

In terms of foreign policies, world peace must in the long run radically transform all foreign politics into world domestic politics, thus requiring all powers, even the greatest, to renounce their sovereign right to wage war. Some central world political organisation, a "world government," however federative and limited in its rights, seems to me absolutely essential. Every plan that seeks to make do without it seems to me to be unrealistic wishful thinking. The most important short-term step towards such an organisation is to create worldwide awareness of its necessity. As, however, there is not the slightest chance in the short term of realising this world organisation, a short-term and medium-term change in the structure of society and awareness is necessary, one which will affect all other fields of life and be derived not from the ultimate goal of a world organisation but from the individual requirements of the time, while, however, being explicitly consonant with this ultimate goal. As regards international politics, we must in the short term support the current truce between the great powers with all the means at our command, although in so doing we are consciously supporting false structures, ultimately hindering final peace. But we must give this support, for otherwise the risk of a war between the great powers is too great.

The present-day difference between the industrial countries and the economically underdeveloped countries must in the long term be levelled out without, however, giving rise to completely similar economic systems. This process may begin in the medium term, but unless the industrial countries destroy their own prosperity by war, it will take longer than the creation of a world organisation and may be to some extent a consequence of this creation. Here it should be noted that in a system of competing sovereign states a mercantile alliance of the weaker states against the stronger may be a vital aid to development but will only very rarely lead to complete equality with the stronger states. Furthermore, in a world continually faced with the danger of war, a certain striving towards autarchy is so eminently reasonable that it would be senseless to wish to hinder it. However, a world organisation achieved in the long term could bring the danger of exploitation of economically weak areas by strong ones, either brought about centrally or automatically resulting from the system of competition. The world organisation cannot help but impose a strong element of central planning in the world economy. On the other hand, I am convinced that the more possible it is to preserve or create free markets, bearing in mind the demands of the common interest, the more successful (and more satisfactory) the world economy will be. Even in the short term, economic policy can and must be oriented towards finding such a compromise between two equally essential components. In the sense of the term "unity in freedom," world society must, to use current terms, take on the form of a liberal socialism.

These obvious and easily stated requirements are, however, sensible only if the conditions for their fulfillment are realisable, and these I have discussed from anthropological and philosophic perspectives. I consider that a post-industrial society oriented towards happiness and pleasure will be incapable of mastering the ambivalence of the systems it will permit, systems designed not to interfere with happiness. If it is inevitable that the guiding principle of the majority of men will be subjectively felt personal happiness, this state of affairs will require a society with an elite structure, in which the elite are oriented towards that truth whose body is world peace. In the short term this structure exists already, insofar as only a minority is facing up to the problems involved and exercising a pedagogic function with respect to the rest of the population.

The guiding words of this development are freedom and self-realisation. Freedom is essentially freedom for self-realisation, and only self-realisation is essentially freedom. Thus everything depends on understanding what self-realisation is. I have said that happiness is an indicator of realised values and that suffering can be an incentive for their realisation. The indicator is not always reliable: We distinguish true happiness from a questionable, partial, compensatory, false pleasure. I believe that happiness is ultimately an indicator of the stages of self-realisation. This realisation occurs in stages, and hence we here use terms such as progress and coming-of-age. What was happiness in early stages is at a higher level a means or perhaps must be sacrificed in order to reach the higher level. The ultimate decisive perception concerning mankind is the distinction between the happiness-seeking I and the Self. The ego in all its mental wealth is one of the stages on the way towards the Self. When a man fails to sacrifice ego-rooted resistance to change, he fails to realise his personality and integrate himself with society. This sacrifice also occurs only in stages, as does the realisation it permits and the happiness this realisation brings. It occurs only with individuals, and perhaps in history.

This self-realisation has been throughout the whole of human history the theme of religion. In concrete historical terms it was the theme of religions in their plurality. The social body of the realisation achieved found its form in the various cultures. Each such culture was the relative peace of a truth of human self-realisation. If it is possible at all, world peace is peace between cultures that meet. The culture compelling it today, western culture, compels it through unharnessed progress of knowledge and power and, as it has reached no goal of recognised truth, is essentially nonpeace. This culture in its modern form is an ambivalent secularisation of its own religion. World peace may provisionally be kept as an outward coexistence of cultures. But at its present stage our own culture cannot coexist with itself, let alone with others. Paradoxical as it may seem from purely political or social analysis, I am convinced that our actual task, on whose success the possibility of a true world peace stands or falls, is the realisation of the human Self. One of its forms is the achievement of religion in its truth, to which the meeting of cultures and religions may contribute. The achievement of truth means the realisation of what is actually meant in that truth; it means coming-of-age. Political efforts are a part and a consequence of efforts towards this realisation.

Men very well understand the requirement of a sacrifice of the ego. If we consider political values, it is everywhere central, for the side of these values in which the ego and its needs are confirmed requires no emphasis. The unity of absolutism is the compelled sacrifice of particular interests. The freedom of liberalism is essentially the freedom I grant my fellow citizen. The solidarity of socialism everywhere demands the sacrifice of selfish interests for the interests of the community. The perversion of all these values always occurs when the ego transforms them into demands made on others instead of on itself. The limit of insight of these political valuations lies mostly at the point where they replace individual egoism by a collective egoism in which the undifferentiated values of an I still underage are merely reproduced.

Such demands are extraordinarily far removed from what is called reality. They are therefore not requirements for current political actions, but represent a criterion. May I be proved wrong in naming this a sceptical contribution.

NONTERRITORIAL ACTORS
AND THE PROBLEM OF PEACE
Johan Galtung

Some Assumptions About Peace

This is an essay dealing with the problem of peace from one particular angle: *nonterritorial actors*. This important angle merits the attention of the peace analyst, and the following is an approach to the problem of how nonterritorial or transnational actors can influence war and peace.

It is customary today to talk about peace as at least a two-sided concept. It still makes sense to define peace as the absence of violence, but one has to use a sufficiently extended concept of violence. One way to extend it would be through the following two definitions. First, there is what may be referred to as direct violence, the violence committed directly by persons against persons. It takes various forms, depending on whether it attacks the human body anatomically in war, in torture, by piercing, tearing, crushing, burning, and poisoning or physiologically by controlling the inputs to the human body through suffocation, starvation, and dehydration or by controlling the output from the human body through chains, imprisonment, detention, or more modern weapons affecting the higher nerve centres. This kind of violence is well known; it is dramatic and, literally speaking, deadly significant.

Second, there is what could be referred to as structural violence, which is built into the social structure. It may take the form of an exploitative pyramidal or feudal structure, something like the diagram as shown on next page. The arrows in the diagram stand for some kind of exploitation, such as net capital transfers from poor to rich nations. Moreover, the underdogs are fragmented, kept apart; only higher up is there contact, even "integration." Everybody knows this structure from personal experience; it is found within and between countries; it is an embodiment of violence. This structure is reproduced in the agricultural, industrial, commercial, and administrative sectors of society in such a way that surplus is extracted from the lower levels and trans-

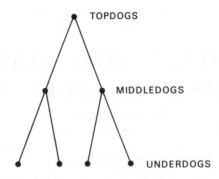

ferred upwards, making the higher levels richer and richer at the expense of the lower levels, producing the famous "gaps" in development. The result is often highly differential morbidity and mortality rates between rich and poor countries, districts, and individuals. But the impact is not only in such concrete terms. It also takes more psychological forms —as when all interesting work, problem-solving included, is reserved for those at the top, leaving tedious work to individuals, districts, and countries lower down through what is euphemistically called "division of labor," depriving them of chances of growth and expansion of freedom in a broad sense. This structure persists, because it is difficult for underdogs to organize and overthrow the structure; the low levels are atomized and their interactions mediated by the higher levels.

In short, *structural violence is based on a combination of exploitation and fragmentation,* often placing those at the bottom below a minimum existence and always at a disadvantage. But sometimes there are confrontations, even revolts, and these display the linkage between direct and structural violence. Imagine a revolt against the higher echelons of a social structure, whether truly feudal, capitalist, state capitalist, or what-not and whether the revolt intends the substitution of present underdogs for topdogs or a truly revolutionary end to the exploitative structure. It is generally assumed that the topdogs will react to defend not only the structure but also their own position in it. Ultimately they may use direct violence, but usually as a response; they do not have to before the underdog throws the first stone. In that case, the underdog can be labelled an aggressor; there are laws and legal institutions that can then utilise all types of direct counter-violence. We get three stages of violence: structural violence benefiting the topdogs; direct violence initiated by the underdogs to change the status quo; and the direct, repressive counterviolence to preserve the status quo. Imagine further that the revolt is very feeble, very easily crushed. It would still be registered by the attentive observer, and even reported as "trouble" by newspapers and on TV. But if one extrapolates further, one may picture the revolts that never come to the take-off simply because they have been crushed in advance, because the underdogs are sufficiently manipulated, apathetic, and fragmented. One then sees how continuous these two types of violence are with each other.

Structural violence is only continuous with direct violence between unequals, in the *vertical* or asymmetric conflict built into the structure just depicted. Between equals, in a *horizontal* conflict, the structural violence element is by definition absent or negligible, and if there is violence it is of the direct variety. It may, however, result from structural causes inside the actors. If to work for peace is to work against violence, it means to work for the absence of both types—more concretely, to work not only for the reduction of direct violence but also for egalitarian structures. By that we mean, roughly, structures, where no party is exploiting the other; where no party is dependent on the other but each possesses sufficient autonomy to carry on alone; where parties are not kept apart but may cooperate, in solidarity, with each other. *Equity, autonomy,* and *solidarity* would be the necessary characteristics of such structures.

If we now study peace in its more classical sense, simply as absence of personal or direct violence, then there seem through history to have been two major trends in peace thinking; we shall refer to them as the *dissociative* and *associative* trends. According to dissociative thinking, actors who may be on a collision course should be kept apart from each other, whether by geographical (oceans, mountain chains, natural borders) or social (prejudices, stereotypes, deterrence) techniques. According to associative thinking, the best plan is exactly the opposite: to keep them together in cooperative relations. A typical example of the first is alliance formation, polarization, and balance-of-power policies; equally typical examples of the second are exchange and cooperation across conflict borders and the creation of supranational organizations.

At this point, it is interesting to introduce the two concepts of violence. It is often held today that dissociative strategies are somewhat old-fashioned, custom-tailored as they were to a world with slow speeds of communication and transportation. But since the middle of the nineteenth century, these speeds have been on an exponential increase, with a corresponding increase in transnational and supranational bonds. Geographical as well as social barriers between countries are being broken down; consequently the objective situation calls for extensive use of associative rather than dissociative strategies. A good example is the relationship between France and Germany. Three invasions of one by the other in 70 years could have led to a final dissociative answer, but what today is being molded between the two within the framework of the European Community is certainly an associative solution. It is certainly not impossible that large-scale direct violence between the two will be eliminated for the foreseeable future. For the ties between France and Germany within the European Community are very different from the exploitative relation that the community has with African countries: they are nonexploitative, horizontal ties that do not produce deep conflicts.

How does structural violence relate to the distinction between dissociative and associative peace policies? Dissociative policies have the advantage of killing two birds with one stone: they often produce the absence of violence, if only in the short run, and at the same time solve the problem of exploitation and injustice *in vacuo*. Where there is no interaction, there cannot be any exploitation. With associative strategies exploitation becomes a major problem—*not only because exploitation may lead to direct violence and hence is not stable but because it is violence in itself.* Clearly the problem is to bring parties together to prevent direct violence without at the same time creating structural violence. This is the general problem of peace politics in our time: how to practice associative policies as a bulwark against direct violence without at the same time getting into the pitfalls of structural violence.

How then should one conceive associative peacemaking? There seem to be five factors or conditions that are at least heuristically very helpful and also seem empirically to play a considerable role:

Symbiosis: a relationship based on needs that lead to real interdependence, so much so that both A and B know that if they destroy each other they hit themselves;

Symmetry: a relationship that is really egalitarian; no party enriches itself at the expense of another. In other words, absence of structural violence is in itself a condition;

Homology: as the two parties are reasonably similar in structure, cooperation is easy because each actor knows where his opposite number is to be found;

Entropy: all interaction channels are used—if not equally, at least in such a way that heavy concentration on one (usually elitist) channel is avoided;

Transcendence: moves in the direction of integration, providing a medium in which conflicts can be articulated and resolution attempted, the medium usually being some kind of nonterritorial actor, governmental or nongovernmental.

A typical example of a region where these conditions exist reasonably well is the Nordic countries. They are among each other's biggest trading partners, not only of commercial goods but of cultural goods and manpower as well. This exchange and cooperation takes place in a reasonably nonexploitative way, partly because these countries are not very different in size, Iceland excepted. The countries are institutionally very similar and have become increasingly so through processes of harmonization. An impressive number of channels of communication exist and are used; and there is a certain superstructure, the Nordic Council, with its various ramifications. There is *peace,* by and large, in the double sense of this term. Although one example proves nothing, it serves as an illustration, particularly if it is compared with other regions of the world such as the Western Hemisphere or Eastern Europe where the second condition, symmetry, is typically not satisfied. The Soviet Union dominates the Eastern European countries (except Albania), and the United States the Latin American countries (except Cuba) and Canada. The famous 49th parallel is a border of peace only for him who is satisfied with a very narrow peace concept. With at least two thirds of the Canadian economy in U.S. hands, this is a border of structural violence, so far without any corresponding direct violence in either direction.

What then does one do in the case of an associative structure that satisfies all conditions but symmetry and entropy, in other words a structure without direct violence but embodying structural violence? One simple answer is: in a first phase, one destroys the structure by means of dissociative policies, by severing ties between high and low, by withdrawing cooperation and association—for instance, underdog countries would sever ties with the big power concerned, whether military, political, economic, cultural, or all four—to gain autonomy and independence and build one's own institutions. In a later second phase there may be a change from fission to fusion policies, from dissociation to association, but this time on a basis of equality. In other words, *for horizontal conflicts, associative techniques may be most appropriate; for vertical conflicts, a first phase of dissociation is probably needed before association can come into play.* Association is not ineffective, being probably the most effective bulwark possible against direct violence, but exactly for this reason it may be too much, too effective. Whereas dissociation may buy freedom from structural violence at the expense of isolation, association very often buys freedom from direct violence at the expense of structural violence. A glance at the world today gives ample testimony that this price is too high. Look at all the "law and order" there is, all the "tranquility"—in so many cases it is based on the subordination of many to the big, rich, and powerful.

In political thinking, there are those to the right who say that the human animal can be kept nonviolent only in a structure of law and order, embedded in a basically hierarchical set-up; there are those to the left who hold the view that the human being can set himself free from structural bondage only by means of direct violence. According to these ideologies, freedom from one type of violence can be bought only at the price of accepting the other. According to the present author's ideology these are false dilemmas, which represent a political and intellectual capitulationist view of human affairs: the task is to strengthen those institutions and forms of action that try to maximize both types of peace. One approach lies in the direction of nonviolent forms of revolution and nonmilitary forms of defense. Another approach points towards the use of nonterritorial actors, the approach to be developed in this essay.

What then is the role of such traditional peace strategies as arms control and disarmament in all this? One view is that most conferences and negotiations on disarmament fail not because of ill-will or lack of skill but due to something much more basic. What they try to do is to square the circle, to disarm a highly dissociative structure prepared for the violent cataclysm called war and refer to the result as peace. But a disarmed dissociative structure is still a dissociative structure, only an unprotected one. It has neither the peacebuilding effects of the associative structure that ties parties together in a web of exchanges and cooperation nor the peacekeeping effects of the dissociative structure that keeps opposing parties apart by the threat of the severe punishment called retaliation. One little incident, and the disarmed dissociative structure will crumble; one party will prevail over the other, or there will be a quick arms race up to and even surpassing predisarmament levels.

Disarmament in a dissociative structure can take place only in an atmosphere of distrust, for the reasons already mentioned. If the parties could fall back upon geographical distance and forget about each other, there would be no problems, but technology has outdated that possibility. In our day the alternative to a dissociative peace structure maintained by the threat of direct violence is an associative structure. It is probably far more likely that such a structure will lead to disarmament than vice versa, for in an associative structure weapons may cease to be targeted on the other party and remain only a capability until they wither away. Strictly speaking, they do not even have to wither away. Norway and Sweden have more than enough weaponry to stage a respectable war: *the reason there is no feeling of threat is not disarmament but distargeting.* On the other hand, the chance that disarmament by itself will lead to an associative structure seems low or negligible. Disarmament is hardly the road to peace; rather, peace in a real sense seems to be the road to disarmament, by way of distargeting.

Quite another thing is arms control aimed at reducing the chances of war by accident or escalation. One may say that all wars are caused by some escalation and are accidental and, further, that human frailty or madness is usually found not at the level of the soldier, sergeant, or trigger-happy officer but much higher up. The topdogs are the definers of madness and sanity, exempting themselves from accusations; and it is built into the structure that they can make others accept their definitions. Nevertheless, there is some virtue in such measures: they do aim to perfect a dissociative peace structure, even though we would certainly rank them low in effectiveness relative to an associative peace structure.

In short, the problems of attaining peace are manifold and the solutions many, and they may look contradictory at the first glance. But in this regard, peace research does not differ from, say, medical research. Only if illness or peacelessness are seen as unitary phenomena can they be dealt with in a unitary way. What we have indicated is that there are two basic forms of violence, direct and structural, and two basic strategies of peace, dissociative and associative, yielding a total of four possible combinations. Dissociative ways to counteract direct violence— by means of natural borders, balance of power and so on—are waning in significance because they are ineffective and too costly. Dissociative policies to counteract structural violence through some kind of decoupling and associative strategies to counteract direct violence without leading to new forms of structural violence are all on their way up.

Some Assumptions About Nonterritorial Actors

We now turn to the nonterritorial actors. The question is, what role can they play? That role is certainly not necessarily a peace-building one. As these organizations are themselves an important part of the current structure, no simplistic conclusion to the effect that "states make wars, organizations make peace" is warranted. The opposite conclusion, that nonterritorial actors are simply the instruments of states, particularly of the dominant states, is not correct either, as it makes no distinction between the present situation and what these organizations could become.

Which are these nonterritorial actors? This section will present a brief resume of the basic characteristics of nonterritorial actors and particularly of their growth. Their growth is the growth of the world's sixth continent, *the invisible continent of nonterritorial actors.* It is a continent that does not show up on any map, yet one of the most significant of them all in world politics.

Underlying any analysis of this sixth continent is one fundamental factor: the variable of communication/transportation speed and capacity. Basically constant for a million or two years of human history, it has increased exponentially since the first successful attempts early last century to install steam engines in ships (Fulton) and in locomotives (Stephenson). The system of territorial actors (Ts) developed in the first phase with spatial contiguity as a basic and undisputed assumption. With slow mobility, contiguity was a necessity. That the ensuing exponential growth of transportation/communication should lead to the emergence of nonterritorial actors (NTs) is hardly strange, but it should be pointed out that we are at just the beginning of this process. Even though the monastic orders were forerunners, and ethnic groups or nations have always been split between states at least to some extent, NTs as we know them today are the result of the speed revolution initiated in the 19th century. Even the colonial empires, noncontiguous as they were (and are) owed their tremendous growth partially to the fact that the means of mobility were quite unevenly distributed.

The standard typology that breaks NTs into international governmental organizations (IGOs), international nongovernmental organizations (INGOs) and business international nongovernmental organizations (BINGOs), usually called multinational corporations, will be used in the following exposition. It should be pointed out that this general system of NT actors now seems to have gained sufficient momentum to have reached a stage of self-sustained growth. By this is simply meant that the NT system has its own dialectic, its own sources of growth; it is much less dependent on what happens in the system of states than before.

In the first phase of the development of NTs, powerful governments come together—first bilaterally and ad hoc, later multilaterally and in an institutionalized form—and the result is an IGO, such as the postal union or the League of Nations. Correspondingly, nongovernmental organizations come together—also first bilaterally and ad hoc, later multilaterally and in an institutionalized form—and the result is an INGO, such as the international professional association. Corporations expand, establishing or using local companies—which result in BINGOs. In the second phase IGOs and INGOs and BINGOs start directly and develop immediately into the multilateral, institutionalized form, often using a strong base developed in one nation. Instead of using existing elements in other countries, they create these elements. Intergovernmental organizations lead to new offices in national governments (for instance, in the field of environment); new associations, even professions, are created to serve as a local base for an INGO (Rotary Clubs being an example); and multinational corporations breed daughter companies everywhere. But then comes the third phase, when the system has become more autonomous, more detached from its territorial base. Thus, there is the formation of super-IGOs, super INGOs and super-BINGOs, organizations comprised of IGOs, INGOs, or BINGOs, because of the need for coordination, articulation, and conflict solution. There is also the formation of links among the three types at any level of complexity. Examples are the coordination of UN Specialized Agencies, unions of international scientific associations, and organizations of multinational corporations in the field of oil. Very often this cooperation takes the form of contact and cooperation rather than a new organization: we are still in the early phase of second-order nonterritorial organizations.

Each IGO, INGO, and BINGO tends to foster, through the usual social dialectic, a competitive counter group, vying for political, sociocultural, and economic markets among the territorial actors. Economic cooperation leads to cooperation in the field of environment; if radical political parties internationalize, so do conservative parties. In fact, they may often cancel each other out like matter and antimatter, leaving behind only a lot of noise, as in the dialectics of international student activity in the cold-war period. Above all, there is the equally dialectical differentiation inside the NT system along its own class lines. As it is now, masters and servants are emerging, and although the smaller, younger, and less powerful NTs are badly organized, they will soon see the need for some kind of trade union. All international youth organizations, for instance, might join together. A stratification may sooner or later crystallize into a class system, and the result may be gigantic super-IGOs, super-INGOs and super-BINGOs pitted against each other. It is not at all inconceivable that a conflict may emerge between the IGOs within and those without the UN system, between INGOs representing professions and all the others, and between BINGOs using technologies harmful to the environment and all the others. Modern transportation and communication facilitate many kinds of alliance-formations, not only between organizations within countries, but also between nonterritorial actors, regardless of the locations of their headquarters. As we shall see, location usually represents no obstacle: most NTs have headquarters in a limited part of the world, relatively close to each other.

Finally, within each NT there is formal equality between members from rich and poor countries. Dominating and dominated are found side by side. But in most instances the world territorial structure is simply reproduced. Not only are NTs usually organized with national chapters, but dominant countries outside tend also to dominate inside the international organization. Hence revolutions inside NTs are to be expected, and they will produce new NTs. Dominated countries will find it increasingly in their interest to have their own international organizations rather than being manipulated inside "universal" organizations, but this tendency will, of course, vary from field to field.

In other words, the invisible continent will grow, and unlike the visible continents it has no fixed border. One cannot postulate any upper limit if communication/transportation speed and capacity continue to develop as they have, except perhaps a limit resulting from the number of human beings involved and the time they can spend to make the organizations meaningful.

Let us turn to some data to illustrate this discussion. Fortunately, one specialist on nonterritorial actors, Chadwick Alger, has recently synthesized much of the information available (in a paper at the International Political Science Association, Montreal, 1973). We shall draw on his material in what follows, starting with figures showing the growth of IGOs and INGOs, as displayed in Table 1.[1]

The INGOs now outnumber the IGOs about ten to one and have

[1]Werner Feld, Nongovernmental Forces and World Politics: A Study of Business, Labor, and Political Groups (New York, Praeger Publishers, Inc., 1972) p. 177. Excerpted and reprinted with permission.

TABLE 1

Number of IGOs and INGOs, 1860–1970

	1860	1870	1880	1890	1900	1910	1920	1930	1940	1950	1960	1970
IGOs	1	2	5	10	11	13	9	31	38	81	142	242
INGOs	5	9	21	37	69	135	214	375	477	795	1321	2296

done so for most of this century. The "private" sector has about ten times as strong an internationalizing capacity as the "public" sector, which is not strange, taking into consideration how little of social life is in fact made governmental in most of the world. Of course, in the socialist countries the distinction between IGOs and INGOs may become meaningless, unless it is interpreted to mean something like "direct or indirect governmental control".

However that may be, the growth rate is high, well above 50 percent for both categories for many decades. What would this mean if we extrapolate to the year 2000? It might mean more than 1,000 IGOs and 10,000 INGOs, if the growth rates do not show any pronounced downward or upward trend in this century. The finding is important not so much in itself as in comparisons with the number of territorial actors, the states. In the territorial system there will appear some new states, other states may integrate into one, and some—perhaps not so few—may disintegrate into two or more; but it is highly unlikely that the change in number will be of the order of magnitude indicated by a straight-line extrapolation.

Of the many simple reasons, one is particularly important. Territorial space is finite and clearcut; if a new territorial actor is to be carved out, it will be at the expense of somebody else's power over that slice of territory. But nonterritorial space is without limitation: a new actor can usually be created just by proclaiming itself. What rules of recognition exist—for IGOs (for instance, ratification by member states) and for BINGOs (which have to be incorporated somewhere) —are not nearly so dramatic as for the state system, where new actors usually have to shoot themselves into recognition. This is one of the great strengths of the whole nonterritorial system, leading to growth that is still exponential. Sooner or later, it will have to taper off, however.

What, then, about the BINGOs, the multinational corporations, whose growth is by and large also exponential? Distinctions must be made—first, among industrial corporations, banks, and insurance companies; second, between the number of corporations or "parent systems" and the number of foreign subsidiaries. Thus, of the 185 most important U.S. industrial corporations in 1967, all were active in Europe, 182 in Latin America, 174 in Canada,117 in Japan, and 62 in Black Africa. This high level of penetration around the world becomes much more impressive when the total number of foreign subsidiaries is considered: 3401 in Europe, 1924 in Latin America, 1048 in Canada, but only 233 in Japan (the main office in Tokyo and one more?) and 166 in Black Africa. Seen over time, since 1900, both trends in most parts of the world show exponential characteristics, but more so for the number of subsidiaries than for the parent systems. In other words, it may be that international corporations from now on will grow much more in depth and breadth than in number.

The number of banks with foreign branches and the number of these branches, as well as the size of the deposits, also show signs of exponential growth. In 1968, for instance, some 27 major banks had 450 branches abroad, a rise from 2 banks with some 90 branches in less than a decade. Moreover, their activity abroad is a significant part of their total activity, foreign deposits making from 26 percent to 46 percent of all deposits. Whether there will be the same tendency for banks —that the increase in the number of banks will tend to slow while subsidiaries continue exponential growth—remains to be seen, but it is likely.

We should now have presented some information about the total number of multinational corporations of all kinds operating in at least three countries, but that is not so easy. Numerical estimates tend to vary between two and five thousand, depending on definitions. What is quite clear, however, is that their number far outstrips the number of states and that there is an increasing gap between the number of states and the number of nonstates—of nonterritorial actors—leaving the former behind.

It may be objected that numbers are not the same as power and that the significance of nonterritorial actors will depend on their power more than on their numbers. Where do the nonterritorial actors stand in power relative to the states? One could compare the total number of members of INGOs (with national chapters) with the population of states and the economic strength of industrial corporations (sales), banks, and insurance companies (assets) with the economic strength of states as measured by GNP. Although it is far from obvious that these factors are comparable, if we rank these four entities on the basis of economic strength, the top 50 include 31 states, 11 banks, 4 industrial corporations, and 4 insurance companies, according to the research carried out by Arosalo and Väyrynen at Tampere Peace Research Institute. An earlier report, reproduced among other places in War/ Peace Report (October 1968), compares states with corporations only and finds that among the 40 biggest economic entities 8 are corporations. More important, the biggest corporation, General Motors Corporation according to all lists, had only 17 states ahead of it on the list. Then follow Ford, Standard Oil, Royal Dutch/Shell, General Electric, Chrysler, Unilever, and Mobil Oil—almost all of them involved in the nonterritorial *sine qua non,* transportation and communication.

Thus, the NTs increase in number, they proliferate, they grow economically, and they eat themselves upwards on the list of states. They are not only comparable with states, they are on the same footing in many regards and above them in one very important respect: They show more dynamism. All this, however, does not show that they constitute a system alternative to, or even opposed to, the territorial system. For it might well be that the nonterritorial system is to a large extent a reproduction of the territorial system at another level and that all these IGOs, INGOs, and BINGOs mainly are the conveyor belts that carry the political, military, cultural (in a broad sense), and economic power of some states over others.

To explore the nature of the NTs, let us look at some other aspects of the nonterritorial system. The crucial question is simple: *Are they really nonterritorial?* To be nonterritorial they should be universal or at least symmetric. The territorial system should not be reflected too much in the members; in the organizations' locations, for instance, in terms of headquarters; and the home states of their most important officials. But from the data it immediately becomes clear that these organizations *as we know them today,* however impressive their numbers, their power, and their growth, are at best *potentially* nonterritorial actors.

Have a look at the membership pattern. Essentially it is a question of comparing the world Northwest,—Northern America and Western Europe,—with the rest of the world. Among the IGOs, the Northwest predominance in the membership of the total number *is* decreasing— from 100 percent at the very beginning, through 61.4 percent in 1900, 49 percent in 1925, 47 percent in 1950, 39 percent in 1960, and down to 36 percent in 1966. But this is more than equitable, for that part of the world has only 16 percent of the world population. The trend tells us one thing, above all: other states are joining the system. But the picture is immediately less symmetric if one looks at the INGOs: From 1959 to 1966 there was a decline in Northwest membership of the total INGO system from 66 percent to 54 percent, but that is a slow decline and still far above any proportionate representation. What this tells us is, of course, that the whole idea of formal organization and international association is a Northwestern one.

The predominance of the Northwest becomes much more pronounced in the location of the headquarters of the international organizations. In 1906, 97 percent of them were located in the Northwest, in 1962 still more than 90 percent (90.8 percent to be precise), and in 1968 down to 87.1 percent. As to headquarters, the center of power is Western Europe rather than North America, although North America has by far the highest number of multinational corporation headquarters, with only a scatter of headquarters located elsewhere.

As to the nationality of the people on the executive organs: in 1960 88.4 percent of them were from the Northwest for the INGOs, 80.5 percent for the IGOs. Although they could in fact hold most of their meetings elsewhere, in 1966 still as much as 76 percent of the meetings were held in the Northwest (down from 87 percent in 1951). Secondary offices were also predominantly located in the Northwest (58 percent of them in 1968, as against 77 percent in 1958). In short, there are trends toward greater symmetry, but these trends are usually weak and have far to go.

It is very difficult to escape the conclusion that the structure of the nonterritorial system is very similar to the colonial pattern, with a centre located in the world Northwest, so richly endowed with superiority complexes, spreading out to the world periphery and capable of exploiting and fragmenting it.

Not only is the centre of gravity of power located in the Northwest, but the invisible continent is also anchored there in other ways. The whole conception underlying nonterritoriality will have a northwest colour or imprint. Dominant personnel will be taken from that region, sources of finance will have to be found there, and so on. But this should not be seen as a deliberate, Machiavellian plot to engulf the rest of the world, using nonterritoriality as the machinery of neocolonialism just as territoriality was used for colonialism, with a chain of bases and supply points reaching out to the colonized periphery. One should rather see it structurally, in terms of the postindustrial Northwest having to expand to make the neomodern socioeconomic system meaningful at all. In this need to expand lies the reason for the net of structural violence thrown over the world, not in the stated intentions. The intentions are usually benevolent, like "bringing the fruits of Western civilization" and "technical assistance."

TABLE 2
The First Nations in terms of INGO per Capita and IGO per Capita

Rank	INGO per capita	IGO per capita
1	Israel	Panama
2	Norway	Costa Rica
3	Switzerland	Nicaragua
4	Denmark	Mauritania
5	Finland	Liberia
6	New Zealand	Paraguay
7	Panama	Central African Republic
8	Ireland	Israel
9	Uruguay	Norway
10	Austria	Honduras

Another aspect to this pattern should be pointed out. In the rich and capitalist Northwest, one group of nations probably benefits particularly from the development of the invisible continent: *the small nations.* If we calculate the number of INGO memberships per capita by country, excluding territories with less than one million population, the ranking list is as shown in Table 2.

The two lists are quite different, and the reason is simple. As already mentioned, there are many IGOs in the world today to which a state simply has to belong in order to be a state; hence the states topping the list are the smaller ones. That does not mean that we do not have the same postcolonial pattern in the IGO system. Even for UN agencies, only one has headquarters in the east or the south, the UN Environment Program in Nairobi. Other UN headquarters are either in the militarily organized West or in nations "neutral to the West." But as the INGOs do not mobilize all states, the INGO membership reproduces a well-known structure, this time with the small, rich, and capitalist on the top. Both the absolute number of members and the relative number per capita are significant. It is not unreasonable to assume that for the same number of memberships the smaller of two nations is more penetrated, more people are affected, and the invisible continent is more visible.

The invisible continent is the continent that the small, developed, and capitalist nations try to colonize, particularly as all other continents have to some extent been colonized by the big powers, capitalist or socialist. The importance of this factor, and the validity of this general hypothesis, can be further appreciated by studying Table 3.[2]

---

[2]"Who's Who in International Organizations" by E. S. Tew, "International Associations-Associations Internationales," Union of International Associations, 1 rue aux Laines, 1000 Brussels, Belgium.

165

1. Switzerland	86	6. France	22
2. Belgium	55	7. Norway	19
3. Netherlands	42	8. Britain	16
4. Denmark	25	9. Italy	9
5. Sweden	23	10. North America	4

The site of an organization is definitely an important factor in determining the nationality of its officials. The small, rich nations have made use of this resource.

Nonterritorial Actors and Peace

Having seen the present state of affairs, we face the question of what potential there is in the nonterritorial system, how it can be transformed to serve peace, in both senses, as the *absence of direct violence* and as the *absence of structural violence*. But, many will object, we still live fundamentally in a world of states. True, but what has happened inside countries may also happen between them: organizations (e.g., parties) may become more salient, more powerful than territorial units such as districts. Hence, in discussing this general problem we shall consider three different assumptions: the nonterritorial system is (1) lower, (2) equal to or (3) higher than the territorial system in salience. Varying this factor will permit us to discuss increasingly radical strategies, starting from the situation today. For there are also possibilities within the existing system; what matters is to make use of them to prepare the ground for more progressive, more peaceful structures.

(1) Nonterritorial System Lower than Territorial System in Salience

Today the nonterritorial system is lower in salience, and the question is how it can be improved from the point of view of peace theory—assuming that the territorial actors will still be the foci of decision-making and that the NTs will to a large extent still depend on Ts for their existence. Although they may be granted some extraterritorial rights, NTs will be controlled by Ts and be financially dependent on national organizations, governmental or nongovernmental. In this general setting NTs will continue to grow and have ample opportunities for growth, but as we have seen undirected growth will not in itself change the world structure in a direction that automatically favors peace. New NT organizations must be created with more relevance in this particular field of peace, old and new NTs penetrate more deeply into the territorial system, and this entire nonterritorial system be more symmetrically distributed over the territorial system. We shall look into these three points in more detail, starting with the INGOs, proceeding to the IGOs, and ending with the BINGOs.

New, More Peace-Relevant NTs

As to *new INGOs,* one suitable point of departure may be the already existing international organizations of parliamentarians and of international civil servants. These INGOs unite people who have a particularly direct concern with peace problems; and although the participation usually is very asymmetric in terms of the T system, the first group is undoubtedly an efficient channel of communication and the second an instrument for the internationalization of a real world administration. They should be made more representative, more active, seeing themselves as progress-oriented pressure groups and not as trade unions for high-status privileges. It is particularly important that they develop world perspectives, that they all think in terms of world food budgets, world ecology, and the like.

World perspectives will be the cause as well as the effect of world movements and world political parties; they are not the sum of well-articulated national or regional perspectives. World political parties will be a much more powerful factor than the two organizations mentioned. National political movements find each other and create an international organization, as conservative, liberal, socialist, and communist parties to a large extent already have done. But this is still mainly a nonterritorial coordination for territorial action: The parties are active in an institutionalized form only at the national level. The perspective changes completely when such INGOs can act in an IGO setting, as to some extent they do in the European Parliament and the Council of Europe.

Hence a basic problem is to find institutional settings within which world organizations in general and and world political parties in particular can act. One general formula would be to build on the system of consultative status, tying professional INGOs to the UN specialized agencies and ideological INGOs to the UN itself. But this system will become effective only when INGOs are called upon to do some real decision-making, in later phases of increased salience. In this phase it is more a question of expanding the system of consultative status, in a sense legitimizing politics in the form of political parties at the world level rather than leaving all politics to governmental delegations. Then there are the more informal political movements that have not (as yet?) crystallized into political parties—not even into NTs. Informal world movements may, however, prove to be much more important than the formalized movements, including world political parties, because they serve as vehicles for new ideas, new conceptions. The hippie movement, for instance, has been setting a cultural tone, a style, defining values all over the world, for a long time, and it will have its successors. The anti-Vietnam war movement was an example of loosely coordinated efforts to resist an imperialist war at a world level. In many parts of the world a New Left, less bent on socialist nationalization and planning ideas and more on decentralization, alternative technologies, a sense of ecology, self-reliance and similar values, has been taking shape for some time, challenging bigness and exploitation of man and nature, regardless of whether it passes under the name of capitalism or socialism.

It should be emphasized that these movements are to a large extent youth movements, based on persons who are transnationally mobile and highly explicit in their ideological orientation precisely because they are low on occupational and family identification. But they are *preparing* for occupations and for permanent family life, and the problem is that statuses such as youth or student often do not command lasting attention and organizational potential because they are transitory. The ideological turnover is often very high. But this may change: youth may start working earlier and people may study at later stages in their lives, making larger sections of the population more mobile geographically and attitudinally, more able to cope quickly with new contingencies, less rigid than present power structures make them. In the first phase, however, this type of organizational growth must be seen as a preparation for a later stage when such informal movements can act as direct pressure groups in relevant global decision-making institutions, for instance, gradually taking the form of world political parties.

Turning back to the examples of parliamentarians and international civil servants: *there are many untapped possibilities in this world for tying together people occupationally concerned with the politics of peace and war.* More concretely, we are thinking of international organizatins of heads of state, heads of government, foreign ministers, defense ministers, generals and other top military personnel, and ambassadors and other top diplomatic personnel. The purpose would be clear: not so much to facilitate their communication as to put them in a setting where they are forced to think, and even act, from world perspectives whenever such perspectives are relevant. One is used to thinking of these statuses as highly competitive, playing zero-sum games against each other in the territorial system. But that is a very partial vision indeed:

First, it is well known that such organizations develop every day on a regional and subregional basis, partly because of opposite-number diplomacy: a decision-maker in one country seeks his opposite number in another country rather than using the cumbersome road involving two foreign ministries and two embassies. Such contacts may start as bilateral and ad hoc and end up in a multilateral and institutionalized form, as with the Nordic meetings of foreign ministers.

Second, it is of course trivially true that such informal or formal organizations derive much of their significance from the circumstance that they define who are the regional or subregional actors engaged in zero-sum games with counterpart regions. But not all political games are of that type at the world level: the very existence of the UN is a demonstration of this fact. In any case there is a need for regulation of competition and for direct, efficient channels of communication to increase the level of predictability in the system. Summit meetings serve this function to some extent, but they also preserve the feudal structure of the world by facilitating interaction at the top of the international system among the big powers. For who meets at the summit? The big, of course, and some neighbors like in the European community.

For that reason summit meetings, including one or more of the three top statuses on the list above, should be really universal and institutionalized, for instances, linked to the opening of the General Assembly every year and not only to random head-of-state funerals that no doubt also may be useful. They should be accountable to the General Assembly, gradually being forced into thinking and acting in global terms, emphasizing interests transcending at least some of their antagonisms. Problems relating to the finiteness of the world might be suitable for global top-level consideration, forcing top-level actors from countries particularly responsible for depleting and polluting common world resources to explore new forms of production. The use of oceans and the scarcity of food and energy are obvious topics of general concern.

Third, such organizations probably will proliferate in the near future as a response to the rapid growth of the nonterritorial system. General secretaries—the heads of government on the sixth continent—will easily find each other because this type of highly mobile interaction is the *sine qua non* of their existence. In the near future the world will probably see the first clear signs of general secretaries pitted against prime ministers, almost forcing a tighter coordination among the latter. They will have common interests in their relations with the system of NTs, perhaps even in fighting it in the first phase, after they wake up to discover that the baby created to serve territorial interests has outgrown many of its parents. But if heads of governments come together to discuss how to cope with transnational bureaucracies, such as the UN and the European Community, they themselves will form a transnational actor. The adequate response to the NT challenge will hence be continued growth of the NT system, one more indication that this system is invincible because it is the only one compatible with the technological infrastructure in communication and transportation. Of course, countries may isolate themselves and withdraw, as China did for a long period. That is probably a very wise strategy in a certain phase of development, but if you want to change the system you have to become part of it, one way or the other.

Of equal significance would be institutionalized cooperation among military people and among diplomats in all countries. The World Veterans Association is an approximation to military cooperation, the Quaker seminars held all around the world for diplomats a very informal but significant start for the second type of association. But much more can be done, and in all probability will be, to give an organizational basis to the articulation of common concerns.

Military people all over the world can meet on a basis of a shared resentment against civilians. They can define civilians and politicians as ignorant and develop a certain professionalism around a nucleus of arms control (not disarmament) ideology: "If it only were left to us there would be no problem; we know how military systems work." Our experiences are not too good with this type of cooperation, but the nucleus is there for thinking and even acting in a more transnational way than before. Moreover, in a world that somehow will have to head for some form of disarmament, including heavy reduction in the number of military personnel, military people will have extremely difficult and also often humiliating transition problems, which will probably also drive them together. There will be a premium on military from countries with experience in demilitarizing armies, giving to the military increasingly civilian functions. No doubt much of that transfer of experience will be in the theory and practice of military coups d'etat and in how to thwart efforts to move towards some real form of disarmament. But some can also be used in international peacekeeping forces. Some transnational organization must absorb much of the military know-how, and international peacekeeping forces are almost a necessary consequence of steps towards disarmament.

Diplomats will have corresponding problems. As the system of NTs grows at the expense of Ts, bilateral diplomacy will recede into the background and multilateral diplomacy will constantly increase in salience. Many of these problems will be handled by foreign ministries, which will gradually have to transfer personnel from the bilateral to the multilateral sector, reducing the size and number of embassies and increasing the size and number of delegations to IGOs. This will mean that an increasing number of diplomats will have their horizons extended from a bilateral to a multilateral view, and some of them may de facto, if not de jure, become rather like international civil servants. Thus they will have trade union problems in common and a gradually increasing communality in their views on world affairs. Their views will tend to be correlated less with national background and more with other factors such as personality, experience, and ideology.

With military and diplomats organized in a more transnational manner the idea of national interest will recede more into the background and global interest will be better articulated. This process is to some extent already going on: you take the zero-sum people and put them into a cooperative context. Some of their old roles as defenders of national interests will then be seen as outmoded or ridiculous, even be resented. But as the seabed issue shows: there is still a long way to go.

What is the possibility of *creating more IGOs* with direct relevance to peace and war? We shall not go into much detail here but only mention that the following organizations seem to our mind particularly relevant:

a system of regional security commissions, parallel to the system of regional economic commissions, under the UN;

a UN arms control and disarmament agency;

a UN space agency;

a UN space communication agency;

a UN seabed agency;

a UN food agency;

a UN energy agency.

The rationale of these agencies would be partly to see to it that space, space communication, and the seabed are demilitarized, at least below an acceptable threshold, partly to see that benefits from these activities accrue to all mankind, partly to secure for the UN independent sources of income to be spent in accordance with standard UN procedures, and above all to start globalizing what have so far been the monopoly of the big powers, particularly the superpowers, and what are two of the basic economic concerns of all of us: food and energy.

All this is envisaged within the UN system and will probably come sooner rather than later. But the UN, with its Security Council and generally strong big-power dominance not only reflects but also to a large extent maintains a status quo in the international system of stratification of nations. Hence there is a need for an *organization of nonaligned countries* to challenge the bloc system; an *organization of poor, often formerly colonial, countries* to challenge world distribution; and an *organization of small countries* to challenge the system of big-power dominance.

These three types of organizations would not be universal or regional in a geographic sense, and consequently cannot be accommodated in the UN system. There is also the important argument that this system tends to gloss over and usurp the three important contradictions: the UN becomes to a large extent an instrument of bloc politics, of the rich nations, and of the big powers. This argument is certainly not made against the UN but rather in favour of organizations to supplement the UN for efficient articulation of basic conflict, for new power groups to emerge unimpeded by the status quo orientation of the present system.

Of course, these groups are already emerging to some extent: the Bandung, Belgrade, Cairo, Lusaka, Georgetown, and Algiers Conferences are examples of an organization of nonaligned countries gradually involving also European nonaligned countries. The Havana-based Tricontinental and the Algiers Group of 77—but certainly not the entire UNCTAD system—are examples of organizations of poor countries. Organizations of small countries, as such, do not as yet exist. In this type of organization, countries like the Dominican Republic and Czechoslovakia would join each other side by side, in a shared interest, to be protected against protection from certain big powers. The very circumstance that their situation is handled by the respective big powers inside a regional framework dominated by those big powers (the Organization of American States and the Warsaw Treaty Organization) to the exclusion of the UN is a solid indication of the need to develop new instruments in this sphere.

In short, we are arguing both for associative and dissociative policies, both for integrating the international system by strengthening the UN so that it can offer more services and enter more effectively into the security field and for disintegrating the international system by new organization of the uncommitted, the poor, and the weak. Although we do not see any contradiction here, we are aware that most people probably do. Most people tend to be either integrationists favouring the first course of action or disintegrationists favouring the second because they do not make any distinction between horizontal integration of equals and hegemonic vertical integration.

But, to take a nation-level parallel, in certain stages of social development there is value both in trade unions for workers only, pitted against employers' unions *and* governmental organizations where the two parties meet. It may well be that this course of development leads to the elimination of one or other of the groups (socially, not necessarily biologically), but that is another dimension of the total problem. The basic point here is that a necessary condition for the poor and the weak to attain autonomy and identity is to do it alone, to be without strings, without crutches, without aid, and later on the basis of equity re-establish ties with the rich and the strong, who are then less rich and strong, as these terms express structural relations of exploitation, not only absolute resources. Solidarity and autonomy among the poor and the weak are negations of the old structure and the beginning of a new one.

Nonterritorial Penetration of the Territorial System

Let us then look at the possibility of more penetration of the T system by the NT system. An immediate proposal that comes to mind is:

establishment of UN embassies in all member-states with sections for the various UN and Specialized agencies' programmes, and a UN ambassador from a different region;

internationalizing the moribund bilateral *corps diplomatique* (CD) by making the UN ambassador *doyen* of the CD, ex officio, and using the CD gradually as an instrument for articulating UN agenda points concerning the host nation in a multilateral form, a local general assembly in miniature;

penetration into the local executive and legislative branches by UN personnel as observers on foreign relations committees, as personnel in bilateral technical assistance agencies and even in foreign ministries, gradually internationalizing the foreign affairs of a country, transforming classical foreign ministries slowly into local branches of a (so far not existing) world internal affairs ministry.

The rationale behind this kind of proposal is simple. In past centuries, with a relatively low degree of mutual interpenetration of nations and a low level of interaction or coupling in general, foreign affairs were perhaps more bilateral in their consequences and less significant, affecting peoples' lives less than today. Today we are faced with the anomaly that decision-makers in a democratic country discussing *domestic* affairs would have the representatives of all parties built into the decision-making machinery. A parliament discussing communication and transport programmes would do so with due weight to the districts affected or not affected by the programme. It is a travesty of democracy to believe that a decision to bomb Indochina taken by a national assembly, or even through a plebiscite, was somehow more democratic than when taken by an executive authority alone. Democracy means that all concerned participate in the decision-making —and Indochinese peasants had some concern in that connection. Hence, to extend foreign policy decision-making intranationally only serves as a camouflage, a way of making others co-responsible.

To many the idea of having the receiver-countries permanently represented on the boards of the bilateral technical assistance agencies with the right not only to listen but to speak and vote might seem somewhat utopian. But it is not. The United Nations Development Programme Resident Representative acts de facto very much as a UN ambassador would in some countries, and his staff has important reporting functions both ways. However, the *corps diplomatique* is not directly built into this relationship and we feel there should be some possibilities along these lines, particularly because of the factors mentioned. Structures of this kind may start developing any year, and there is no reason that all member states should embrace the total package at once. Some countries might go further than others along this scale of UN penetration, and although this would introduce certain asymmetries it might still be a highly valuable contribution to the internationalization of foreign policy.

But the nonterritorial system does not consist only of IGOs; there are also INGOs to consider. How can they become more international? One way of doing this is structural, another is more attitudinal, and they can easily be brought to work hand-in-hand. The classical way was to make an INGO a weak coordination centre for national associations. If all nations were not represented there was, as mentioned, a second phase of looking for organizational bridgeheads into non-member nations. In this case the initiative would come from the international centre, but it could also come from interested persons in non-member states or from groups in any number of member-states. Throughout this phase the idea however is still to have national associations, although they may be more chapters than associations because of increasing strength of the international centre.

One can imagine a third phase, of direct individual membership of the INGO, which then becomes an association of individuals and not of national associations. Obviously such an INGO may easily find itself operating in a vacuum when there is no other organization at the international level, for instance, no IGO with which it can have institutionalized interaction, or at the national level, where such organizations may have no local chapters and only consist of individuals connected internationally. This type of INGO is ahead of its time: it is an actor in search of a counterpart at the right level of operation, which is the *world* level and not the international level, but its transcendence. Of course, INGOs will always find some roots in the NT system but will generally be too weak to convert organizational investment into real social action.

It is important that this type of structure with direct affiliation, or affiliation mediated through very weak national chapters only, should be combined with a global pattern of identification, for if the basic identification is still at the national level the incongruence between structure and attitude will lead to basic friction. As an example, take scientists, in both the natural and social sciences. With war becoming increasingly technical, these sciences become increasingly important and relevant to the national cause, and there is a very basic contradiction today between the international nature of scientific research and the national application of scientific research. In times of crises, scientists employed by national universities and academies of science are supposed to rally to the national cause and may even be pledged to do so by oaths of loyalty. It is therefore important to work for new loyalty patterns that do not tie scientific loyalty to supposedly value-free science (such a thing never existed and will never exist) but to a more global identification, that the benefits of scientific activity should accrue to all mankind. Organizational structures that would correspond to this conception might be the UN university, or a UNESCO university, or a proliferation of nongovernmental, transnational world universities, perhaps even defining national universities as national chapters. The Inter-University Centre in Dubrovnik is an example of this.

The Pugwash Conferences and the International Peace Research Association are examples of efforts to internationalize the scientist interested in war and peace. Such organizations may or may not have national chapters: the important factor is whether their members are dominated by national values and loyalties or by more universal international loyalties. Scientists are important examples, but they are not the only ones whose work transcends national boundaries, if not national interests. This is also to a large extent the case of businessmen; so let us now turn to the BINGOs—probably the strongest nonterritorial actors when it comes to structuring the world.

Symmetry Through Disintegration and Through New Power Structures

The third point of our discussion of this first phase is how to guarantee a more symmetric distribution of the nonterritorial system over the territorial system. This is a general problem, since the NT system is so biased in favour of the northwestern corner of the world, which serves to preserve and maintain a certain structure with highly feudal and exploitative aspects. The question is what to do about it.

The first step is very simple: disintegration, as already mentioned. The whole system of NTs reflects and supports too much of the exploitative characteristics of the T system to be permitted to grow as it has done so far. There has to be basic disintegration within many of the organizations, with the national associations or chapters of nonaligned, poor, and small nations simply detaching themselves from this type of fake internationalism and constituting international organizations of their own. Clearly these organizations would not be world organizations, but they might serve the needs of poor nations much better. To take an example: it is hardly in the interest of poor nations to reproduce the medical structure found in rich nations, with a division of labour between highly specialized and highly paid physicians and nurses, when what they need may be medical technicians, barefoot doctors, and the like. In the BINGO world this is even more clear. If the exploitative international division of labour is reproduced *within* the BINGO, one way of changing it is to break up BINGO. The world cannot continue with "daughter companies" providing raw materials, performing production according to ready-made blueprints, and doing "marketing" and "mother companies" making all key decisions, doing the research, and defining for the rest of the world what constitutes a product.

In other instances the existing asymmetry may be dealt with in a less disintegrative manner. There are two basic approaches to the problem, both of them aiming at reducing the predominance of the northwestern corner of the world. One has to do with the territorial location of the central focus of decision-making and the other with the ultimate power over that decision-making. The two approaches are heavily related, as it is obvious that territorial location means a lot. The host country will contribute not only site and housing but also very often personnel, patterns of work, basic concepts of work, and sometimes capital and the power that flows in its wake. It *may* change the concept of what constitutes a product, e.g. as something satisfying fundamental needs rather than satisfying the frivolous demands of the upper and middle classes to take an important BINGO problem.

Though the location of the NT system is extremely biased, much can be done if there is serious concern about the problem. In general it will not be so easy to move old headquarters, nor is this so crucial. New headquarters should however be established as far as possible in the East and the South; as communications become better, old objections to this decentralization should decrease in significance. This is particularly true of the new specialized agencies under the UN, such as the examples mentioned earlier, or an agency for housing, which is today not handled by any one of these agencies. The number of UN agencies may potentially become vast, especially if more non-UN INGOs are converted into such agencies, as they very well could be. The borderline is often artificial. Some of the oldest IGOs, for instance, dealing with postal communication and telecommunication, could very well become members of the UN family in a decentralized manner. There are also other solutions than symmetric distribution of location; the classic ones would be rotation of the location, not very practical, and the creation of world federal territories. This is a much more attractive solution, provided that the territory was located outside the Northwest. Thus West Berlin would not be a good choice, although it might very well function as a site for agencies of all-German and all-European cooperation. It may well be that some important present or future conflict over disputed territory could be solved by federalizing it and getting into it a large number of NT organizations. Another possibility would be to create new world territory such as floating cities, reclaimed land, and the seabed.

Much of what has been lost so far because of asymmetry can be regained by focussing on the super-IGOs, super-INGOs, and super-BINGOs. They are bound to come in increasing numbers; and because they will control to some extent the lower level of organization, it is very important that their location should be closer to the ideal of symmetry than the distribution at the lower level. According to the second basic approach to the problem of symmetry, location is a superficial aspect and does not imply control: Control itself is the essence. If one wants symmetric control of IGOs, INGOs, and BINGOs the lasting solution is not symmetric territorial distribution but symmetric power distribution. This is rather similar to the problem of land reform: the old model was equality by means of territorial distribution according to the one-family, one-farm principle; the more modern approach is to distribute power to decide on large farms, in other words industrial farming with industrial democracy. The People's Commune in China may be one example, being democratic and autonomous.

In the field of BINGOs such power distribution is referred to as coproduction, whereby two countries agree to coproduce something. "Co" stands for symmetry, although often more in theory than in practice. Often an ad hoc organization is created to manage coproduction in order to start from scratch with something that is sufficiently symmetrical. Thus one form is a bilateral ad hoc IGO, a joint commission, managing BINGOs between the same countries, although we should use these terms only for multilateral relationships.

But our point here is rather the possibilities of generalization implict in this scheme. The general principle would be to concentrate ultimate power over the NT system in the most representative, most symmetric NTs. This is probably the way it will have to develop anyhow: so why not get started, in a modest way, as soon as possible?

There are many possibilities. In the first phase there will probably be many instances of BINGOs being put under IGO control. *The multinational corporations are globalized just as the national corporations were nationalized before them.* Exactly what forms this will take are not easily predicted. But one beginning could be a tax levied on all BINGOs by and for the UN, by the rationale that these BINGOs operate on the international level. The basic point is that the operation of a BINGO concerns not only the nations in which mother, daughter, or sister companies (are these feminine terms used in order to appear more innocent?) are located but is of basic interest to the whole international system, to all of humankind.

In the second phase there will probably be many instances of IGOs being put under INGO control, and there will also be instances of the opposite. All nine combinations of IGOs, INGOs, and BINGOs controlled by similar organizations could be explored. But we focus on the pattern of INGOs controlling IGOs for the simple reason that this is our model of democracy: People must control government and not vice versa, at least ultimately, and so associations of people should control associations of governments. Thus one is led gradually towards a model of a world central authority with worldwide elections based on worldwide parties—all of them INGOs—to a worldwide parliament tied in with a worldwide executive, perhaps an improved version of the UN Secretariat and specialized agencies. Clearly, however, much of this would belong to the second and third phases of NT growth. There is a considerable distance to go. For instead of INGOs controlling IGOs controlling BINGOs it seems descriptive of our situation today to say that we have BINGOs controlling IGOs controlling INGOs. But much of this belongs in a sense to the second and third phases of the growth of nonterritorial actors. All we can say here is that this first phase will, and to our mind should, witness, the first efforts to control the asymmetries in the system of nonterritorial actors—sometimes by breaking them up, sometimes by making them more symmetric, less violent in their structure, and sometimes by making them penetrate more deeply into the states themselves. This should apply not only to IGOs and INGOs but above all to the BINGOs, as soon as possible.

(2) Nonterritorial System Equal to the Territorial System in Salience

When the nonterritorial system equals the territorial system in salience, the three basic patterns of influence are about equalized:

NT commands about as much *loyalty* (normative power) as T:

NT renders about at much *service* (remunerative power) as T; and

NT has about as much *force* (coercive power) as T.

Obviously this condition of equality will not come into being simultaneously all over the world, nor is that essential. Moreover, these three aspects of power will not be equalized simultaneously. For instance, as most T-oriented people probably are prone to believe that ultimate power is coercive power, they will not surrender this kind of power monopoly easily, especially not when they see that NT actors command more and more loyalty and render more and more services to increasing fractions of the world population, thus threatening regional and class privileges. They will not understand that the *ultimo ratio regis* is not necessarily the *ultimo ratio* of the secretaries-general, or they will understand this too late, when the NTs have taken over with their softer power—like it has happened inside the nation-state before.

Hence we proceed on the assumption that there is some kind of equal balance between T and NT where loyalty is concerned, and that this loyalty is not merely an attitude but is tied in with services of all kinds. The individual exchanges loyalty for services in both directions, and there will be intermediate phases in which he will be overrewarded by T and underrewarded by NT. What does all this mean to the prospects for peace?

Theoretical approaches to the problem can lead to rather different results. In this future world, for instance, a man's loyalty will be shared between his own government and people with whom he identifies in some other country because they belong to the same race, ethnic group, class, profession, or general association. The problem arises when his brethren in the other country are suppressed by their own government. To this man nonintervention now becomes meaningless. Whether his own government joins him in his effort to help or not is not so important. Whether the response takes the form of governmental intervention or rank-and-file infiltration is of less significance: he cannot refrain from doing something. The whole doctrine of nonintervention is based on the assumption that territoriality dominates in salience so that governments can hold their people at bay with soft, normative strings. It also presupposes bad means of communication and a generally low level of political consciousness and information. In this phase the doctrine of nonintervention will have to go or take on new forms; it cannot survive when patterns of loyalties work completely against it. It will be interesting to see how international lawyers tackle this problem. For instance, when will international law become as sensitive to structural violence as it has been to direct violence? When will structural violence be defined as aggression—structural agression—and a revolution as an act of defense? A balanced crisscross of loyalties may in some instances break down the impediments of the past against intervention and infiltration. But it may also lead to a higher potential for communication, mediation, and arbitration for neutrals who can withdraw and serve as bridges between the belligerents than when the NT system has very low salience. Just as wars to help brothers abroad may increase, wars against whole countries will probably decrease for the simple reason that they would also be wars against people with whom there is solid identification because of nonterritorial bonds. The conclusion is that this phase will be dominated by other types of wars. We are there already: international relations are characterized by internationalized wars of liberation rather than by national wars of conquest. The old territorial system fails to come to grips with the realities of this world. It is still dominated by the idea that a regime can only be recognized when it has territorial control, not because it represents the legitimate interests of the people. It is still dominated by the idea of governmental power monopoly inside the country in defiance of all the transnational forces and concerns.

But there are many other aspects to this world of equal salience. First, most of the trends we have mentioned in the preceding section will continue, most of them at an increasing rate. Sooner or later this will lead to a stronger crystallization of relations between IGOs, INGOs, and BINGOs. More particularly, we assume that in this phase BINGOs will be controlled by IGOs much more than in the first phase and that IGOs will be controlled by INGOs increasingly. One way of achieving this could be as follows.

There are many ways of conceiving a future UN, particularly the General Assembly and the Security Council. To us it does not seem unreasonable to assume that in this phase the trade unions of the poor, the nonaligned, and the small powers will be able to reduce considerably the power of the rich, the aligned, and the big, particularly that of the superpowers, the U.S. and the Soviet Union. Today we have some kind of upper-house, lower-house system in the UN: the Security Council based on ascription and the General Assembly more on representation. The Security Council is modernizing itself a little, but it is still based on the concept of the victorious great, Allied powers of the Second World War. To make the Security Council reflect present-day realities better, by exchanging the present five permanent members for the frequently mentioned pentagon consisting of the U.S., the European Community, the Soviet Union, China, and Japan would clearly be a step backwards, not forwards. To make the UN isomorphic with the present world order is to strengthen that order, and that is not what the present order needs most. It needs defeudalization, democratization. Give or take a decade or two: the Security Council and the veto system will have to go. The year 1789 will ultimately come to the international system.

But there is need for a two-chamber system in a new UN because the world is complicated; it is certainly not unidimensional. In this phase one might therefore think in terms of a General Assembly with two chambers, one representing nations more or less as now and one representing international organizations. In other words one chamber for T and the other for NT. This idea contrasts with the most current proposal at present, to have one chamber as now and another corresponding to the House of Representatives in the U.S. Congress representing people more directly in proportion to their number, for example, with one representative for every million inhabitants. This proposal is more democratic than the present but it is also basically territorial, assuming that people primarily identify with their territory. Hence an alternative model might be as follows.

One chamber represents territoriality, leaving us with two problems. Are we to continue with the old one-nation, one-vote system or should we move to a one-man, one-vote system? Should we accept one of the many proposals for weighted voting? Second, how shall the delegations be constituted? Should we continue the old pattern of appointment by the executive and/or legislative branches of government or strive for more democratic procedures encouraging direct election? How would we guarantee that emerging states containing suppressed minorities, which are often majorities, can also articulate their demands and be heard?

If we combined these two ideas we would in reality have a world parliament, as this reorganization could hardly happen without the crystallization of present and future formal and informal INGOs into political parties. As this will not happen at the same time, the changes will both be traumatic and dramatic, certainly not synchronized for the world as a whole.

But right now we are more concerned with the second part of the parliament representing the NTs. This smacks of the corporate state, which to Europeans and Latin Americans alike has rather unfortunate connotations. But it looks as if we have to leave such reservations aside, because we simply cannot go on forever pretending that territorial foci dominate all others in relevance and salience. Hence it may be a question of building on the existing institutions of INGOs with consultative statuses of various categories. The nucleus exists already and could be expanded and given more formal power. As did the inclusion of mini-states in the UN, it would raise the general problem of standards for inclusion; and if seniority and level of crystallization are accepted as criteria, the system will be severely weighted in favour of the existing establishments of all kinds, in favour of the topdogs in the topdog nations. It is very important to find some way of articulating the interests expressed in very new and very informal INGOs. Hence we have exactly the same problem previously mentioned: not only emerging states but also emerging organizations must be given some possibility of articulation lest the system become rigid, capable only of reflecting the past.

In this chamber the principle of voting would probably be *one organization, one vote*. It may be objected that this system would indirectly give multiple votes to individuals with multiple memberships and no votes to those who do not belong to any organization. But the world has had a tremendous capacity so far for accepting unequal de facto voting distributions, the UN itself being a major example, and voting could also be weighted according to the size of an organization, and there could be direct election of delegates. There is no reason why only the territorial system should be democratically represented.

Nothing has been said about the relative power of the two chambers, and here a host of possibilities are open to us. We are inclined to think that in this phase the NT chamber should perhaps have more than a consultative, deliberative role, but less power than the T chamber. The major function of the nonterritorial chamber would be to serve as an additional forum of articulation, of grievances, conflicts, and problems —as a reservoir of human and other resources and as a network for the implementation of decisions.

A third aspect of this world is the real power some of the NTs will now acquire. We are not thinking so much of the IGOs but of some INGOs. The point is simply this: just as a national trade union organizing workers in some key occupation such as communications or energy can paralyze a modern nation and throw it back to a pre-industrial stage of development in a well-organized strike, an international organization will in time be able to do the same to the international system. And this applies not only to such IGOs as OPEC. More effective than international associations of longshoremen will probably be such organizations as the international pilots' associations. Their effort to strike against the Algerian government over the capture in 1968 of an El Al plane is a telling foreboding of things to come. The question is to what extent these strikes will be for peace and not only for higher salaries or in the interests of certain nations dominating the INGOs, which latter point underscores again the importance of equalizing power over the NT system.

What would be the impact of a worldwide strike by the future INGOs of heads of state, heads of government, foreign ministers, and defence ministers, not to mention the organizations of diplomats and the military? This type of strike seems to be related to the prospects for peace, but how? If all military went on strike all over the world— but that is perhaps a too utopian hope for the near future! More likely would be the emergence of other forms of defence, e.g., nonmilitary forms based on transnational noncooperation and civilian defence. In this second phase they would not be organized on a national basis alone but transnationally, as popular movements against the repressive use of military force, nationally and across borders. It is one thing to argue in favor of, say, the Norweigian nonmilitary defence against the German attack in 1940; quite another to argue in favor of both that and antimilitary mobilization in the attacking country. For that, high NT salience is needed, and forms that were ineffective in earlier phases of world development may gain considerably in efficiency.

(3) Nonterritorial System Higher Than the Territorial System in Salience

A world in which the nonterritorial system is higher in salience is hard to imagine for many, but it should not be hard to imagine for people living in nation-states where local district identification is quickly decreasing, where territorial mobility is high, and where identification with nationwide organizations and associations, e.g., parties and trade unions, is correspondingly high. *This world is that nation-state writ large.* Actually we already have a system in the world that can serve as an illustration: *India.* As a nation-state this continent is badly integrated; but as an international system, and it really is an inter*national* system, it is very successful. Of course, there are local protests against super-system, Delhi, penetration, and these protests might conceivably one day accumulate and lead to a new and looser India more reflective of the world as a whole. But India today is somewhere between the second and the third of our phases—the separate states are highly visible, but there are overriding concerns and loyalties crisscrossing with them. Hence this is no unrealistic utopia—it exists.

Identification with the local district will seldom decrease to zero, partly because local life is a form of life that will remain dear to many for a long time or forever and partly because exploitation across territorial borders will appear and reappear and will call for some kind of territorial organization to counteract it. But a world of small social units, self-reliant and nonexploitative, with high mobility between them, is also perfectly conceivable and would be an ideal version of our world in the third phase.

In this system, to stick to our image of a two-chamber UN, the chamber representing the territorial subunits would recede into the background, as it has in many countries. That would leave us with two possibilities: to develop that chamber into a *world parliament* based on world political parties and movements and the *chamber of organizations.* But it is not a question of either/or. Inside the nation-states of today the need will probably arise to give the organizational-associational system a better opportunity to articulate itself, instead of only the old territorial system based on district representation. One might think in terms of retaining two chambers but using countries in the first chamber only as administrative subunits to organize worldwide elections locally. Another possibility would be to proceed as under the second phase just outlined but giving all real power to the NT chamber and using the T chamber, which we then assume to be of the one-nation, one-vote variety with appointed delegations, as an ornament, something like the House of Lords.

In this system territorial war as it is known today will be considerably less probable simply because it will be less feasible. There is a very simple reason for this: people live together in such a way that friends and enemies are too spatially mixed to permit the free, unimpeded use of explosives. Explosives, from the smallest dumdum bullet to the fusion bomb, are effective means in warfare. But they presuppose low entropy in the spatial distribution of people: a bomb is to be placed at points of maximum enemy density and minimum friend density. If such points do not exist or are not satisfactory because of the mixing of friend and foe resulting from general NT growth, bombs simply cannot be used.

It may be objected, however, that people fought religious wars under such conditions using cloak-and-dagger techniques, selective poisoning and the like, and that therefore there is the possibility of such tactics as placing homing devices for mini-missiles on the backs of enemies. We are in no doubt that military techniques and ingenuity, to which large numbers of scientists and technicians always seem to be willing to prostitute themselves, will be able to overcome this setback to the "bigger bang for the buck" enthusiasts. More kill for the buck will simply have to be obtained without so much bang.

The question is, however, whether this condition will not offer a relatively good basis for *nonmilitary defence,* as that type of defence by its very nature is social rather than spatial. It is not a question of keeping territory clean from enemies but of retaining values and forms of life and organization. As mentioned, this type of defence can best be organized on a transnational basis, the people against the military, and the third phase should be good for that purpose.

Our general conclusion is that in this world both loyalty entropy and geographical entropy will be so high that we very much doubt major world wars will be feasible. There will be local violence, and it may well be that this world will be so complicated and so taxing on individuals because the simplicity of spatial organization is lost and functional organization is much more abstract that there will be *more* micro-level violence than before. In other words it may well be that what we have gained at the macro-level will to some extent be lost at the micro-level. Nevertheless, if a major world war leading to total elimination or major setbacks of human civilization were the result of any system with low entropy, the price may not be too high to pay for high entropy, for more mixing in the world. Correspondingly, if continued structural violence is the price to pay for the present centralized territorial and nonterritorial systems, they will have to be decentralized into smaller, more self-reliant units one way or the other—and in that case symmetric NTs will have to be the integrative force.

In this world there will sonner or later be a transfer of many kinds of power towards a single centre. There will be some kind of world central authority, not necessarily a world government, based perhaps on the development of the UN we have traced in various phases. According to this model some world centre could also serve as a repository of the means of coercive power, of arms of all kinds; and a number of transfer models could be imagined in this field.

For example, *nonterritorial actors may get arms themselves* for wars among themselves or with territorial actors. This may possibly provide a crisscrossing balance as indicated in our analysis of the second phase, but it is also possible that it means only that future disarmament will have to comprise nonterritorial as well as territorial actors. In short, the acquisition of arms by world political parties as well as by states is not the model we would favor.

Also, *arms could be transferred from territorial to nonterritorial actors.* This is not inconceivable if the point of gravity of decision-making in general is moving from territorial to nonterritorial actors, for then it would not be strange if weapons followed the same power gradient. There are two subcases:

Transfer to several nonterritorial actors. In this case everything would be set for armed conflict between non-territorial actors and one is back to religious wars in Europe, for instance. It is difficult to believe that such weapons possessed by NTs would not be either the cause or the consequence of conflict.

Transfer to one nonterritorial actor. In this case the NT would have the power monopoly so often aspired to by nations. The transfer, according to classical thinking, would not have to be complete before it would be sufficient to overpower any conceivable coalition of territorial actors.

But then we would, in a certain sense, be back to the beginning: Instead of a set of nation-states we would get a world organized as one giant nation-state, a world state. Many others have arrived at this conclusion, but the standard scenario is to see this process in terms of city-states that coalesce to form nation-states, nation-states that co-alesce into superstates (regions), and superstates that coalesce to form a world state. Our point is that that scenario is *not very probable* be-cause there will also be disintegration and secession; and NT growth, which does not respect territorial contiguity, will occur much more quickly than territorial coalescence into superstates. *Nor is it very desirable because the last step towards the world state is very dangerous,* as the superstates will have important grievances against each other and will have a tendency to fight superwars; and it is *not very desirable be-cause a highly centralized and strong world government may be one more instrument of structural violence and of extreme direct violence* out of power and self-righteousness.

Some international peacekeeping is in order, but in general the road to peace consists in making arms less necessary, not in transferring them to a world center. We feel that the present scenario, gradually playing up NTs rather than building on ever-bigger Ts, is just as likely or more likely. And for that reason we feel one should from the very beginning stop thinking in terms of an *international* system, because the term itself has a territorial connotation, and talk about a *world system* embracing both Ts and NTs.

Conclusion

Characteristic of this scenario is that it does not see the coming world as a nation-state writ large, for every nation-state today has built into it some porcupinelike defence against other nation-states, which we would not like to see carried over into higher levels of organization. Rather the idea is set forth in terms of a complex world with nonterri-torial organizations crosscutting self-sufficient territorial units; non-territorial units so strong they can serve as a base for a world central authority with the capacity not only to articulate problems and con-flicts transcending these territorial units but also to solve them.

This organization would not be one big worldwide pyramid but would permit all kinds of looser associations in all directions—T with NT, T with T, NT with NT— all of this combined with a high level of individual mobility and a high level of diversity among the basic units. Phrased in the terms of this analysis, *the ideal phase is probably not the third phase.* In that phase the structure would too easily play into the hands of those who can make use of the nonterritorial organizations;

and the total structure would too easily crystallize into some kind of centralised world state, even with tremendous means of destructive power at the disposal of the center. *Nor is it the first phase,* in which the system of states with their impenetrability, their relations of direct and structural violence, and their utilization of the nonterritorial actors for their own purposes is much too dominant.

Hence, our preferred world, *where this dimension of nonterritoriality is concerned,* would be more similar to the second phase: a balance between the two ways of looking at and organizing the world; a balance between association and dissociation, to conquer the evils of structural and direct violence.

TOWARD GLOBAL IDENTITY*

Yoshikazu Sakamoto

The future has a twofold implication for human beings. On the one hand, the element of *indeterminacy* enables man to make free choices. As the future does not exist independently of the orientation of human beings to it, it may be more precise to say that the very fact that man has a capacity to choose and a range of choice makes the future indeterminate. On the other hand, there is an element of *uncertainty* that makes human beings uneasy and insecure, stemming from the fact that the future involves factors and conditions beyond man's capacity to foresee. Or to put it more precisely, the shortage of information on the range of possible developments that go beyond the range of deliberate choice makes the future uncertain. This uncertainty will become terribly wide when, as today, society undergoes a rapid change giving rise to developments that defy cognizance based on precedents.

In light of the existential ambivalence towards the future rooted in the human condition, the cardinal objective of our future-oriented intellectual exercise is to minimize the uncertainties and to maximize the range of positive choice.

It is as a consequence of our positive choice in a rapidly changing world that we explicitly presuppose world-order values. We take a world perspective for two reasons. First, we believe that world interests and universal concerns should precede national or parochial interests. We do not see why a baby who happens to be born in Vietnam should be exposed to the danger of warfare while an American baby sleeps in comfort. We do not see why a black African peasant should lead a poverty-stricken life while an Australian farmer enjoys a living standard of the well-to-do. We believe that the gap between human beings' essential equality at birth and the actual inequalities into which people are born should be minimized and that this can be done only by view-

*Part of this essay was submitted to the UN Institute for Training and Research for comments by its research staff.

ing the problem from a global humanitarian perspective. This idea is very old but still crucial.

Further, we believe that the world is moving toward increasing interdependency, which provides a structural foundation for a world perspective. It is therefore not only its time-honoured philosophical validity but also the growing feasibility of the principle that enable us to espouse world-order values.

Core Values

What then are the world-order values? What are their interrelationships? Obviously one can immediately point to such basic values as peace, freedom, justice, dignity, and so on. Although there is no question that they are the principal values contained in a world-order perspective, these concepts are so basic that they require further specification to be free of ambiguity and clearly linked to concrete world problems.

Different interpretations of the symbol of peace by different nations have frequently contributed to the aggravation of conflict. Or the danger of the "population explosion," which is widely regarded as a matter of global concern, may be generally related to all these values, and yet may not be specifically related to any one of them.

We shall therefore define our world-order values in more specific terms, that is, in terms of five objectives that any human society and, for that matter, the world as a whole are required to attain if they seek stable development. These objectives are functional specifications of more basic values. They are ecological balance, economic well-being, communication development, human development, and peaceful change.

The first objective, ecological balance, refers to the self-sustaining interactions of the human species with its environment, which consists of a primary natural environment and a secondary human environment, the second represented by the industrialized urban setting.

The second, economic well-being, refers to goods and services as products of interaction between the human species and the environment, and also within the species itself. It concerns growth and production on the one hand and equitable distribution on the other.

The third, communication development, refers to improvement of the flow of meaningful information as a product of man's ecological and social interactions. It also has two aspects, the quantity and quality of available information and the degree of free choice the flow of information can enhance. While the first aspect centres on the improvement of access to information, the second concerns the problem stemming precisely from improved access to information such as information overload, political and industrial espionage, and invasion of privacy.

The fourth objective, human development, refers to the increase of chances that the individual can find his life positively meaningful as a member of society. That is, the chances for equal participation in decision-making and for self-realization on personal and spiritual levels as well as within the context of social actions, are increased.

Finally the fifth objective, peaceful change, refers to nonviolent allocation and reallocation of the four values previously listed. In view of the fact that human society constantly calls for reallocation of values in accordance with changing conditions, it should be recognized that peace is essentially a question of nonviolent change. There are two modes of peaceful change—dissociation of parties in conflict and association for common goals.

In the light of these five objectives, we can identify the world problems we have to solve in order to attain these objectives:

Ecological balance:
In the primary environment: pollution, resource shortage and depletion, energy crisis.
In the secondary environment: urban deterioration (for example, slums, traffic accidents).

Economic well-being:
For growth: poverty, unemployment, fluctuation and instability (unstable terms of trade, monetary crisis, inflation).
For distribution: disparity, transnational deprivation (multinational corporations, migrant labor).

Communication development:
For free access to information: information control and restriction.
For free choice of information: information overload, communication infiltration (invasion of privacy, industrial and political espionage).

Human development:
For participation: discrimination.
For self-realization: alienation.

Peaceful change:
By dissociation: interstate and civil war, arms race, foreign intervention, subnational violence.
By association: North-South gap, isolationism.

It may be noted that every one of these five objectives is independent in the sense that it is not a subcategory of any one of the other four. As our world order should seek optimal realization of these objectives, the degree to which any of them is attained affects the realization of world-order values as a whole even if the requirements of the other four objectives have been fulfilled. For instance, if the first four objectives are achieved by force at the expense of peaceful change, that in itself would inevitably hamper the fulfilment of world-order values.

It goes without saying that the five objectives and their associated problem-clusters are closely interrelated. Merely to state that there are interrelations among these clusters of values and problems is insufficient. What is more crucial is to know how they are interrelated. Theoretically, there are two modes of interrelationship, trade-off and synergy. For instance, it is generally recognized that there is a trade-off between economic development and ecological balance; on the other hand synergistic mutual reinforcement is observable between human development and international cooperation. But the problems are not so simple. For instance, it is true that industrial development contributed to the creation of an environment better in many respects than was attained in pre-industrial societies. Preoccupation with human development at the domestic level has frequently led to isolationism in foreign relations. Even economic development and communications advancement, which normally go hand in hand, may have trade-offs under certain circumstances, such as the negative implications of the demonstration effect of the life style of high-consumption societies on the development of the emerging nations. Obviously the communications advance could have adverse as well as positive effects on human development. These facts invariably suggest that there is a saturation point beyond which mutual reinforcement will turn into trade-off relations. Such an insight leads to the following two points:

First, we should make careful identification of these trade-off relations in respect to each set of variables that cuts across the problem-clusters of the different objectives. It may also be recalled that the saturation point varies from one society to another according to the level of socioeconomic development and the value system peculiar to each culture. The difference in the reactions to environmental issues between developed and developing societies is a case in point.

Second, as long as there are trade-off relations between different objectives we shall have to decide on the priorities we give to competing demands. In this connection it may be noted that what we are expected to achieve is not the maximal attainment of individual objectives but the optimal fulfilment of the entire set of five objectives.

Organizational Lag

The identification of interrelations and the decision on priorities in regard to these five clusters of values and problems are naturally a task so complex and disputable that the whole operation calls for a machinery of coordinating authority at various levels of decision-making. Even within a national society that is normally based on a relatively high degree of consensus the complexity and disputability of the task calls for the creation of governmental machinery. Small wonder that international society should also require a coordinating body. Imagine what would happen if more than 130 sovereign states should pursue their policies independently on the basis of individual determination of trade-offs and priorities in regard to the five categories of variables. Further, the degree of conceivable confusion and conflict is bound to be high because of the rapidly growing interactions and interdependence among nations. The need for a global coordinating actor is unquestionable.

At the same time, the lag between need and achievement is also unmistakable. It would appear that the lag is largely due to man's tardiness in creating a new system of identification that transcends the nation-state. In other words, what may be called an *organizational lag* can generally be attributed to two causes: a lack of common interests among the parties concerned and/or a lack of common symbols of identification among them. As there is an objective need for a global coordinating body, the interests of parties should be served by its creation. Nevertheless, the formation of a global coordinating body lags behind the need, not so much because of a lack of common interests (from the viewpoint of the people as a whole, not of those who have a vested interest in international conflict) but because of the slow emergence of new symbols of common identification.

This point is best illustrated by the arms race. From the viewpoint of the interests of the parties involved there is no reason that they should not convert arms production into peaceful purposes through arms reduction. The major obstacle, as the Prisoner's Dilemma game model indicates, is the lack of a system of common identification. Yet another illustration is the problem of environmental pollution. International regulations on the emission of pollutants began to be considered only after the pollution of air and water had gone far beyond the control of individual nation-states. Even from the viewpoint of the interest of individual states, international measures should have been taken earlier. The international response tends to lag behind primarily because of the delay in the transformation of the system of identification. It is only because a species of identity has in fact begun to emerge that the UN's Stockholm conference on human environment could have taken place in 1972. The same is true of the United Nations conference on world population in 1974.

In sum, the organizational lag at the international level frequently stems from delay in formulating a new system of identification. How is the system of identification changing today? How is it possible to promote the formation of new types of actors whose sense of identity will conform to the world-order values?

Problems of Identity

Strictly speaking, the empirically observable entity in human society is the individual. The collectivity or group can be regarded as an empirical entity only because the individuals act in the name of the collectivity and identify themselves with the collectivity by regarding the decision made in its name as if the decision were their own. A change in the system of identification must therefore stem in the final analysis from change in the value concepts and behaviour at the level of the individual. The focus of our analysis will thus be placed primarily on the individual in his or her relations to society.

It goes without saying that in the modern world the nation-state is the frame of reference of overriding importance for the social and political identity of the individual. Except for a small minority of pacifists, revolutionaries, and others who have had a strong sense of transnational identity, most people have been prepared to sacrifice their lives for their country in times of war and crisis. This classic pattern is however undergoing several modifications.

Let me begin with spelling out what identity means in this context. Identity has two aspects, positive and negative. Positive identity refers to the chances of man's being and *becoming* himself, both as an individual and as a member of society. In other words, positive identity in its sociological context refers to the two basic aspects of man's mode of existence—his chances of meaningfully relating himself to others through such acts as participation, identification and cooperation and of meaningfully relating himself to himself through autonomy, self-determination, self-fulfilment, and the like. The importance of 'becoming oneself' should be stressed, because the notion of identity tends to have a static connotation of being the same and continuous. As is indicated by the reference to becoming oneself and a member of society, the process of identity formation is closely intertwined with the developmental processes of social structures, whether incremental or drastic.

By using the term chances we hope to operationalize the concept of identity in terms of statistical probability, such as chances of school enrollment, medical care, and employment.

What then are the major problems encompassed by identity? Table 1 is a checklist of the major manifestations identity problems generally take:

TABLE 1

Manifestations of Identity Problems

	Negative Identity	Positive Identity

Outward:
   Society-oriented
	Aggression:
	   discrimination
	   violent action
		Participation:
		   inclusion
		   contestation

Non-interfering	Apathy:
	   indifference
	   resignation
		Autonomy:
		   independence
		   nondominance

Inward:
   Individual-oriented
	Self-destruction:
	   addiction
	   suicide
		Self-realization:
		   lifelong education and
		   self-education

It may be noted that the six types of manifestation refer to the behaviour of individuals and/or groups, not to their psychological motivations. Thus aggression, depriving others of values, may be committed out of defensive motives.

Inward-oriented behaviour is essentially a matter of individual concern. But if the inward-oriented, negative pattern of behaviour is shared by a considerable number of individuals, such behaviour should be regarded as a social problem.

Negative identity refers to the pattern of behaviour that is oriented to "what I am *not*" or, "what we are *not*" rather than "what I am" or "what we are." Obviously those patterns of behaviour most commonly recognized as problems—aggression, apathy and self-destruction—are on the negative side.

The major focus of analysis in this essay will be placed on the two modes of aggressive behaviour—discrimination and violent action—because of their special relevance to the world-order values. The focus will be particularly on discrimination by the privileged, whether nations or other social groups, against the underprivileged in denying the underprivileged equal opportunity for self-realization, and next on violent action, normally but not exclusively at the subnational level, taken by the underprivileged against the privileged and at least professedly aiming at equal opportunity for self-fulfilment. Here the question of violent resistance is taken up in combination with that of discrimination for a simple reason. The popular discontent with discrimination, inequality, and social injustice will not take a violent form until they reach a critical point. If we focus our attention only on the violent manifestations we tend to overlook the wide range of discrimination and injustice that exists below the critical point.

Apathy is another form of negative identity: indifference on the part of the privileged and resignation on the part of the underprivileged. The problem of apathy, particularly of indifference, will increase in its importance both domestically and internationally, as will be discussed later. Still another form of negative identity, self-destruction, may be self-evident. It is exemplified by the abuse of and traffic in drugs, which obviously is more than the problem of the individual concerned and has international implications. The so-called issueless violence, as distinct from civil violence originating from specific grievances concerning institutionalized discrimination, may well be interpreted as one form of suicide.

Turning to the positive side of identity, we find two aspects of participation. One, inclusion, refers to the institutional guarantee of equally shared opportunity to take part in public decision-making. If it signifies only inclusion, participation may turn into conformism. Under fascism for instance everybody was urged to participate in street demonstrations, rallies and parades organized under the leadership of the party; in fact many people were convinced that their desire to participate was satisfied. There is no doubt that inclusive participation, if it is not combined with the right of public contestation, will easily turn into conformist pseudo-participation.

Autonomy is a positive form of noninterference—independence from external interference and abstention from dominance over others. Self-realization can include physical self-realization in which ecological balance and economic well-being are involved. But special attention is drawn here to the question of intellectual and spiritual self-fulfilment. As a UNESCO report on the future of education suggested, this is essentially a search for the complete man in anticipation of the emergence of a learning society (*Learning to Be,* 1972).

While discrimination, violence, resignation, participation and independence primarily centre on the problem of *lack of opportunities,* the concept of identity will be sufficiently extensive to comprise such problems as drug abuse, suicide, issueless violence, aimless leisure time on the one hand and intellectual and spiritual self-fulfilment on the other. Both of them are concerned essentially with the *lack of a sense of direction* rather than with objective opportunities. We must be on guard however against the danger that those subjective problems tend to be treated as if they were a subject of clinical psychology divorced from the structural conditions of society. It may be equally noted that these subjective problems are likely to gain importance in the future world.

Negative identity and positive identity are not unrelated. The most familiar instance is the case in which the realization of positive identity is accompanied by the exercise of violence. It is frequently only by resorting to force that an underprivileged class or a colonized people are able to set up a new political system or state where they can participate in the decision-making process. This has happened so often that one is inclined to think that the end justifies the means. But there is no doubt that violence, whatever the ultimate goal it is expected to serve, is in itself a manifestation of negative identity because it is an act that deprives others of values and is committed on the ground that a clear distinction can be made between we and they. One must recognize this fact regardless of whether or not one subscribes to the principle of nonviolence. As Machiavelli aptly observed, one has to be aware of the evil one commits even if one takes the view that there is no alternative to evil means under certain circumstances.

What is most important in terms of human development is to transform the individual's relations to others and to himself from manifestations of negative identity into those of positive identity. In reality however he quite often tends to confirm his identity by discrimination against the outgroup rather than by recognizing the other's right to dissent. Or he tends to take refuge in apathy and privatized comfort rather than attain autonomy.

In a sense the ultimate value of world-order objectives depends on the formation of positive identity, of which the manifestations are participation, autonomy, and self-realization. In other words, from the viewpoint of the individual all the other four objectives—ecological balance, economic well-being, communication development, and peaceful change—can be considered as the societal prerequisites for human development, the fifth objective.

What then are the implications of trends and developments in world politics for the attainment of a positive identity for mankind? Let us examine the trends of the world political system, as it will provide a framework for the optimization of world order values.

Trends in World Politics

What are the discernible trends in world politics that are relevant to the realization of world-order values in general and positive global identity in particular?

We can identify three main trends that in varying degrees will modify the nation-state system as it has existed in the last quarter of the century. They are depolarization, denationalization, and increasing interdependence.

Depolarization refers to a political change that has two aspects. First, in terms of the world power structure it involves the transition from a bipolar to a polypolar structure and even to depolarization. That is to say, as there is now a growing rapprochement between the U.S. and the U.S.S.R., and between the U.S. and China (and even Sino-Soviet relations are unlikely to get worse than they are today), the principle of coexistence among the three superpowers is being established. But this does not mean the establishment of a system whereby the world will be partitioned, as in the 19th century, into three segments. In fact, the anticipated detente among the three superpowers will strengthen the demand by other nations for independence both within and without their spheres of influence.

Second, the multipolar coexistence system will undermine the primacy of the issue of military security and thereby decrease the dependence of smaller nations on one or another of the superpowers for such security. The strategic gap between the superpowers and the smaller nations will remain but will count for less. The major issue will shift from military security to socioeconomic security. As the strategic gap diminishes in importance, the developmental gap will become the dominant focus of attention, particularly in the developing areas, although there is the danger of arms races among the developing nations. Depolarization will not, however, lead to a situation in which a large number of self-contained sovereign states coexist. The diffusion of power that will evolve among nation-states will also develop within these states, cutting across them transnationally, that is, there will be denationalization. This process will take place at two levels of society: There will be increasing transnational interactions. The prime mover of transnational interaction is technoeconomic development, of which the obvious example is the multinational corporation (MNC). The classic notion of the nation-state and national sovereignty is based on the presupposition or myth that the scope of the *national state* coincides with the scope of the *national economy* and the *national culture*. But MNC indicates that the scope of economy has already surpassed, and will increasingly surpass, national boundaries.

The near-exponential increase of the transnational nongovernmental organization (NGO) may be seen in the same light. As most NGOs come into existence by acts of spontaneous organization and cease to exist when unnecessary, they may be considered a much better index of the functional needs of world society than intergovernmental organizations that have a tendency to bureaucratic self-perpetuation.

Another aspect of transnational interactions is increasing transnational social communications, which promote the emergence of a universal culture on the one hand and the reinstatement of subnational ethnocultural communities on the other. Although these communities may be another form of nationalism, while a universal culture is essentially transnational, both tend to erode the authority and legitimacy of the established nation-state as the primary cultural reference group. Even countries in the process of nation-building will not be entirely immune from this twofold impact. Further, as the principle of equality is accepted by an evergrowing majority of mankind to be a component of the emerging world culture, not only specific forms of authority structure such as the nation-state but authority in general will tend to be eroded.

In sum, depolarization and denationalization will contribute to the proliferation of political actors in a variety of dimensions and will not be confined to national governments.

Third, if we were to see only depolarization coupled with denationalization, our image of the world would be one of fragmentation. But as the trend toward increasing transnational interaction indicates, there will also be a growing interdependence. In other words the world is characterized by increasing functional interpenetration, while power is becoming more diffuse. Interdependence refers to symmetrical interactions, not to asymmetrical dependence-dominance relations.

Concretely, the over-all political, if not military or economic, relations among the big powers will increasingly become interdependent, taking the form of competition and cooperation rather than confrontation. On the other hand, the relations between North and South will continue to be far from interdependent. Their political relations will however probably become *less* asymmetrical if the developing countries diversify their dependence on the developed countries by taking advantage of the competition, but no longer the confrontation, among the big powers. This change would be aided further if those developing countries endowed with natural resources utilize them as a lever for bargaining to induce the developed countries to provide positive assistance and cooperation and if the developing countries, through reform of their political and socioeconomic structures, reinforce their self-regulatory, shock-absorbing mechanisms, including their systems of regional or subregional integration.

A combination of these three trends—increasing depolarization; denationalization, and interdependence—will give rise to a situation with these two characteristics: each actor on the international scene will have a greater range of options than it has today; conversely, no single actor will be able to dominate the system of world politics as a whole. What is likely to emerge is a system similar to the market model. In political terms it will approximate the liberal image of community, which consists of the free interplay of individuals and interest groups. Unless we believe in the myth of natural harmony assured by the invisible hand, we have to accept the need for regulatory machinery. Thus there will be more need for a world organization entrusted with guidance and coordination of the whole system, particularly in view of the increasing inadequacy of the nation-state system for that purpose. But if the global regulator should become too powerful, there is a danger that it will itself turn into a dominant actor. That is why the liberal image of community has been associated with the notion of weak government. If the liberal democratic model evolves at the international level, it will have very interesting and significant implications for the future of the world organizations represented by the UN system. In the absence of dominant actors the function of systemic coordination and guidance can be performed by this system even with the limited amount of resources at its disposal. In such a situation, a weak government will be able to function not despite its weakness but because of it.

But the problem remains of who will compose the global and subglobal actors, who will make decisions, and who will control the decision-makers. In other words, how will the liberal democratic model, extended on a global scale, really work? How can we create a new system of identification that will serve as the groundwork for such a structure of global authority? Here we must turn to another set of trends that are of a sociological nature.

Trends in World Society

There are three trends with crucial implications for the future development of the positive identity of man: the increasing depersonalization of society, the development of a post-modern type of discrimination, and the increasing dysfunction of democratic majority rule.

Increasing depersonalization of society. The revolution of rising expectations will continue in the coming decade. Because social strains generally stem from the gap between what people expect themselves to be and what they are capable of doing, the continuous rise of the level of expectations will cause serious strains and tensions.

These strains and tensions may take somewhat different forms in the developed and the developing societies. The development of technological capabilities will continue to exceed human expectation in developed societies. This phenomenon is best illustrated by the creation of nuclear weapons and the appearance of large-scale environmental pollution, which have turned out to be extremely dehumanizing. On the other hand, the level of expectation tends to surpass the level of feasible technological development in developing societies as illustrated by the frustrated youth, in particular, who have experienced the demonstration effect of the technology of developed societies.

But whatever the differences in the manner of their manifestations, there *are* discrepancies between expectations and capabilities, which will lead to the increasing spread of a deepening sense of frustration and dehumanization and away from the attainment of positive identity.

The combined effects of technological development and rising expectations will accelerate temporal change, spatial mobility, and the transience of interpersonal relations. Underlying these currents is the basic trend toward the increasing functional differentiation of society, the process often called modernization. This trend will promote the erosion and disintegration of traditional value constraints and facilitate the process of equalization in social relations. It will also lead to the depersonalization of society, in the sense of dissolving, differentiating, and reorganizing human relations on a functional and instrumental basis and not on the basis of man in his whole integrity. Man increasingly becomes replaceable and interchangeable because it is not his personality but the function he performs that counts.

This tendency to depersonalization will create a new problem. While the people's sense of frustration will become increasingly keen, the channels of sociopolitical communication, through which the grievances stemming from the infringement of man's integrity should be turned into constructive organized action, will become all the more

201

diffuse and ineffective because the process of communication itself is becoming depersonalized. The resulting sense of frustration is occasionally noticeable in the protest movements of youth and the liberation movement of women, which while fighting specifically against discrimination by adults and men actually resent not only the power and privileges of these groups but also the depersonalization that affects adults and men as well as youth and women.

This trend toward the depersonalization of society will be particularly pronounced in urban areas, and urbanism will be the dominant style of life in the future. To quote the *Report on the World Social Situation, 1970* of the UN (1971, p. 190):

> It is estimated that the world's urban population, which was 33 percent of the total world population in 1960, will be 46 percent in 1980 and 51 percent in 2000. Other estimates of this trend are that at the beginning of the twentyfirst century, the urban population of Latin America will include 80 percent of the region's total population, making that region more urbanized than Europe, while the urban population of North America will reach 87 percent of the total.... In the year 2000, it is projected that 62 percent of the world's urban population will be living in the regions now described as developing.

Thus there is an unmistakable tendency towards urbanization on a global scale. Problems of depersonalization closely linked with the urbanization process will therefore become matters of serious concern to the large majority of mankind, whether East or West, North or South.

Development of a post-modern type of discrimination. The trend towards global urbanization has two implications: First, as an increasing proportion of social conflict involving discrimination and violence will be linked with the process of urbanization and mass migration, at both the domestic and the international levels, it is not difficult to foresee that discrimination based on racial and ethnic distinctions will worsen. The large-scale encounters of culturally heterogeneous groups with increased mobility will inevitably lead to mounting social tensions. Further, it is no easy task in urban areas, for even a culturally homogeneous group to integrate itself into a community based on a sense of positive identity. Under such circumstances only a sense of negative identity will be fostered when a group is faced with the inflow of strangers.

Because this mounting discrimination will develop in depersonalized urban areas, the conflict is not likely to take the form of a clear-cut confrontation based on intensive group cohesion but will tend to be diffuse, subtle, indirect, and unorganized in its manifestations. Moral inhibitions against explicit racism and other forms of discrimination will reinforce this diffusiveness.

A broad and bold generalization may be made about types of racial and ethnic discrimination as they emerge in the course of historical development. We shall call them traditional, modern, and post-modern respectively.

The traditional type of discrimination originated in most cases from conquest or colonization by force, with the conquering or colonizing group, whether it constituted a majority or minority, having a strong sense of group solidarity and a high degree of discipline and with the conquered being divided and unorganized.

The modern type of discrimination emerges when the conquered themselves have come to possess a clear sense of group identity. In this type of situation, two or more units of nationalism come into conflict or competition. Most of the cases we normally call minority problems fall within this category. We have had this situation till recently in many developed countries, and we find it in most developing countries now and will do so in the decade to come.

After a brief interlude of development in some of the developed societies in which the underprivileged become quite group-conscious, for example, Black nationalism, while the privileged began to lose their nationalist or racist fervour, the third type of discrimination emerged. This post-modern type of discrimination, which may be expected to become increasingly prevalent in the developed societies of the future, is a conflict in which both parties have been so depersonalized and fragmented that not only the privileged group but even the under-privileged one tend to fail to articulate their grievances and organize their actions effectively.

These developmental stages of discrimination may also be observed in the history of class conflict. In traditional societies the underprivileged classes tend to remain divided, unorganized and apathetic. They become class conscious and are mobilized in workers' and peasants' movements in the process of modernization. When societies reach the post-modern stage disorganization and fragmentation will affect the movement of the underprivileged as well. A similar pattern of change may apply, *mutatis mutandis,* to discrimination based on sex or age.

We thus envisage in post-modern societies organizational fragmenta-tion of the movement of the underprivileged as well as the counter-movement of the privileged for three reasons. In contrast with the urbanization of nineteenth-century Western societies, which were es-sentially oriented to industrial production, in post-modern societies urbanization and urbanism as a pattern of behaviour and life style will be geared predominately to consumption, which represents privatized behaviour. Second, most post-modern societies will take the form of welfare states, which can afford to meet in part the demands and grievances of some of the underprivileged, thereby tending to keep the underprivileged divided and respective minority groups isolated. Finally there will be increasing resentment and distrust of functional differentiation and depersonalized organization, so much so that even organized movements against depersonalization will tend to be regarded as depersonalizing. In other words the inner fragmentation of society will be so deepseated that protest movements will themselves be fragmented. Gone will be the days when protest movements were guided by a great cause and unifying ideology as many great nineteenth century thinkers envisaged. Anarchistic tendencies and internal splits have already begun to undermine the formation of unified movements by youth, women, racial minorities, and even industrial workers.

This development naturally has significant implications for political organizations, whether global or sub-global, designed to channel popular discontents through organizational frameworks.

Most discriminatory practices in developing societies will be of the modern type, and their pattern of urbanization will more or less resemble that of nineteenth century Western Societies. The underprivileged, particularly minority groups, formerly subject to traditional forms of discrimination will be exposed increasingly to transcommunal interactions and flow of information both nationally and internationally which will facilitate the articulation of new feelings of group identity. It must be noted however that this process of modernising discrimination will not be quite the same as in nineteenth-century Western societies, in that the flow of information promoting modernization will bring with it the impact of post-modern societies (especially in the urban sectors) unless the governments of developing societies are able to keep their populations insulated from this inflow.

Increasing dysfunction of democratic majority rule. Fragmentation of underprivileged groups will call for a serious re-examination of the democratic processes through which grievances should be remedied. We may be standing at a historic turning-point in the development of patterns of political processes and social configurations.

Almost from time immemorial there have been men and women who devoted themselves to realising democratic goals such as equality, human rights, and social justice. What they fought for amounts to eliminating disparities in value allocation between the privileged minority and the deprived majority. This has long been the major task of the democratic government and humanitarian political leadership. Many societies in the northern hemisphere now called welfare states have however reached a stage where the large majority of people are becoming beneficiaries of the system of egalitarian redistribution of values while various minority groups remain underprivileged.

Under these circumstances, majority rule, the principal form of democratic decision-making, will prove inadequate. It may even be counterproductive because it will only aggravate the distrust of minority groups in the principle of majority rule and the procedures of parliamentary decision-making, including perhaps that of parliamentary diplomacy.

For analytical convenience we may translate the three stages of discrimination into a typology, with particular emphasis on the political implications of majority-minority relations (see Table 2).

TABLE 2

Political Typology of Discrimination.

	Underprivileged	Privileged
Traditional oligarchy	passive majority	active minority
Modern democracy	active majority: bourgeois revolution proletarian revolution peasant revolution nation-building	counteractive and/or passive old minority and active new minority based on active majority
Post-modern democracy	active minority: revolt autonomy secession	passive majority

Under the post-modern democracy there will be less tendency for the eruption of discontents and protests of minority groups to take the form of revolution in the classic sense of the term (transformation of the social system in which the underprivileged perceive themselves to be an integral component). Disruptive protest increasingly will be bound to take the form of abortive *revolt* if it fails or *secession* if it succeeds, although there will possibly be room for the incremental attainment of *autonomy*.

The majority will not be quite responsive to the grievances of the minorities. The diffuse dominance of a passive silent majority will become the normal pattern of future democracies. This type of society will also be characterized by postnationalism, that is, denationalization.

The emergence of modern democracy is linked with the process of nation-building, although the reverse is not necessarily true. As illustrated by many emerging nations, what is called nation-building is the process aimed at forming an active majority called the nation. While the developing countries will continue to pursue the goal of nation-building, post-modern democracies will tend to be denationalized, a process which will also contribute to weakening social cohesion.

We have previously pointed out that the world political structure is likely to come closer to the liberal type of community. If majority groups tend, however, to be diffuse and minority groups fragmented, how can a liberal democracy and nationalism of the classic type function as an institutional framework for popular mobilization and positive identity formation? In view of the inadequacy of the democratic system at the national level, what should be the appropriate structures of world authority? What should be the symbols of identification to promote world-order values?

We can suggest two answers to correspond to the two trends discussed above.

Transnational Participation

One way of reflecting the views of the people would be to utilize, in addition to such intergovernmental organizations as the UN, transnational organizations that would serve to restrain the power of nation-states and promote functional interdependence in world society. For instance, the transnational organizations of business, industry, labour, professions, religions, youth, women, and the aged could send representatives with a consultative status to the UN and the specialized agencies. Even if their status remains consultative in legal terms, their actual influence on international decision-making will grow as the role of transnational organizations increases within the functional interactions of world society. This functionalist formula will contribute to multiplying and diversifying the channels of communication, which national governments have tended to monopolize.

But this outlook has two important limitations. First, the influence of transnational organizations depends to a much greater degree than that of national organizations on the funds, resources and facilities available for their operation. Thus business, particularly big business, will be in a more favourable position than labor; the influence of doctors, lawyers, and professors will outweigh that of nurses and school teachers. In this sense transnational organizations are not necessarily suited to represent the views and interests of the underprivileged.

Second, transnational organizations are apt to be large and impersonal, and they tend to breed gigantic nongovernmental bureaucracies. Further, most of them exist for specific functional purposes and are not therefore appropriate remedies for depersonalization. Reinforcing identification with particular functional bodies may on the contrary even intensify negative identity in some of them, for instance, the attempt of multinational management to evade the pressure of national and international labour movements.

Another variation of this transnational formula that deserves consideration is the idea that the UN should create a Consultative Assembly composed of representatives of the major political parties of each country. Any political party that gets more than 10 percent of the popular vote would be entitled to send delegates to Consultative Assembly on the basis of proportional representation. One important advantage of this arrangement would be that opposition parties not represented in the present UN system could exert influence on it by organizing a transnational coalition, or minority groups in specific countries could have the opportunity to turn themselves into a transnational majority. Such a device could serve to channel the views and interests of the underprivileged and minorities into the international decision-making process.

Even if the role of this assembly were to be confined to consultation, the creation of a forum where transnational identities could emerge at the political as well as the functional levels would lay the foundation for the future development and reform of the UN system in a direction that reflects more realistically the political configuration of world society. Ideological bloc voting in the UN, particularly in the General Assembly, is one form of party politics at the international level. But the Consultative Assembly would differ in that it would institutionalize representation of subnational minorities and other underprivileged groups. And yet this body would not be immune from the problems of large-scale transnational organizations.

It is for this reason that we suggest another approach, designed to link the global coordinating body with communities at the grassroots level.

If the major basic obstacles to the mobilization of people in the future to eliminate discrimination are depersonalization and fragmentation of social relations, what a global coordinating body such as the UN should do is to involve people in community-building so that they may attain the positive identity of a cohesive social group while preserving their diversity. To avoid the danger of giving the world an image of the UN as yet another gigantic bureaucracy that will ag-gravate the depersonalization of society and the fragmentation of the horizontal ties of the people, it is important for the UN system to initiate in many parts of the world relatively small-scale model projects to promote community building. If the development of a sense of identity and dignity is demanded by racial or ethnic minority groups, the UN system should serve as a centre of community-building to help such groups develop cultural autonomy. If integration is the goal racial or ethnic groups strive for, the UN system should help them build model communities where the achievement of racial or cultural inte-gration can be visibly demonstrated.

To set up nondiscriminatory UN universities in member-states that accept them will serve to help the transnational faculty and student bodies influence local educational systems away from discrimination, whether racial, ethnic, sexual, or gerontological. Model community-building for the aged would be a fascinating intellectual challenge to the UN system, as it is one of the least-explored areas of human de-velopment. With respect to the professional careers of men and women, worldwide adoption of nondiscriminatory practices by the UN and related agencies would serve as a model for national and private organizations.

The crucial point here is that the UN system should act as a nucleus of community-building by serving as a vehicle for the creation of small-scale but open communities throughout the world, which while pre-serving indigenous elements of identity and diversity would share in common a universal humanitarian concern about discrimination and violence. This might be called the UN's "sociopsychological presence," and it will contribute to the attainment of positive identity by mankind perhaps much more than any other form of UN presence.

When these community-building programmes call for improvement of economic conditions, especially an upgrading of the living standard of underprivileged groups or discriminated-against classes, UN eco-nomic assistance should be extended with a view to eliminating dis-crimination that is linked to economic disparities. To encourage bal-anced development between the more advanced and the less advanced sectors of a country, the UN system can set an example for all donors of economic aid by including among its criteria for approving country programmes and projects an equitable distribution of projects among various regions and/or sectors of a country, with a major emphasis on the need to eliminate the economic foundations of discrimination.

Underlying this suggestion is the following idea: Most of the economically backward regions and/or sectors of developing countries (and of developed countries as well) suffer from underemployment, low rates of literacy, inadequate vocational training, and urban drift. In most cases, migration to urban areas will only aggravate the depersonalization and alienation of the migrants, especially if it is coupled with racial or ethnic discrimination. The same pattern applies on a global scale to the North-South gap. Serious consideration should therefore be given to formulating and implementing a development programme under which no government should deprive an individual of his right to increased social and geographical mobility. Every effort should be made to assist the populations of less developed regions or sectors to remain in their areas by spreading small cities and industries into rural areas and by developing communities in a way that permits people to enjoy the fruits of urban as well as rural life-styles.

An obvious additional measure to help underprivileged groups and regions would be the widespread technical and professional training of local people to form the core of community-building activity. Community-building by definition depends heavily on forming indigenous leadership groups. Evidently, then, the transfer of skills, knowledge, and culture for nonprofit humanitarian purposes is one of the most appropriate roles the UN system can play as an organization whose major resource is information.

Having thus gained footholds at the level of local communities in a great many parts of the world, the UN, as an organization for transmitting information, can encourage the underprivileged to participate in formulating its policies on discrimination and human rights by inviting them to send representatives to assume a consultative role to ECOSOC. However, as a report of the UN Secretary-General, *Channel of Communication with Youth* (9th August 1972), has pointed out, not too much emphasis should be placed on the role of established organizations to the exclusion of ad hoc groups generally concerned with specific issues. In the developed societies of the future there will be a declining sense of identification with big established organizations. In the developing societies, which are undergoing increasingly rapid change at every level of social organization, ad hoc groups for social movement may play a much more important role than established organizations.

The increasing activating of consultative functions among the underprivileged and the UN system would no doubt contribute to reinforcing the following three roles of the UN system:

Through participation in the consultative processes of the system, the underprivileged would be able to influence those decisions and recommendations that have a direct bearing on their fundamental rights as human beings. By serving as a channel of continuous communication through the consultative process, the system will be able to perform the function of a clearing-house of information on discrimination, assisting those engaged in community-building by giving pragmatic information on the projects, efforts, and achievements of their co-workers in other parts of the world. Finally the system will thereby meet the crucial needs of mankind by acting as a symbolic vehicle by which man's personal identification with the community of his own choosing will be linked to his identification with humanity without falling victim to the depersonalizing effects that a big global organization such as the UN might bring forth.

TOWARD A NEW WORLD ORDER: MODEST METHODS AND DRASTIC VISIONS

Richard A. Falk

Introductory Comments

The basic objective of this essay is to put forward a vision of a new, improved system of world order that could come about by the end of the century.

These proposals are not predictions. On the contrary, we seek to provide an intellectual framework capable of guiding efforts to realign the predicted future with a specifically depicted preferred future. At this time in human history a world-order movement is needed to overcome the basic drift of the present world-order system, based on the primacy of sovereign states, toward positions of danger, a general deterioration, and an uncertain prospect of disaster. We believe the sooner such a movement built around these concerns takes shape in the principal societies of the world, the better the prospects for constructive human interventions in the decades ahead.

At present, world-order reform movements must operate mainly within the limited arenas of principal states and select regions, building transnational and glcbal links in only the most preliminary and haphazard fashion. Only now do we see the first glimmerings of a genuinely global movement for world-order reform, one impetus for which is arising from the continuing efforts of the World Order Models Project (WOMP). Such a movement requires an agreed ideology, and the United States section of WOMP (WOMP/USA) hopes to provide such an ideological statement. It should be noted here that ideology is being used in an affirmative sense to denote a body of thought relevant to the pursuit of a series of explicit social, political, and economic goals.

The label world order causes difficulties. To some it is too idealistic, suggesting a kind of dreamy utopianism; hence, in this view, world-order studies are irrelevant to practical men of action and influence in the real world. To others, for almost opposite reasons, the phrase is mere rhetoric, associated with appeals for world order that are routinely worked into Law Day proclamations by power-wielders who scarcely bother to disguise their hypocrisy. To still others, talk of world order sounds uncomfortably similar in spirit to domestic promises of law and order; it is the serious talk of the powerful who seek higher budgets for police departments to keep the poor and the weak in line, to find instruments to control disorder, and to discourage demands for change.

In WOMP we support major reforms of the world political system capable of contributing to the prospects for peace, social and economic well-being, human dignity, and environmental quality. This conception of world-order reform concentrates upon a search for political, social, and economic arrangements that will achieve these four goals as fully as possible. In this phase of WOMP we have emphasized the prospects for *structural reform* that might reasonably be achieved *by the end of the century.* WOMP/USA has shaped its inquiry to avoid some weaknesses of world-order studies in the past. In this regard three features of our inquiry may be identified: *systemic scope, normativity,* and *orientation to the future.*

Systemic Scope

By systemic scope we mean a genuinely global orientation that serves as a basis for disciplined inquiry; we do not propose a transplant of national governmental structures into a global setting. Hence it is possible and desirable to consider a range of structural arrangements in relation to our world-order goals. Indeed, throughout this effort we seek to reconcile notions of planetary guidance as the nexus of a new system of world order, with wide dispersals of power and authority based on minimum bureaucratic build-ups and maximum human participation at every level of social organization.

Normativity

The success or failure of a world-order system—whether past, present, or future—depends on its capacity to promote the realization of the four WOMP goals. In this sense a world-order system is not necessarily valued because it achieves peace unless it also makes sufficiently important contributions to the reduction of poverty, repression, and pollution. We seek a system of world order that is peaceful, just and protective of the ecosphere, and in this search we are concerned with man's relations over various time horizons as well as across national boundaries. A world-order system must hence heed the claims of future generations, especially in relation to the use of scarce and finite resources, but also with respect to the preservation of our cultural and natural heritage.

Orientation to the Future

World-order inquiry needs to be concerned with grasping the predicted and probable future; a careful study of trend projections is part of the developing field of world-order studies. At the same time, futurology should not be regarded as a substitute for speculation and appraisal, nor should the work of futurology be conducted according to the characteristics of computers and other high-status technological apparatus. We need to *envision* the future as well as to *project* it, and hence the energies of the imagination are at least as relevant as the printouts of the computer.

The essence of our project for global reform involves shifts in political consciousness (value change), mobilization of energies for action (active politics), and the transformation of structures (building the preferred world order of the future). In very schematic terms we can correlate these three phases with time zones:

1970s: The Decade of Consciousness Raising

1980s: The Decade of Mobilization

1990s: The Decade of Transformation

Of course the three stages are not so mutually exclusive or temporally precise as this sequence seems to suggest. Consciousness-raising needs to persist throughout the entire transition process, transformation begins now for certain issues such as ocean resources and environmental protection, and mobilization will have to go on during the whole process. Nevertheless, we believe it helpful to suggest a model of transition based on a series of stages, provided that each stage is understood as a matter of tactical priority and that its duration of a decade is understood more as a metaphor than a prediction.

We should also make it plain that the work of world-order reform will never end. We are seeking a substantially improved system of world order by 2000, not its perfection. Indeed, the integrity of any human society depends on its capacity to keep re-envisioning a preferred future; human fulfilment presupposes an ongoing *process* of moral growth that influences individual and collective aspects of existence. Past conceptions of a preferred system of world order have seemed dreary, in part because they tend to presuppose a stoppage of history, a perfection so complete that no improvement thereafter was needed or sought, in effect the creation of a *closed political system*. The WOMP/USA models of future systems of world order are decisively *open*, and a sense of political realism indicates to us that even the most successful world-order movement can do no more than begin the work of realizing the planetary potential for human development by devising beneficial arrangements of organizing power and authority as our generation now perceives them.

A first step toward commitment to drastic and mainly nonviolent world-order reform is to build a consensus about the properties of a preferred world-order system that could be attained by relatively peaceful means in the next few decades, quite conceivably by 2000. Thus, we need representative statements of world order positions—the shape of a preferred world and the tactics and strategies of transition—from different ideological, regional, development, cultural and personal perspectives. It is very likely that at the present time such representative statements can be most usefully prepared by those without deepseated attachment to the existing world order.

Those with views and values at variance with the prevailing world-order consensus need to be particularly imaginative and dedicated to obtain a fair hearing. Governmental efforts all over the world to induce media to conform to official ideology suggest the difficulty facing those who seek to promote changes in the state system by peaceful means. Without communication within the large states and across their boundaries, it is very difficult to offset the official manipulation of human desires and beliefs and thereby loosen the regressive hold of vested economic, political, and social interests on the human imagination. We therefore attach great importance to securing national and international protection for civil liberties to facilitate the internal and transnational mobility of ideas.

In this connection also, prospects for consciousness-raising depend on the degree to which a new conception of world order begins to attract domestic and transnational support. In the years ahead a primary priority for world-order education is to assure that domestic, change-oriented, progressive elites understand the relevance of the larger world setting to their more specific and local programs of reforms. Thus movements associated with the status of women, minority rights, labor reform, population policy, environmental protection, and consumer protection need to be linked to an interpretation of the total world order and its dangers and deficiencies, and to be made part of the emergent debate about a direction and program of response. Such a domestic emphasis—complemented because of the nature of inter-dependence by a transnational emphasis—reflects the judgment that proposals for reform of the world-order system should take account of the present realities of power and authority. The continuing global dominance of national governmental actors, reinforced by domestic economic and social leaders, is the proper starting-point for any analysis of prospects for world-order reform. *Without substantially changing the orientation of these leadership groups (governmental and nongovernmental) there is no realistic hope either for adjustment (except in a post-catastrophe period) to the hazards of the present world order or for use of the opportunities for transition and reform.*

Most national leaders are to varying degrees entrapped by the ruler's imperative, which entails a *competitive* participation in the world system to *maximize* the relative shares and absolute levels of wealth, power, and prestige of each state. Because the world's resources of air, land and water are neither infinite nor equally distributed, not all groups of national leaders can succeed. The industrial societies of the world have fostered an ideology of continuous economic growth that embodies a faint promise of eventual affluence for all societies, though poorer societies achieve affluence later—as if they are trains proceeding down the same developmental tracks as the richer societies but handicapped by a late, slow start. With such an image of the future it seems sensible for every actor to seek a steady expansion of productive capacity—annual increments of GNP—to overcome problems of mass misery and poverty. Put more definitely, the system of states provides a coherent and moderate way to overcome the *absolute* problems of inequality even if it does not provide much hope of erasing its *relative* aspects. As the richer societies continue down the track, perhaps even accelerate their velocity, the slower pace of modernization by poor societies will not overcome inequality. Indeed, the gap between rich and poor is currently increasing.

Within this system of separate states, each maximizes its relative interests; the weak and poor cannot hope to challenge directly either the economics or politics of international stratification.[1] Leaders of poor countries are no longer pinning national aspirations on major voluntary capital transfers from rich countries. Third World leaders are becoming increasingly apprehensive of the neocolonialist and interventionary features of foreign aid and are wary of its distorting economic impacts, skeptical about its continuity and magnitude, and hostile to implications of dole.[2] Some argue that the growth of the rich countries is essential for the growth of the poor, namely, that without expanding export markets for their primary products the poor countries will not be able to develop, prices for their main exports will decline, and foreign exchange available for imports will shrink. That is, as many economists in the developed countries argue with great vigor, those who decry growth for the affluent countries are renouncing the only feasible basis for alleviating misery in the poor countries. For instance Carl Kaysen writes: "...it is difficult or even impossible to conceive of substantial economic growth in the poor countries in general taking place in a context of economic stagnation in the industrialized world."[3]

But suppose the limits of expansion are approaching in a way that places severe ecological constraints on development.[4] Sustaining our imagery of railroad tracks that lead beyond the land of poverty, suppose the engines pulling the development trains of the poor societies are threatened by fuel shortages? Suppose rather that the railroad as a whole has only enough fuel to run some trains at maximum speeds. How are the fuel resources to be allocated? Are there emergent ecological constraints on a growth-for-all laissez-faire system?

In a prescient essay the novelist Kurt Vonnegut, Jr., associates the intuitive grasp of these issues by leaders of American political and economic life with the rise of a neo-Darwinian ethic:

> The Vietnamese are impoverished farmers far, far away. The Winners in America have had them bombed and shot day in and day out, for years on end. This is not madness or foolishness, as some people have suggested. It is a way for the Winners to learn how to be pitiless. They understand that the material resources of the planet are almost exhausted, and that pity will soon be a form of suicide.[5]

The other side of the Winners' effort to maintain their gains will be the Losers' efforts to disrupt, threaten, and challenge. In a future setting of increasingly easy access to nuclear capabilities and of great opportunity to employ well-conceived tactics of terror and disruption, the potentialities for destructive conflict are awesome. Beyond this, the moral degeneracy implicit in consigning two thirds to three quarters of the world's population to a condition of permanent misery makes it virtually impossible to work for other kinds of significant world-order reform. If the ecological crunch consolidates the position of the neo-Darwinian strategists by giving coercion and hierarchy a seeming rationale in *necessity*, then the near future is likely to be one of the grimmest chapters in world history.

Conceiving of alternatives to neo-Darwinian patterns of behavior requires a drastic re-envisioning of the future of man, of his social relations, of his participation in the natural milieu, and of his attitudes toward violence as an instrument of control and change.[6] Our conception of world order is based on this central need for a re-envisioning of the future in a non-Darwinian manner, along lines charted by an ecological imperative that fuses a concern for the durability of natural habitat with the sort of humanism that rests upon the importance of upholding the life chances of everyone, including the unborn. Ecological equilibrium and planetary humanism provide the guiding ideals of such an orientation towards the future of world order.[7]

We believe then that three propositions follow: (1) The equilibrium of the ecosphere is subject to breakdown by cumulative pressures (wastes, depletions) and by human design (disruptions, accidents, wars); (2) these limits tend to induce drastic forms of behavior on the part of those who act to maintain or alter the existing system of world order; and (3) there is an urgent need to create a world-order counter-strategy that repudiates neo-Darwinian solutions without underestimating mounting social and ecological pressures.

On World-Order Reform and Reformers

There is intense disagreement at present about the proper scope and pace of world-order reform. The prevalent mood is established by world-order *gradualists,* who are convinced that there is no alternative to the state system this side of catastrophe and that therefore its safety and fairness depend on grasping its dynamics as clearly as possible to identify potentialities for reform with precision. Increasingly, however, there is a challenge from world-order *radicals,*who regard the displacement of the state system as necessary as well as desirable and are convinced that it is possible provided enough public education, planning, and organizing take place.[8]

Because the radical critique is becoming more serious, being based on an argument of necessity and inevitability that commands growing respect from responsible people, it encounters more and more direct hostility from world-order gradualists.

The dividing line between gradualism and radicalism in the United States involves opposite responses to three questions that stem from a shared agenda of central concerns:

Is drastic disarmament, including denuclearization, possible, and if it is, would it be a desirable alternative to deterrence?

Is it possible to evolve an effective strategy to eliminate poverty nationally and internationally within 25 years or so that does not depend on an indefinite continuation of economic growth?

Do present pollution and resource-use trends pose serious threats to the ecological stability of the planet or to the life of future human and animal generations?

World-order radicals tend to answer "yes" to each of these three questions, especially if they live in advanced industrial countries.[9] World-order gradualists answer "no" because the very posing of the system-changing question is deemed irresponsible. In a typical assertion of gradualist sentiment, David Calleo writes: "to succeed, an international organism must be based on the common interest of the participating national governments"; he adds that this "is surely the only sensible basis for progress toward a more rational world. As such, it is a welcome relief from the flabby utopianism of so many American enthusiasts of the UN."[10] There are several revealing features contained in Calleo's formulation—that the interests of governments are to be identified with the perceptions and values of present leaders, that this is the "only sensible basis" for world-order reform, that the goal of such reform is a "more rational world," and that the alternative to this sort of statist realism is "flabby utopianism," which in turn is somehow associated with enthusiasm for the UN. WOMP/USA disagrees with Calleo on each of these points.

In a world system where violence remains endemic and pervasive on virtually all levels of social organization, where deep grievances are felt by desperate persons in many portions of the world, where vested economic interests display little willingness to accept voluntary restraints based on public interest, where the technology of destruction and the capacities for disruption are increasing, we believe ample grounds for alarm exist. This sense of alarm is further justified by the basic data on population growth, hunger, political unrest, government reliance on torture, arms spending, and deterioration of oceans.[11] The burden of demonstration seems to have shifted decisively to those who still, as if by habit, interest, vocational orientation, or sheer perversity, insist on regarding statements of concern as so many false alarms. But to sound the world-order alarm is not to decry gradualist methods, as long as these methods are not used as a pretext for avoiding response to the underlying challenge. The gradualist counterattack becomes a menace only if it engenders a defensive reaction from world-order radicals or a tranquillizing reassurance to the public. Gradualist achievements that strengthen the capacities of the present international system extend the adjustment period available for drastic world-order reform, that is, the period available for the value shifts and mobilization efforts needed to organize a response to rescue the planet from its present course of deterioration and entropy, a collision course that promises eventual catastrophe. In this sense WOMP/USA reconciles world-order gradualism and world-order radicalism, especially in its conception of the transition interval between world-order systems.[12]

A radical perspective underlies the diagnosis of the present trends, the projection of an authoritative set of world-order goals, and a vision of facilitative mechanisms needed to sustain such goals. The gradualist perspective—especially efforts to conclude world-order bargains among national governments on issues of resource allocation and use and conflict management—is essential if we are to defer the day of reckoning and avoid a premature and unplanned transition to a new world order. We insist only that such an endorsement of gradualism be explicitly related to the wider setting of planning for a new system of world order.

World-order radicals must be as concerned with *achieving ends* as with visualizing them. Again, the proper fusion of means and ends emphasizes issues of transition. The least we should expect from a world-order radical is that he give serious attention to the process of transforming structures of power and authority. Without such attention, any new vision of human relations organized around values antagonistic to the present arrangements fails the first test of political relevance, sincerity. At the same time, we would emphasize humility. We lack tools to assess the future in satisfactory ways, given our concerns. There is virtually no tradition of inquiry into the transition process when it comes to world-order reform. Hence it is very important to avoid dogmatic attitudes toward either the shape of a preferred world (our relevant utopia) or what the most direct and humane transition path should be.

More than others, world-order radicals will have to be active participants in a continuous political learning process and hence give up the moralistic pretension of the liberal pedagogy that they are only part of the teaching process. Obviously an interplay between learning and teaching will underlie the continuous process of reformulation integral to the transition strategy.

What New System of World Order?

The world-order consensus fashionable among world leaders presupposes the persistence and adequacy of the state sytem. Constructive efforts at world-order reform will, in this gradualist view, be directed towards making the state system operate in a more moderate fashion rather than in transforming it into something quite different. Moderation is associated with clamping down on conflict among principal states, making their relations less likely to degenerate into periods of crisis and confrontation as well as outbreaks of war. To assure moderation it is desirable to evolve a framework for communication and cooperation, an atmosphere in which the existence and legitimacy of rivals is confirmed, and an international mood conducive to the compromise of disputes and rivalries. The Nixon-Kissinger efforts to bring "a generation of peace" are premised on establishing an international framework in which these forms of moderation could flourish. The attainment of moderation in the world-order system would clearly be desirable provided that it does not prevent attempts to overcome more fundamental frailties and inadequacies.

There is nothing objectionable in seeking to avoid destructive forms of great-power rivalry. However, there are serious inadequacies associated with regarding moderation of statecraft as a world-order solution rather than a stopgap. First of all, moderation of conflictual behavior tends to produce toleration of poverty, repression, and environmental decay as well as acquiescence in extreme forms of inequality. Second, the ethics of moderation are extensions of statist logic under altered international circumstances where a more direct protection of world-community interests is necessary; as such, laissez-faire patterns of behavior and maximization of state power and wealth continue to flourish. Third, moderate views of world order, by their stress on the sufficiency of traditional great-power diplomacy, tend to diminish, if not altogether displace, visions of planetary unity derived from the Apollo mission, of human solidarity derived from the prophets of world culture, or of ecological and nuclear vulnerability on a global scale associated with interdependence and the absence of a central guidance mechanism.

The human species may be better prepared for transition to a new system of world order than is generally evident, especially to those accustomed to thinking about change in the short time horizons of power wielders. Teilhard de Chardin and Sri Aurobindo, among others, have discerned a shift in human sentiment toward solidarity and altruism, and we believe that this shift is one significant feature of our generally bleak modern situation. Just as the collapse of colonialism was comprehensible only after it happened, so might the collapse or displacement of the state system become visible only when we get a chance to look backward. The call for a world order more responsive to bioethical requirements—species survival, including habitability of the planet—represents a new impulse in human history, itself a hopeful sign.

We believe it necessary to delimit the contours of a relevant utopia before urging any specific lines of action in the present situation. Our preferred system of world order therefore precedes *in analysis* our conception of transition, even though the transition process is earlier *in time.* It is like deciding where one wants to go before selecting the route or mode of conveyance; it is not only a question of choosing effective means to reach preferred ends. There may be other motivations as well. We may need to reach our destination by a certain time, or we may have only limited money at our disposal, or we may have a phobia about heights or tunnels, or we may be willing to take longer or pay more if the route is scenic or the mode private and comfortable. Means and ends are not neatly separable in world-order thinking or action, despite the importance of concentrating both on a model of an alternative system and on transition tactics and strategies.

In world-order speculation we also, as a traveller with a tight schedule and a fixed budget and some keen curiosities, have constraints and biases that condition our approach. To orient the approach, we enumerate those biases that seem relevant:

We should like to bring the new system into being by the year 2000 or shortly thereafter.

We should like to reach our destination without relying on violence or intimidation.

We should like to make the shifts in organization and priorities result from preference rather than necessity.

On a more concrete level such a world-order budget places a premium on limiting expectations. We cannot hope to achieve all our goals by the year 2000, assuming survival without catastrophe until then, even if developments are very favorable. We might however reach a world-order destination that overcomes the worst features of the present situation and initiates a process of change that builds momentum in the direction of further positive developments.

The first leg of the journey is long and difficult, beset with dangers, uncertainties, and adversaries; the odds of getting through do not seem high. World-order expectations involve a comprehensive response to rising danger and deepening decay in the present context. Our concerns can be enumerated:

The planet is too crowded and is getting more so.

The war system is too destructive, risky, and costly and is getting more so.

An increasingly large number of people live at or below the level of subsistence.

Pressure on the basic ecosystem of the planet is serious and growing, as is the more tangible pollution of air, water, and land.

Governing groups in many societies are repressing their own people in an intolerable manner.

Human and material resources of the planet are wasted and depleted in a shortsighted way, and at increasing rates.

Technologies are not adequately managed to assure planetary and human benefit.

On the basis of these concerns we seek by the end of the century, a world system that:

achieves and moves beyond the norm of zero population growth;

moves toward dismantling the war system, including putting into effect a plan for drastic disarmament;

moves toward a world economic system in which each individual is assured the right to the minimum requirements of body, mind, and spirit and in which food, clothing, housing, education, health, and work are regarded as collective as well as personal responsibilities;

moves toward an integrated and coherent system of dynamic equilibrium so far as human impacts on the biosphere are concerned;

achieves and moves beyond a minimum bioethical code based on human survival, planetary habitability, and species diversity;

moves toward a conservation policy that is sensitive to the life chances of future human generations and protective of natural wonders and species diversity;

achieves an effective system of global oversight on the side-effects of technological innovation.

Although these objectives are extremely ambitious, they are mainly designed to plug leaks and improve man's prospects of survival. These reforms are designed to overcome the worst features and tendencies of the present world system and stabilize the results without discouraging further world-order reform. We expect the shape of the relevant utopia for the first generation of reformers of the twenty–first century, assuming prior realization of WOMP goals, will involve liberating people from various sorts of bondage—work, mores, anxieties—so that more and more of them can participate more fully in a life of dignity, joy, and creativity that mobilizes the full energies of self-development. Putting this sense of potentiality differently, we believe that on the average human beings are now able to make use of 5 percent or so of their potential for development and that our preferred world-order system might reasonably expect to raise the average to 20 percent or so, but the challenge and opportunity will remain immense after our initial program of world order reform has been completed. In this first phase, WOMP/USA is seeking to deal only with the establishment of *minimum preconditions* for tolerable human existence, free from high risks of catastrophe and misery.

Our focus is on the *organizational framework* of collective human existence. We believe it will be necessary to modify the present structure of world order, but that it will be possible only after a considerable effort of persuasion, planning, and mobilization in the principal parts of the planet. One ingredient of this effort involves the design of the sort of organizational framework that will realize our minimum goals and support the continuing pursuit of the objectives of personal development.

To economize on space and focus response we shall rely on some visual representations of design structures for new world-order systems. The rationale of our preferred system will become clearer in the exposition of the transition strategy in the next section, but at least its principal properties may be indicated at this point in the discussion.

We begin with several general considerations:

First, conventional world-order thinking has tended to proceed on the basis of a stark alternative between virtual anarchy and virtual world government. We seek to explore the *numerous* intermediate world-order *options,* as well as the many variants of world government and anarchy.

Second, our design of a system is put forward as a tentative sketch that will be frequently revised as the world-order building process unfolds. It is therefore misleading and trivial to make highly detailed institutional proposals, which would exhibit *the fallacy of premature specification.*

Third, our design of a preferred world system is not confined to *external linkages* of principal actors but also encompasses the *internal linkages* of national governments to substructures and to the population as a whole, thereby reflecting the hypothesis that a progressive world order is not reconcilable with regressive systems of domestic order, at least in principal societies.

Fourth, our design is intended to convey a sense of *organizational pattern* rather than embody *precise measurements* of relative actor roles and capability.

Fifth, preferred organizational solutions will involve simultaneous dialectical movements towards *centralization* and *decentralization* of authority within and among states.

We shall now consider these types of systems: the existing system; a five-power world; a regional system; a transnational functional system; a world-government system; a world-empire system; and a WOMP/USA central guidance system.

Our purpose is to depict the principal alternative futures of the world-order system. This presentation emphasizes the form and distribution of capability and authority among principal bureaucratic actors. The description of various status patterns for actors in different systems is as yet a primitive mapping technique, involving highly selective and imprecise features of the overall context. Nevertheless, we believe that such visual displays of power/authority patterns encourage thinking about a range of constructive world-order alternatives. First of all, comparative features are stressed. Second, the variability of any type of world-order solution—the array of world structural arrangements—is easily grasped. Third, more sophisticated mapping can gradually provide visual analogues to configurative analysis of the political setting.

1. The Existing System. Figure 1 displays the basic interplay of actors in the existing international system. The predominance of state actors is readily apparent, as is the emergent role of regional and universal functional actors. Such actors would not have been represented at all on a comparable display of actors in 1900, when colonial clusters would have been prominent. Only the rather insignificant Portuguese colonial cluster remains at present, although a fuller display that attempted to depict hegemonic relations or spheres of influence might suggest a new series of neocolonial clusters of significance. Also omitted in Figure 1 are alliance clusters, which have considerable importance in creating patterns of cooperative behavior in the war/peace area as well as in establishing alignment and interaction patterns embracing the whole spectrum of transnational relations.

Nevertheless, the statist character of this system is apparent, as are the hegemonic and condominium potentialities arising from the inequality of state actors and the predominance of the two superpowers; this predominance is especially apparent in relation to military affairs. Figure 1 makes no effort to consider variations in internal political arrangements as a factor in the capacity of state actors to realize WOMP values.

Figure 2 represents a crude attempt to take account of the internal political arrangements of state actors in the present system of world

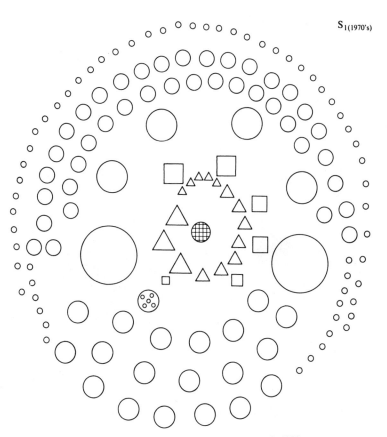

$S_{1(1970's)}$

Figure 1. Existing world-order system, early 1970s.

KEY TO MODELS OF WORLD ORDER

⊕ Global Governmental Actor   ⬡ Corporation as World Actor

△ International Institution (Global)   ⬢ Corporation as Statist Actor

▲ International Institution (Regional)   ⊗ World-Empire Actor

☐ Regional Actor   (88) Colonial Cluster

○ States

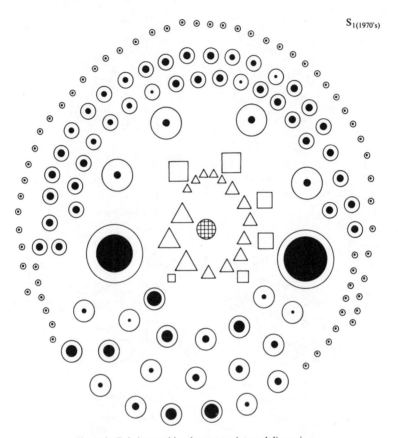

$S_{1(1970's)}$

Figure 2. Existing world order system: internal dimensions.

order. The smaller the diameter of the internal black circle the more directly the prevailing governing perspective is regarded as committed to the promotion of WOMP values, and vice versa. The size of the inner black circle expresses the degree of militarization (size of military budget, military budget as proportion of national budget and of GNP), the extent of social privation (proportion of population at subsistence level or below, provision of basic life necessities), the extent of political privation (number of political prisoners, protection of civil liberties, existence of an active opposition movement), and the extent of ecological privation (extent of pollution, responsiveness to ecological consequences of policy).

226

Our contention is that the values around which existing governmental centers of power and authority are organized directly correlate with their capacity and willingness to participate in a peaceful transition to a more beneficial arrangement of world-order values. Simplistic views as to the responsiveness of national actors to WOMP values are bound to be misleading. We recognize that a given government might have a good record on social welfare and a poor one on political liberty or peacemindedness. We also recognize that a domestic disposition toward or away from WOMP values does not *necessarily* correlate with attitudes towards the direction and preferred character of world-order reform, but we believe the following propositions are generally accurate: that the value priorities of domestic governments are relevant to prospects for world-order change and that there is a tendency for attitudes toward world-order reform to reflect domestic value priorities. Thus Figure 2 augments Figure 1 by contending not only that states dominate the existing world-order system but that their distinctive influence significantly reflects their domestic orientation towards the four WOMP values.

2. The Five-Power Variant of the Existing World Order System. Figure 3 represents an effort to display the Nixon-Kissinger (-Brezhnev?) world-order design based on the contained or moderated competition of five principal actors (the U.S.A, the U.S.S.R., China, Japan, and Western Europe). This model of world order is premised on maximizing certain oligopolistic tendencies in the existing system. It attempts to diminish the destructive risks of rivalry, to adapt to an emergent condition of multipolarity in economic and security affairs, and to simplify the procedures for mainstream cooperation in a world of increasing complexity and interdependence.

The five-power variant of the existing system is basically an intergovernmental managerial notion without contemplated normative reforms. The main world-order objectives are to eliminate destructive forms of political and military rivalry by encouraging moderate relations among existing centers of power and wealth. Ideological differences are respected and minimized; a condition of efficient global management is ideological tolerance. Supranationalism is diminished in status and role beneath even current levels, although particular functional tasks may be assigned to specialized institutions under the effective control of principal government actors.

The agenda of world-order issues does not accord priority to values of social welfare or political dignity. A five-power scheme is fully compatible with toleration of high levels of poverty and repression within the system as a whole. Even violence outside the framework of

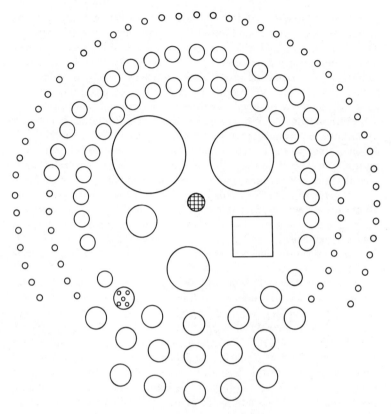

Figure 3. Nixon-Kissinger design.

great-power relations is acceptable, and no major emphasis is placed on peacekeeping or nonproliferation of weapons. Environmental quality is a fit object of inter-actor cooperation, but again it is presumed to be manageable if dealt with by cooperative undertakings of the dominant international actors.

The five-power design is in significant respects an improvement on the cold-war years, provided it does not encourage an era of complacency and does not itself degenerate into a two-power condominium arrangement. SALT and the Brezhnev-Nixon Declaration of Principles in 1972 provide some grounds for fear that the nuclear superpowers are seeking to impose their will on the rest of the globe. The five-power design also fails to affirm ideals of human solidarity or to seek ways of overcoming the immense inequities and miseries endured at present by such a high proportion of the human race. This five-power conception also tends to underestimate the ecological constraints and risks arising from continuing patterns of uncurtailed economic growth in a decentralized world system. Finally, principal actors excluded from significant management of world-order concerns, such as India, Brazil, Nigeria, and Indonesia, may be led to organize rival groupings. A concert of principal actors that denies participation to many other important actors in the global arena is likely to provoke reactions of bitterness and opposition.

3. Regionalist Modification of the Existing World Order System. There are definite potentialities—functional and political—for developing stronger regional actors, both as an offset to the degree of fragmentation associated with the state system and as a protection against the sort of homogenizing centralization associated with a direct move toward world government. The progress of regionalist approaches in Western Europe is irreversible in many respects and provides an example to the rest of the world of the possibility of reconciling national autonomy with rather advanced forms of regional integration with respect to economic and security sectors. In Latin America, Eastern Europe, the Middle East, and Africa it is possible to envision considerable regionalization or subregionalization of national activity over the next three decades. There are major obstacles in each region to embarking on a regional or subregional course, but there are also major incentives relating to efficiency and bargaining leverage vis-à-vis other major actors.

The basic appeal of regionalism over the short run is that it appears to safeguard two principal goals of the foreign policy of weaker and poorer countries: first, it improves the capabilities for national development by taking better advantage of the international division of labor arising from varying national capabilities; second, it gives poorer and weaker governments a better chance to defend themselves against interventionary pressures mounted from outside the region and provides an increased prospect of access to and participation in various world decisional contexts such as world monetary policy, ocean resources, and skyjacking regulation.

As such, regionalism has considerable appeal as a world order halfway house. It seems more feasible in the near term as a step beyond state sovereignty that can be used to dilute nationalist sentiments during a period when global loyalties need to grow stronger. Also such

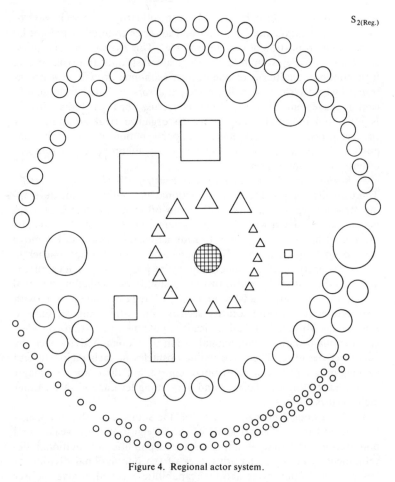

$S_{2(Reg.)}$

Figure 4. Regional actor system.

regional tendencies could overcome some inequalities of the existing system without requiring the principal state actors to alter their formal role in any way.

Figure 4 illustrates a regional plan for world order. This plan is one of many variations on the fundamental notion that regional actors could become very important centers of decision and control by the end of the century. The basic assumption of this model is that functional, global, and large state actors are all diminished in their respective roles during the period of regional build-up. The emergent system depicted in Figure 4 might evolve into a Nixon-Kissinger concert of principal actors (see Figure 3), but with regional actors playing a much more significant role.

Further, the structural visions of world-order reforms developed by WOMP/USA are expressive of normative priorities arising from the affirmation of four world-order values. Thus we would associate the outcomes of transition depicted in Figure 4 as a consequence of the impact of WOMP values. As will become clear when we discuss the transition process, changes in prevailing patterns of political consciousness are preconditions for structural modifications.

As a matter of emphasis we believe the world-order reforms implicit in Figure 4 are neither plausible nor responsive enough to the agenda of challenges to warrant primary emphasis at this time. From a problem-solving, value-realizing perspective the regional growth model is far more attractive than the Nixon-Kissinger five-power model, although its attainability is more dubious. Regionalist developments to date, most ambitiously exhibited in EEC, constitute a mixture of world-order reform and a tactical statist program to achieve national priorities in competition with the two superstates. There is no prospect that regionalist movements, even if much more successful than now seems possible, could provide the kind of central guidance mechanisms needed to administer the resource base of the world, to cope with the intricacies of economic and technological interdependence, or to give a sense of direction to the emergent world culture. Regionalist solutions also overlook decentralizing and transnationalizing tendencies that may become as important for solving problems and realizing values as centralizing tendencies.

In sum, the regional alternative has an important place in thinking about reform of the present world-order system, but it does not seem to offer the most promising solution to present problems.

4. Transnational Corporate Modifications of the Existing World-Order System. Figures 5 and 6 suggest the potential significance of multinational corporate actors as reshapers of the world system. Managers of large corporate operations increasingly portray themselves as the new globalists, ardently expressing their commitment to a world without boundaries and to a labor and consumer market of maximum scope. Whether such transnational corporate ambitions are compatible with the interests of major governmental actors remains to be seen.

In Figure 5 we envision the continuing displacement of state actors by multinational corporate actors oriented toward WOMP values of social and political responsibility. In Figure 6 we envision a somewhat

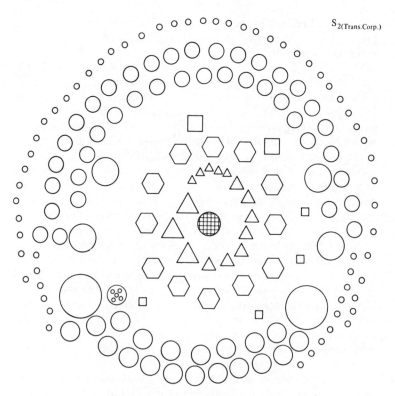

$S_{2(\text{Trans.Corp.})}$

Figure 5. Transnational corporate system.

comparable growth of multinational corporate power but project this growth as essentially an extension of statist logic rather than as a constructive response to it. These polar variations are presented to stimulate reflection about the uncertain impact of multinational corporate activity on the world-order system. Such simplified alternatives are in fact unlikely to develop. The picture is likely to be more mixed and far more complicated. Nevertheless, it is important at this stage of primitive mapping to take account of multinational corporations as actors in the world-order system and to explore their positive and negative relations with the specific program for world-order reform endorsed by WOMP.

Establishment of large production plants by Pepsi-Cola and Fiat in the Soviet Union is a significant indicator of the ability of multinational

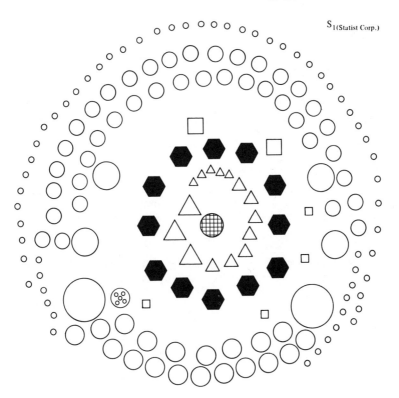

S_1(Statist Corp.)

Figure 6. Transnational corporate system.

corporate actors to penetrate the socialist sector of the world system. No comparable penetrations have been made by international institutional actors. It may be that governmental actors, even of diverse ideology, find it easier to reconcile themselves to the *division* of functions implicit in the world-order reform patterns depicted in Figures 5 and 6 than to the *transfer* of functions implicit in Figures 4, 7, 8, 10, and 11. In this regard, the normatively positive image depicted in Figure 5 would be helped by the formation of comparable socialist economic units which establish bases of operation in leading capitalist societies. Such intermingling might lead to new social and economic orientations for corporate actors. In this regard the recent movement by shareholders to press corporate management to promote social goals alongside growth and profitability goals should be of extreme interest to world-order specialists. In many institutional settings, investment codes are emerging around debates about transnational issues that bear directly on WOMP's concern with peace and justice. For example, the numerous church and university inquiries into the propriety of holding investments in firms doing business in Namibia are indicative of this new trend to bring noneconomic interests to bear in corporate settings. The controversial Polaroid experiment in South Africa represents a corporate effort to satisfy some of these normative demands and signifies the acceptance of their legitimacy. It is time that world-order analysts appreciated the extent to which the corporate arena is relevant to their concerns.

5. *Functionalist Modifications in the World-Order System.* Figure 7 portrays a world-order solution premised on the growth of global and regional functional actors, that is, intergovernmental actors like the World Health Organization or the Food and Agricultural Organization concerned with a specific subject. The basic reform premise is that the most viable compromise between existing realities and future needs and preferences can be achieved by accenting the role of functionalism.

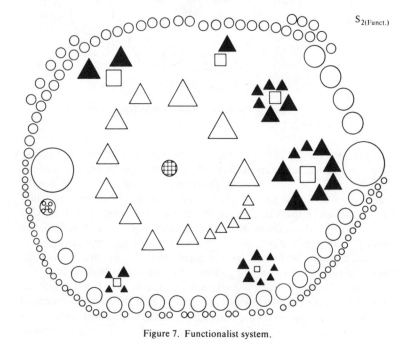

$S_{2(Funct.)}$

Figure 7. Functionalist system.

Technical competence is concentrated in specialized actors, flexibly allocated among regional or global actors as problems, needs and opportunities for institutional development dictate. Political competence is left virtually as it is at the state level. Figure 7 is one example of a *type* of world-order solution that could be varied in proportion in many ways. This solution is attractive because it achieves a balance between the centralizing requirements of problem-solving and the decentralizing goals associated with protecting and enhancing zones of diversity and autonomy on the level of group and individual action.

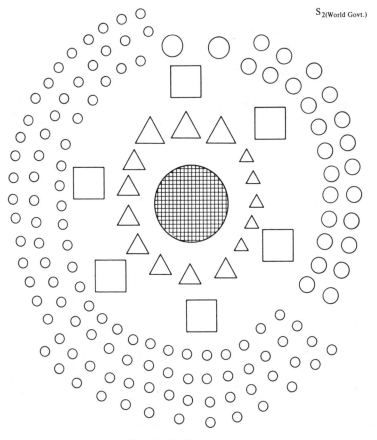

$S_{2\text{(World Govt.)}}$

Figure 8. World government.

Is this reconciliation plausible? Would not functional actors of such importance acquire political roles as well? Would state actors allow their roles to be eroded and bypassed? Would a functional network possess sufficient coordinating capabilities to meet the needs of the planet? If such coordinating capability existed, would the world solution then resemble a weak variant of world government (see Figure 8)?

These questions cannot be understood fully in the framework of the early 1970s. The world-order solution we project presupposes the experience of a transition process that achieves value reorientations generally supporting the WOMP program of world-order reform. As we

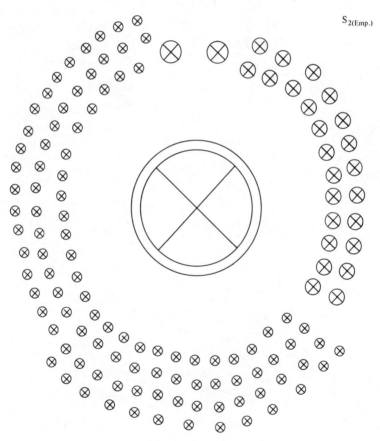

$S_{2(Emp.)}$

Figure 9. World empire.

suggest in Figures 10 and 11, our own recommendation is for a compromise between the functionalist line of development (Figure 7) and
the world-government line of development (Figure 8).

6. *The World Government Modification of the Existing World Order
System.* Figure 8 depicts an intermediate form of world government
in which there has been a substantial centralization of political power
and authority combined with a drastic reduction in the status and
capability of state actors. In this conception of world government,
regional and global functional actors play a much more important role
than they do in the existing world-order system (compare Figure 1).

A world-government solution to the challenges of world order seems
to be the most logical response to the torments of war and interstate
rivalry, although there are important reasons for skepticism. Further,
deep-seated ethical and religious affirmations of human unity seem to
support a movement toward political unification. There has been an

Figure 10. Preference model.

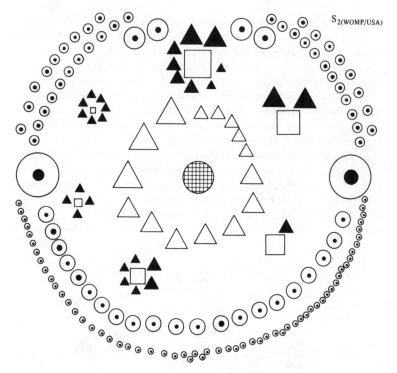

Figure 11. Preference model: internal dimensions.

historical tendency toward larger units in human affairs, although the cyclical build-up and collapse of empires suggests a process more complex than the steady increase in the size of units dominating the international scene. Indeed, it is plausible to interpret recent patterns of political behavior, especially the activity of numerous militant separatist movements, as leading to a period of fragmentation of existing states into units that are ethnically and psychologically more meaningful than larger ones for most of their inhabitants.

Finally, the technology of today relating to communication, transportation, and information creates the possibility (and fear) of an efficient global administrative apparatus, not necessarily one based on hierarchical concepts of organization.[13]

In the decade or so ahead it seems unlikely that any kind of world government can get started. National governments are not disposed to cede their present array of capabilities and roles to a central world

238

actor. Change-oriented groups and individuals engaged in opposing the policies and pretensions of national bureaucracies are unlikely to be attracted in the near future to a project for a superbureaucratic arrangement for the entire planet. A governmental solution to the world-order crisis of the present period is only likely to engender meaningful levels of support in post-catastrophe contexts—after World War III or as a reaction to a fundamental ecological failure. WOMP emphasizes planned, nontraumatic transition potentialities and will not investigate seriously world-government possibilities arising from traumatic transition scenarios.

7. *World Empire or World State Modifications of the Present World-Order System.* In Figure 9 we illustrate the culmination, in organizational terms, of imperial tendencies in the existing world-order system. The present system of rival, unequal states would be supplanted by the complete triumph of a single center of state power. In contrast to the situation shown in Figure 8, concentration of power is achieved by coercion rather than contract. Such a process of transition can be envisioned only as a consequence of World War III or as a sequel to a series of successful infiltrations of principal domestic power structures by members of a global integration movement. In either instance such an imperial solution is neither likely nor desirable, nor would it be likely to persist even if established.

An imperial organization of the planet is likely to require violence and manipulation to maintain itself, and to embody great inequality between the ruling centers of decision and control and the subordinate societies. An imperial or statist solution to the world-order crisis is likely to represent from a WOMP normative outlook a worsening of the existing system. It is true that the failure of planned transition (see Section 5) to proceed at a satisfactory rate may induce desperation or catastrophe, which would make an imperial strategy more attractive and necessary. If adjustment to pressures in the existing system are delayed too long or the magnitude of the pressures is underestimated, the very urgency of the situation may make it almost inevitable that central management will be "arranged" by the strongest concentration of power-wielders. It is possible to envisage a conspiracy to create a world empire constituted by the leaders of the two or three most powerful governments.

As matters now stand, however, we present Figure 9 mainly to suggest what might happen to the global system in the event that planned transition fails to proceed at sufficient speed.

8. *Preferred World Alternatives to the Existing World-Order System.* Figures 10 and 11 provide a structural image of a preferred world-

order system that could be brought into being by a planned transition process sometime around the year 2000. Figure 10 emphasizes the new arrangement of power/authority relations, and Figure 11 emphasizes correlative domestic reorientations of state actors. Both sets of transformation are conditioned by the dominant influence of WOMP values. Without the dominance of this influence in domains of consciousness and aspiration, no process of planned transition could take place.

In Figure 12 we indicate the table of organization for the central guidance system that is entrusted with general functions of coordination and oversight. The specific allocation of institutional roles is discussed elsewhere, but it should be emphasized that the degree of bureaucratic complexity apparent in the diagram does not entail either a highly bureaucratized or hierarchical arrangement of functions and powers.[14] Instead, the high degree of differentiation among institutions seeks to combine considerations of efficiency arising from specialization with the diffusion of authority designed to invigorate a network of checks and balances within the central guidance framework. The institutional arrangement seeks to embody the value priorities underlying proposals for world-order reform as put forward by WOMP/USA.

The basic conception of our preference model is that considerations of what is possible by 2000 suggests a dual emphasis on macrofunctional potentialities and on the trade-off between global managerial build-ups and partial dismantling of national bureaucracies. In essence we anticipate the centralized administration of many realms of human activity—health, environmental protection, money, business operations, ocean and space use, disarmament, disaster relief, peacekeeping and peaceful settlement, and resource conservation. These superagencies will enjoy competence only in relation to their functional domain. Augmented international political institutions less tied to the state system will attempt to assure that normative priorities are upheld and that various functional activities are coordinated. As is any other political mechanism, it will be vulnerable to whatever deficiencies exist with regard to the intensity and clarity of the underlying consensus shaped around WOMP values during the transition process.

Constitutional mechanisms will attempt to mediate between concerns for efficiency and dignity. There will be checks and balances, as wide a participation in decisional processes as feasible, procedural opportunities for review, a code of restraints designed to safeguard diversity, autonomy, and creativity, and a minimization of the bureaucratic role.[15]

The WOMP/USA preference model also allocates authority between the global and regional levels to a considerable extent. This allocation reflects a commitment to diversify control arrangements, to limit centralizing tendencies to real functional requirements, and to offset the decline of the state system in as balanced a fashion as possible. Part of the offset and balance would also be achieved by transnational economic activity organized in a progressive way, as portrayed in Figure 5. Indeed Figure 10 is a synthetic model drawing on features implicit in Figures 4, 5, 7, and 8.

Figure 11 carries forward our fundamental stress on domestic reorientation as a precondition of global transformation. The diminished inner circles reflect the increasing influence of WOMP values on the internal organization of states. As will become evident in the discussion of our transition proposals, this domestic reorientation will be a major undertaking early in the transition process, especially by highly industrialized states; such reorientation of domestic arrangements will proceed unevenly throughout the world system, and the process will go on long after the preferred world order comes into being. The ideal toward which we proceed at all levels of social organization is a minimum degree of coercion and bureaucratization and a maximum degree of spontaneous solidarity, participation, and discipline.

Finally, Figure 10 is not a terminal model. If achieved it will become the system that will in turn stimulate twenty-first century world-order reformers to express new preference models and transition strategies. No world-order solution is acceptable unless it encourages a continuous search for ways to transcend new limits; the dignity of man depends on the provisionality of political and social arrangements, on their imperfectability, except in the imagination. We reject all closed systems of world order as candidates for preference models.

In conclusion, Figures 1 to 12 are offered as images to encourage and orient world-order analysis. Their role is to give visual expression to the notion of comparative systems of order. We believe such mapping operations can be developed with far greater precision in the future. Our goal is to make the idea of alternative futures as vivid as possible in the course of outlining a world-order solution responsive to our value preferences.

The Challenge of Transition

The idea of transition concerns the process of change and engineering designed to convert the predicted future into the preferred future. More generally, the study of transition involves disciplined inquiry into

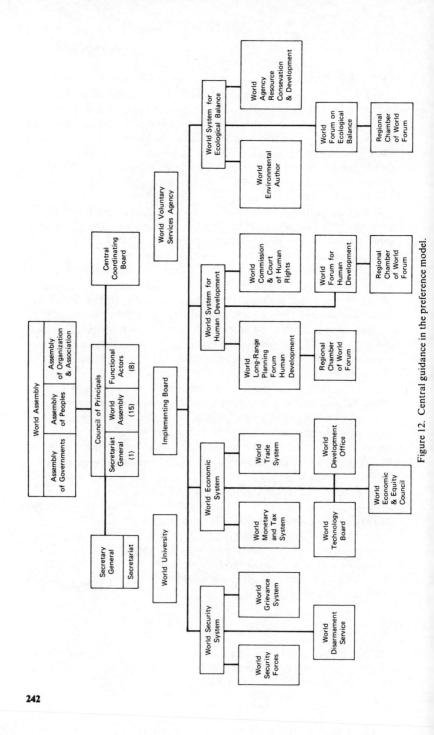

Figure 12. Central guidance in the preference model.

Problem Focus / Change Orientation / Institutional Focus / Analytic Stages	War Consciousness / Domestic Arena	Poverty Mobilization / Transnational and Regional Arenas	Pollution Transformation / Global Arena	Human Rights Transformation / Global Arena
Transition Stages / Temporal Subscripts				
$t_{1970's}$ t_1	*****	**	*	
$t_{1980's}$ t_2	**	****	***	*
$t_{1990's}$ t_3	*	***	****	***

[N.B. The number of stars in each box is roughly proportional to the degree of incremental emphasis in each t interval.]

Figure 13. Transition path $S_0 \rightarrow S_2$.

the process by which social systems change; our interest is confined to changes in world order system, and more specifically to studying the prospects of achieving the WOMP/USA preference model (see Figures 10 to 12 and Table 1) by 2000 or thereabouts. Depiction of a transition path designed to realize a set of social goals should not be confused with prediction or prophecy. Transition planning is at best a style of analysis that might eventually produce a series of statements in the form of "if x then probably y" that would be linked together to establish a coherent framework. As with other facets of world-order studies, disciplined inquiry into transition planning has been initiated only in very recent years.

The study of transition prospects can be separated from historical time. The WOMP mandate to study world-order change over the next three decades imposes a difficult constraint as it presupposes an effort to correlate transition steps with time intervals. Our sense of the future is so imperfect, even at the level of very small social systems, that it seems clear that such a time-bound depiction of the transition process must be regarded in a heuristic spirit, as nothing more than a suggestive metaphor. Our main object is to prefigure the sort of developments that should take place if the preference model of WOMP/USA is to become a reality by peaceful means in the relatively near future.

Traditional proposals for world-order reform virtually ignore the transition process. In that sense even a rudimentary approach to transition engineering seems a distinct improvement, as it underscores the need to activate political energies capable of inducing transformation.

243

Attention to transition, at least and at last, signifies the willingness of world-order reformers to drop anchor in political waters.

In this section we are concerned with feasibility and preference issues as conditioned by constraints of time (the need to complete transition to a new system roughly by 2000) and of modality (as nontraumatic as possible, eschewing violent tactics). We will introduce this approach to transition with a dual presentation; first, a framework for inquiry or a way of thinking about transition; secondly, a set of transition tactics and proposals associated with promoting a responsive world-order reform movement.

To facilitate systematic thinking about the transition process we believe it is useful to develop an analytic framework that organizes material in relation to convenient categories of concern. In this section the basic character of the framework is presented in schematic form.

The first conceptual element involves a designation of world-order systems. Let S_0 represent the present time locus within the world-order system: the subscript 0 is used to indicate the zero point or point of origin. S_{-1}, S_{-2}, S_{-3} and so on refer to earlier periods characterized by distinct world-order systems, whereas S_1 refers to the period of the existing world-order systems and S_2, S_3 and so on refer to periods associated with distinct future world-order systems. Thus S_0 bisects S_1 to indicate whether an observer views the existing system as in an early, middle, or late phase. S_0 is a point, whereas S_{-1} or S_1 are durations or intervals of varying magnitude. S_2 (WOMP/USA) is the preference model depicted in arrangement (Figure 10) and in internal reorientation of state actors (Figure 11). S_2 (empire) (Figure 9) or S_2 (world government) (Figure 8) refer to alternative future world-order systems. On a first level of representation, then, our transition focus can be depicted as follows:

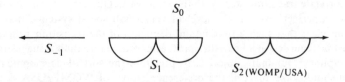

It is important to present a horizon of aspiration that extends beyond S_2 (WOMP/USA) to make it clear that the preference model is itself provisional and transitional and a prelude to the active pursuit of a further program of world-order reform culminating in S_3 (WOMP/USA):

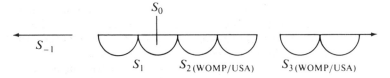

$$S_0$$

$$S_{-1}$$

$$S_1 \qquad S_{2\,(\text{WOMP/USA})} \qquad S_{3\,(\text{WOMP/USA})}$$

Obviously, from the perspective of S_2 there could be as wide a range of S_3 preference models as we considered in the previous section in relation to S_2 prospects and preferences.

On a second level of specificity we believe it useful to divide intersystemic intervals $(S_1 \rightarrow S_2)$ into stages represented as t (transition) intervals. Thus t_0 is equivalent to S_0, but then the space $S_0 \rightarrow S_2$ located in S_1 is filled by t_1, t_2, t_3, and $S_2 \rightarrow S_3$ is constituted by t_4, t_5, t_6:

$$\longrightarrow S_0 \longrightarrow S_2 \longrightarrow S_3$$

$$t_0 \rightarrow t_1 \rightarrow t_2 \rightarrow t_3 \longrightarrow t_4 \rightarrow t_5 \rightarrow t_6$$

These t intervals are *time periods* or *distances* rather than *points* (as are S_0 and t_0). Such intervals can also be projected backward in time to account for the emergence of S_0 and can be represented as t_{-1}, t_{-2}, or t_{-n} depending on the attributes relied upon to identify past transition intervals. It may also be useful to represent transition intervals (anticipated or historical) by chronological subscripts as follows:

$$t_{(1954)} \longleftarrow t_{(1964)} \longleftarrow t_{(1974)} \longrightarrow t_{(1984)} \longrightarrow t_{(1994)}$$

It is possible to correlate the analytic stages with a predicted transition sequence as follows:

$$t_{0(1974)} \longrightarrow t_{1(1984)} \longrightarrow t_{2(1994)} \longrightarrow t_{3(2004)}$$

Each t subscript designates its termination after the elapse of the graphed time to its left; hence, the duration of t_1 is t_0/t_1, of t_2 is t_1/t_2 or ten years as presented above. In WOMP we have been supposing that $S_{2\,(\text{WOMP})}$ could be brought into being by approximately 2000, with a notation as follows:

$$S_0 \longrightarrow S_{1\,(\text{WOMP})(2000)}$$

Hence, t_1 would end in about 1980, t_2 in about 1990, and t_3 in 2000. It should be obvious that such analytic symmetry is extremely unlikely to characterize the actual future. It is unlikely that these transition intervals will coincide with spans of a decade or that they will be of equivalent duration. All modes of historical periodization, even of the past, are arbitrary; and historians question reliance on designations like Middle Ages, Renaissance, and Enlightenment, and even the tendency to study literature or art by reference to centuries. To designate future conditional periods is at most a device by which to organize thought and conjecture; it is a convenience and an effort to establish a convention helpful for analysis and communication.

We accept the notion that the present system of world order is under great pressure and cannot sustain itself for more than a few decades in its present fundamental form. Therefore, some type of transition from $S_1 \rightarrow S_2$ is anticipated, but there is a wide range of alternatives. Even if $S_{2 \text{ (WOMP/USA)}}$ is the goal of transition there are certain planned pathways excluded as unacceptable, namely, transition by trauma and transition by imperial conquest and domination. We regard these two excluded transition pathways as possibly creating a new world-order system, a variant of S_2 capable of dealing with the ecological challenge and of eliminating the prospect of apocalyptic war. However, we reject such potential gains because of the costs and risks we believe such modes of transition entail and because the S_2 framework of control would tend to be too centralized and coercive.[16]

In our conception of transition S_0 is located late in S_1. S_1 is in the process of disintegration and displacement by a variety of internal and uncoordinated pressures. That is, S_1, whose origins can be associated with the Peace of Westphalia (1648), will come to an end in the next 50 to 100 years, at the most, by virtue of its own internal contradictions. The inquiry by WOMP is therefore directed at accelerating this natural process of disintegration and especially at assuring a constructive and progressive world-order sequel, as well as easing the birth pains of S_2; the analogy to preparations for natural childbirth are not farfetched. The prospects of natural transition (i.e., $S_0 \rightarrow\rightarrow S_2$) are dismal, and planned transition is virtually synonymous with avoidance of catastrophe.[17]

In Table 1 we provide a very schematic matrix to convey our vision of planned transition to S_2. The horizontal categories project a sequence of developments relating to values or problems, to the kind of change, and to the critical institutional arena; the vertical categories are concerned with time, as noted in calendar (t_{1974}, t_{1984},) and analytic (t_1, t_2,) categories. The objective is to depict a set of *correlated sequences* as constituting the *political logic* of planned transition to $S_{2 \text{(WOMP/USA)}}$. These sequences can be divided into levels for purposes of easier comprehension:

First level (problem/value):
War $\rightarrow$ Poverty $\rightarrow$ Pollution $\rightarrow$ Human Rights

Second level (change orientation):
Consciousness $\rightarrow$ Mobilization $\rightarrow$ Transformation

Third level (arena):
Domestic $\rightarrow$ Transnational/Regional $\rightarrow$ Global

Fourth level (time/calendar):
$t_{1970s} \rightarrow t_{1980s} \rightarrow t_{1990s}$

Fifth level (time/analytic):
$t_1 \rightarrow t_2 \rightarrow t_3$

In Table 1 we are trying to correlate these five levels of sequenced development during the interval of planned transition to S_2, The number of stars in each box gives a rough sense of the relative degree of correlation. Table 2 illustrates in an even more skeletal form the conception of planned transition from $S_{2 \text{ (WOMP/USA)}} \rightarrow S_{3 \text{ (WOMP/USA)}}$. It should be clear that these images of *sequence* are intended only to identify *patterns of emphasis* and not to convey *mutually exclusive* categories. It would be obviously false to consider t_1 as exclusively concerned with changes in the domestic arena that dismantle the war system as it has evolved in the course of S_1 We are however trying to make the general point that the reorientation of consciousness in the domestic arena and its impact on the war system are the essential preconditions for initiating a process of planned transition to $S_{2 \text{ (WOMP/USA)}}$ as of S_0 or S_{1974}. Given other visions of S_2 or other time/space orientations in S_1, it may be quite likely that a different elemental matrix for planned transition than shown in Table 1 would be selected. At this stage our matrix is mainly designed to encourage a way of thinking about planned transition; the transition path to $S_{2 \text{ (WOMP/USA)}}$ is partly illustrative of the approach and partly prescriptive, embodying the best

TABLE 1

Transition Path $S_2 \rightarrow S_3$.

Temporal Interval	Positive Goal	Creativity	Self-realization	Joy
$t_{2010's}$	t_4	***	**	*
2020's				
$t_{2030's}$	t_5	**	***	**
$t_{2040's}$	t_6	*	*	***

judgments of the author with his knowledge of the means/ends problem in relation to short-term world-order reform.

The idea of planned transition during t_1 should be approached as systematically as possible. We indicate a t_1 framework as well as a series of suitable proposals. Here again our effort is to illustrate and provisionally prescribe in relation to a commitment to realize $S_{2(\text{WOMP/USA})}$. In essence, we are suggesting first steps. One of the features of this kind of world-order analysis is that it takes action possibilities as seriously as it takes intellectual speculation. There must be a continuous audit of action initiatives and a corresponding willingness to revise the concept and substance of planned transition and of the preference model. Although we locate S_0 late in S_1 we do not believe that the world setting is at all conducive as yet to voluntary or contractual transition procedures designed to bring about any positive variant of S_2, including our preferred arrangement $S_{2(\text{WOMP/USA})}$.

In t_1 our emphasis is on changing value priorities within existing centers of decision and control, especially with respect to government operation in principal national societies. Such an undertaking depends on some degree of ideological space in the domestic arena. It may not be possible now to envision relevant reorientations of consciousness in the more *closed* societies of the world, and we may expect even the more *open* societies to experience pressure as a consequence of value challenges. The Nixon Administration's efforts to intimidate the media were partly a defensive reaction against a very fundamental set of pressures for change. We believe, however, that until principal domestic arenas are significantly more receptive to WOMP goals, the prospects for planned transition to S_2 by voluntary means are minimal. In this setting of uncertainty and limited opportunity there are several critical forms of activity that bear on transition prospects during this initial phase of t_1. These activities are approched from the time-space locus of the United States in the mid-1970s and are organized around our broader conception of the transition path to WOMP/USA: Consciousness → Mobilization → Transformation. As we are dealing with early efforts in t_1, the most important payoffs are likely to involve consciousness-raising activities.

To depict the range of our interests we provide some illustrations, some consciousness-raising tactics and programs:

1. World-Order Education. There is a surge of energy in many settings to provide a more convincing account of man's place in the world and of the relation between national well-being and global community. There is a decline of interest in conceiving of world politics purely as an arena for power manipulation and in thinking of global idealism purely in terms of peace. There has evolved a more richly conceived interpretation of social, political, and economic factors that encourages a more comprehensive view of global reform. Many distinct orientations toward world-order studies are being developed. We are already at the stage of allowing a hundred flowers to bloom. Many of these initiatives share globalist, futurist, and reformist goals and thereby share an opposition to an earlier kind of consensus built around nationalism and the war system. As t_1 proceeds, this kind of education revolution is likely to produce a consensus in many national societies and transnational arenas on what is wrong, what is to be done, and what are the most efficient and humane means available. World-order education in all its forms is likely to provide the entire base for the consciousness-raising enterprise of t_1 and to incorporate within itself other notable coordinate developments.

2. *Apollo Vision.* Informing images shape and orient consciousness. To the extent that the Apollo program portrays the earth as an island spinning in space, it conveys a sense of the earth's wholeness and finiteness. By comparison, state boundaries seem artificial and unnatural, although existentially more relevant categories of neighborhood, nationality, race, or religion might not. In t_1 the growth of cross-cutting personal affiliations across and within sovereign states could help shape identity patterns receptive to $S_{2\ (WOMP/USA)}$. An Apollo-type space program usefully connects developments on the technological frontier with at least covert support for a new globalism. Despite the end of the Apollo program, space activities have enormous educational potency with respect to earth activities. Space probes of various sorts provide a dramatic focus of human endeavor, which can be shared through satellite TV by the whole world. Unlike more obvious consciousness-raising efforts, the Apollo world-view penetrates the living-rooms of mainstream America. We may yet discover that the real payoff from American tax dollars devoted to the Apollo program arises from their contribution to the growth of a human identity that is both planetary and species-wide and accepts as fundamental the solidarity of all humans, rather than to deepening cosmological insights derived from samplings of moon dust.

3. *The Drift of the Counter-Culture.* It is difficult at this time to assess the impact, the duration, or even the eventual main orientations of counter-cultural tendencies such as expressed in "The Woodstock Nation," the drug culture, *The Greening of America,* the Jesus People, women's liberation, gay liberation, and the new utopianism. These youth-dominated reevaluations of American culture stand in stark contrast to statist values, especially as embodied in the governing ideology

of the Nixon era. The essence of the counter-cultural resistance is antagonism to technocracy, statism, and moralism. In this sense, the counter-culture leads toward self-definition, self-evolved and experimental personalities, communes, communities, and communication. Implicit in this movement—which has many factions and cross-currents—is a reverence for nature and an antipathy toward artifact and artifice. Also implicit in its embrace of Oriental cultural forms is a significant transnationalism, shaping new belief systems dissociated from the history and traditions of any single nation and especially alien to the ethos of a western industrial nation. Whether the counter-culture takes sufficient hold to stimulate a second effort to assert its central claims remains an open question, but the potentiality is there to infuse those who reject the technocratic and necrophilic drift of American society for a much more life-oriented vision of a new world order. This counter-cultural constituency might yet become an important activist force in promoting a movement for $S_{2(WOMP/USA)}$.

4. *The Limits-to-Growth Debate.* In 1972 publication of two studies caused a major stir: *Blueprint for Survival* by the editors of the British magazine *The Ecologist,* and *The Limits to Growth* by an team of scholars from the Massachusetts Institute of Technology headed by Dennis Meadows and commissioned by the Club of Rome. Both documents emphasized the incompatibility between the growth dynamics of industrial civilization and the prospects for human survival at tolerable levels. Neither document reflected world-order thinking, although the clear implication of the limits-to-growth hypothesis is the need for an increased capacity for planetary coordination and management, which in turn presupposes either centralized domination (Figures 8 and 9) or a more modest capacity for central guidance combined with globalist orientations in principal state actors (Figures 10 and 11).

The limits-to-growth debate has stimulated widespread controversy about the viability of the existing system of world order. The alarmist interpretation of growth dynamics has not yet prevailed, but it has eroded conventional wisdom about the desirability of indefinite and unregulated growth and, more importantly, has set the stage for the presentation of further evidence that pressures on the limited capacities of the earth are crossing dangerous, possibly irreversible, thresholds. Just as the breakup of the Torrey Canyon in 1967 was the Hiroshima of the ecological age, further disasters of an environmental character will strengthen sentiments supporting a movement for drastic world-order reform.

5. *Free-Flow Ethos: Ideas and Men.* The technology of broadcasting, the ease of travel, the moderation of great-power rivalry, and the

universal endorsement of minimum human rights and cultural exchange programs are among the factors favorable to the free flow of ideas and people. We believe that the freest possible mobility of ideas and people will diminish further nationalist inhibitions about world-order reform. The virtual abandonment of passport and customs control in intra-European travel represents a further significant reduction in the symbolic and substantive relevance of national boundaries and hence in national identities. In general, diffusion of reformist thinking might help stimulate convergent demands from distinct regions of the globe, providing the sort of premobilization consensus that must accompany the passage from t_1 to t_2.

6. *The Prometheus Project.*[18] The physicist Gerald Feinberg has pointed to the need for a major attempt to reinvigorate ethical inquiries in response to some very fundamental technological developments—artificial (computer) intelligence and genetic engineering, for example. Feinberg argues that these developments will have a profound impact on human nature and social organization and that we should try to forecast these probable impacts to be in a position to control them.

From a somewhat different perspective Van Rensellaer Potter argues that a new code of behavior based on a bioethical orientation that regards human survival as the prime ethical value is needed.[19] Potter's argument rests on the belief that society is now organized in a bio-ethically regressive manner as a consequence of various outmoded patterns of belief and behavior.

A still different ethical perspective derives from the Nuremberg idea. This perspective rests on the view that all individuals and groups everywhere have a responsibility to oppose governmental crimes of war. In a sense the Nuremberg precedent arising from the World War II war-crimes trials is inverted. Instead of serving accusatory purposes as it has in the past, it becomes the foundation for individual responsibility. Even the war-crimes circumference is not a rigid boundary. One can easily imagine the Nuremberg idea expanded to provide an ethical underpinning for citizen resistance to all forms of governmental wrongdoing wherever they occur. This idea builds transnational bonds, e.g. Canadian citizens and officials have a responsibility to oppose American crimes of war in Indochina. Olaf Palme, Prime Minister of Sweden, assumed a measure of such responsibility when, in defiance of intergovernmental decorum, he denounced U.S. policies of warfare in Indochina as ecocidal at the UN Conference on the Human Environment held in Stockholm in June 1972.

These new directions in personal ethics are part of a broader questioning of traditional patterns of authority and belief. To the extent that this questioning is intensified by the crisis of legitimacy experienced by the state it is part of an inchoate movement for the kind of world-order reform WOMP supports, even if such ethical reevaluation is not so understood by its adepts.

7. *Progressive Governmental Actors.* In t_1 the main consciousness-raising contexts will be nongovernmental, if not antigovernmental in character; there may be indirect, unintentional contributions to transition within main governmental arenas as considered in Step 2 in relation to the Apollo vision. In general, however, principal governmental actors will feel threatened by programs of drastic world-order reform and those reorientations of political consciousness heavily influenced by WOMP priorities.

An exception to this pattern may be governments in small to medium-sized countries that have enjoyed a considerable period of stable rule, have been independent over a long span of time, and have largely eliminated domestic social injustice. Sweden, Norway, and Canada are typical states in this category. A second exception may be some governments in the Third World which have not betrayed their idealistic vision of human and societal potentiality: although there is room for controversy as to a particular case, China and Tanzania seem to belong in this category. These classifications are provisional, as governments and their outlooks may change rapidly in either direction under the pressure of events, including policy conflicts within their own ruling groups.

The main point, however, is that these kinds of governmental actors may themselves assess the need for world-order reform in realistic terms and begin to challenge ingrained patterns of statist logic by their words and deeds within the principal international arenas of the world. Should these challenges coincide with the domestic liberalization of governmental outlook in Japan, the Soviet Union, the United States, and Western Europe, they might create a significant awareness of and support for a program of international reforms responsive to WOMP values, especially with respect to the war system. In this regard governmental arenas might become agents of transition rather than centers of resistance. In the years ahead it is important to disseminate a credible conception of planned transition to S_2 so that leaders of opinion in moderate and progressive states are encouraged to consider world-order reform as a practical project for politics and politicians.

8. *Multinational Corporate Globalism.* Many large multinational corporate actors are seeking to establish an *anational* or global identity for themselves. The search for such an identity is connected with, first,

an effort to avoid neoimperialist stigmatization associated with foreign capital; second, creation of a global milieu as supportive as possible of corporate expansion; third, avoidance of regulatory and safety standards of rich countries, as well as their wage and employment policies. Thus, the self-interest of multinational actors seems to support a globalist thrust, a movement for world-order reform that diminishes the role of state actors.

As we have suggested (Figures 5 and 6), there are two contrary tendencies in multinational corporate development. The large multinational corporation may seek to mobilize the apparatus of the state to protect its foreign investments. The 1972–73 disclosures in the U.S. of the efforts by International Telegraph and Telephone (ITT) in attempted conjunction with the Central Intelligence Agency (CIA) to prevent President Allende's electoral accession to power in Chile suggests the statist facet of multinational corporate behavior. ITT became at the very least an abettor of covert intervention in a foreign society to implement a program designed to foment strife and stifle national self-determination. ITT-CIA links illustrate coalition possibilities among regressive elements in the corporate and statist structures.

Even the globalist aspirations of multinational corporations should not necessarily be confused with a commitment to $S_{2(\text{WOMP/USA})}$. Global mechanisms of coordination and management guided by considerations of market efficiency are not in any sense assurances of support for fairer patterns of economic distribution, for nonrepressive governance, or for the protection of environmental quality. The bulk of available evidence suggests that corporations are responsive to social values only if forced by regulatory and populist pressures.

Mobilization Contexts in t_l.

In contrast to the consciousness-raising contexts of t_1 we illustrate in this section mobilization-for-action contexts that might become significant during t_2. We do not anticipate any transformation of vital structures or patterns of behavior, but we do foresee the active political pursuit of reform programs incorporating WOMP or closely analogous value priorities.

1. Change-Oriented Domestic Reform Movements. Militant minority groups, the women's liberation movement, and progressive factions in political parties and the labor movement are among those groups in domestic society seeking major reforms by mounting a very direct attack on prevailing values. These groups do not in general include world-order issues within their reform platforms, but their outlook and goals are compatible with WOMP, and their access to power or influence would improve greatly the prospects for consciousness-raising. These groups are already mobilized for action, and it is important that efforts be made to encourage their formulation of world-order extensions of their most immediate goals.

2. Peace-Activist Groups. There are groups mobilized for action around war/peace issues. These groups often have no general world-order ideology beyond an opposition to current levels of defense spending, to foreign commitments and bases, and to militarization of foreign policy. Their contributions consist of challenging the dominant groupings of power and wealth within domestic arenas. Such groups can relate strongly to specific antiwar causes (e.g., Vietnam) and exert considerable short-term and special-purpose influence. Their institutional proposals—as for a Department of Peace or a peacekeeping force—are usually well-intentioned but innocuous and unlikely to be realized (and, if realized, likely to evolve in a form enveloped in restrictions emanating from statist guidelines). The fate of the U.S. Arms Control and Disarmament Agency is instructive; its bureaucracy combines an acute sense of inferiority with a very low degree of bureaucratic independence.

3. Transnational Promotion of Human Rights. There is a growing realization that human rights are not domestic questions. Transnational campaigns on behalf of political prisoners are symbolically and substantively important in relation to the growth of the idea of a human community that takes precedence over statist prerogatives. Amnesty International has given some organizational focus to the progressive view that severe deprivations of human rights are not matters of domestic jurisdiction. International psychiatric associations have been protesting Soviet uses of medical detention as a way of quarantining and punishing dissenters. These developments help create patterns of behavior and belief that support planned transition to S_2.

4. Congressional Initiative. The Cranston/Taft initiatives to increase the role and effectiveness of the International Court of Justice suggest an effort in the U.S. Senate to encourage governments to seek peaceful settlement of international disputes; as such, it derives from a posture opposed to statist prerogatives with respect to war and peace. Efforts to impose responsibility on public officials for war crimes by legislative enactment move in the same direction.

Action by Congress is not necessarily likely to be progressive from a world-order perspective, although its representative character makes it the most natural governmental organ to express the outlook and policies of a grassroots or populist movement for global reform. The

Senate has so far failed to ratify the Genocide Convention of 1950 and for years a series of human-rights treaties have either not been ratified or not been submitted to the Senate for advice and consent. Congress enacted the so-called Hickenlooper Amendment, which extended capitalistic views of the sanctity of private property into the assessment of expropriation disputes with foreign governments, even requiring the President to terminate foreign aid if American investors are not fully reimbursed for any expropriated assets, regardless of the extent of their pre-expropriation profits.

5. *The Honeywell and Gulf Campaigns.* There is a fairly extensive set of organized efforts to make corporate management moderate its profit-making by taking account of certain fundamental international policies, such as prohibition of war crimes in the case of the Honeywell firm and repudiation of apartheid in the case of Gulf. These efforts are directed against both ethically responsive shareholders (churches, charitable organizations, universities) and against the corporate managers themselves (shareholder protests, proxy fights, and so on). The goals of protest are not explicitly associated with world-order reform, but the demands reflect a sense of transnational accountability (to the Indochinese or African victims) based on ethical notions of human worth and equality. Such a mobilization context tends to embody an antistatist outlook and could easily be widened to accommodate a comprehensive plan for world order reform such as is embodied in $S_{2(WOMP/USA)}$.

6. *No-First-Use Proposal.* A majority of members of the UN have voted in favor of absolute prohibition of nuclear weapons. A great step forward would involve a renunciation by the nuclear powers of a first-use option in the event of armed conflict. China has unilaterally made such a pledge. It seems important to urge such a policy on the United States government. A no-first-use policy would help denuclearize international politics and establish a measure of reciprocity in arms-control initiatives between nuclear and nonnuclear countries. More significantly, a renunciation of the nuclear option would entail a repudiation of that most absolute of statist claims, the discretion to eradicate civilian populations in the event that a foreign government is perceived as acting in a provocative or unacceptable manner.

7. *Urban Separatism and Secessionism.* The city as the bearer of progressive values is a familiar theme. The city as the victim of an exploitative tax structure and an insensitive political approach is a central affliction of American life. Singapore as a model city-state might encourage other cities to disengage and secede formally from

their suburban and rural hinterland. The 51st-state movement in New York City, although feeble, may be the early signal of an emerging set of claims associated with an urban separatist movement. In any event, it seems critical for world-order reform efforts to become more sensitive to and associated with more drastic conceptions of urban reform, especially given the magnitude of the movement of people from the countryside to the city throughout the world.

Transformation Contexts

As indicated, we do not anticipate significant world order *transformations* in t_1. There are likely to be a large number of international arrangements designed to stabilize economic competition, to cut costs in the arms race, and to make the over-all system less accident-prone. Such arrangements are not, in one sense, transition steps at all, but are rather contributions to the durability of S_1. However, to the extent that the durability of S_1 lengthens the interval between S_0 and the collapse of S_1 through catastrophe, it provides a longer interval within which to effectuate planned transition to a benevolent variant of S_2.

Some institutional reforms are of a forward-looking character that can be conceived of as direct contributions to transition. Some illustrations follow:

1. UN Seabed Authority. There is a possibility that the UN will be given an independent institutional role in relation to ocean resources. Such a role may be modest at first, but it is likely to expand over time until the authority acquires significant status as a world actor. Such an actor might fund other international institutions as well as establish itself as a quasi-autonomous actor within the world system (see Figure 7).

2. European Supranationalism. By late t_1 the institutions of the EEC may possess a significant element of supranationality. A major, genuinely regional participant in the world-order system may thus have importance for transition purposes. Such a regional actor could either stabilize a new phase of S_1 (see Figure 3) or encourage transition to one of a number of variants of S_2 (see Figures 4, 8, 10).

3. Special-Purposes Functional Regimes. One can envision in t_1 a series of institutional developments on a global level dealing with narcotics flow, air piracy, satellite broadcasting, and environmental quality that in their over-all effect will diminish the status of governmental actors in S_1. The need for functional mechanisms on an international plane may reinforce consciousness-raising and mobilization efforts in t_1 and thereby hasten the advent of t_2.

Conclusion

The main objective of this essay has been to suggest new directions of response to the principal challenges of the modern world. These new directions are concerned with three sorts of issues: how to think, what to hope, and what to do. These issues are approached from the perspective of world order, specifically from a conviction that the existing system does not deal adequately with individual and social problems and will become even less capable of meeting minimum human and planetary needs in the future. The existing order is breaking down at a very rapid rate, and the main uncertainty is whether mankind can exert a positive role in shaping a new world order or is doomed to await collapse in a passive posture. We believe a new order will be born no later than early in the next century and that the death throes of the old and the birth pangs of the new will be a testing time for the human species. In this testing time we should not entrust our destiny to the wisdom of national governments, at least as most of them are presently oriented. These state institutions came into being and were generally shaped by much that is obsolescent in the existing world system. We urgently need a spontaneous mass movement for world-order reform that is committed to promoting the four world-order values of peace, economic well-being, environmental quality, and social and political justice, and is skeptical of experts and bureaucrats but reluctant to promise any kind of quick fix for the ills of the planet.

Notes

[1] See Gustavo Lagos, *International Stratification and Underdeveloped Countries,* Chapel Hill, NC, University of North Carolina Press, 1963.

[2] For one representative and moderate non-Western statement see Indira Gandhi, "India and the World," *Foreign Affairs,* 51:65–78 (1972).

[3] Carl Kaysen, "The Computer that Printed Out W*O*L*F*," *Foreign Affairs,* 50:660–669 (1972); see also Peter Passell and Leonard Ross, *The Retreat from Riches: Affluence and Its Enemies* (New York: Viking, 1973); Herman Daly (ed), *Toward a Steady-State Economy* (San Francisco: W. H. Freeman, 1973).

[4] For an important presentation of this position see Edward J. Woodhouse, "Re-Visioning the Future of the Third World: An Ecological Perspective on Development," *World Politics, 25:1–33 (1972).*

[5] Kurt Vonnegut, Jr., "In a Manner that Must Shame God Himself," *Harper's Magazine,* Nov. 1972, pp. 60–68.

[6] For an argument that *social will* is a more relevant constraint that *material shortages* see Robert L. Heilbroner, "Growth and Survival," *Foreign Affairs,* 51:139–154 (1972).

[7] Among prominent visions in this direction see Theilhard de Chardin, *The Phenomenon of Man* (New York: Harper,

1959); Sri Aurobindo, *The Ideal of Human Unity* (New York, 1950); Erich Kahler, *Man the Measure* (New York: Braziller, 1943); for overview see Warren W. Wagar, *The City of Man* (Baltimore: Penguin, 1963).

[8] Radical is used here in the sense of root or fundamental; it is not intended to be associated with any particular historical ideology.

[9] For an extreme statement of Third World response to the effort to emphasize international cooperation to maintain environmental quality and ecological stability, see "Declaration on the Third World and the Human Environment," Oi Committee International, Stockholm, June 1972.

[10] *New York Times Book Review*, Feb. 25, 1973, Sect. 7, pp. 44–45, at p. 45.

[11] For facts and interpretation see Paul R. Ehrlich and Anne H. Ehrlich, *Population, Resources, and Environment* (San Francisco: W. H. Freeman, 2nd rev. ed., 1972); Barry Commoner, *The Closing Circle* (New York: Knopf, 1971); Lester R. Brown, *World Without Borders* (New York: Random House, 1972); Richard A. Falk, *This Endangered Planet: Prospects and Proposals for Human Survival* (New York: Random House, 1971).

[12] For discussion of transition see Section 4; a more complete conception is contained in Chapter V of the full WOMP/USA document, published under the title *A Study of Future Worlds* (New York: The Free Press, 1975).

[13] In this regard the forthcoming work of Ervin Laszlo is especially promising. Professor Laszlo uses a cybernetic orientation to design world-order models with normative objectives similar to WOMP. See Laszlo, *The Systems View of the World* (New York: Braziller, 1972); but especially Laszlo, *Norms for the Future: An Application of Systems Philosophy to the Study of World Order* (New York: Brazillier, 1974).

[14] Such nonhierarchical patterns of organization become increasingly possible as a result of modern information technology, which is capable of both decentralizing decisional activity and co-ordinating widely scattered inputs into an over-all decisional process.

[15] These principles of constitutional restraint are crucial to the normative acceptability of our preference model. They are elaborated in Chapter IV of the full WOMP/USA document.

[16] This conclusion is more fully developed in Falk, "Statist Imperatives in an Era of System Overload," AAAS Symposium, Dec. 28, 1971 (mimeographed).

[17] I have tried to depict this assessment in Chapter IX of *This Endangered Planet*, pp. 415–438.

[18] This rubric is borrowed from Gerald Feinberg, who develops a persuasive rationale for "the Prometheus Project" in his stimulating book *The Prometheus Project: Mankind's Search for Long-Range Goals* (Garden City, N.Y.: Doubleday, 1968).

[19] See Van Rensselaer Potter, *Bioethics: Bridge to the Future* (Englewood Cliffs, N.J.: 1971); cf. also Garrett Hardin's provocative book *Exploring New Ethics for Survival* (New York: Viking, 1972).

DEVELOPMENT GUIDED BY VALUES:*
COMMENTS ON CHINA'S ROAD
AND ITS IMPLICATIONS

Paul T. K. Lin

I

This paper is not an exposition of a Chinese "model" of development. It merely attempts to sum up some observations and reflections on a wide range of issues arising out of China's experience. It represents an interpretation and extrapolation of that experience. It is offered as a modest contribution to discourse, in response to the suggestion that an examination of this particular experience, of its strategies and policies and the conceptual approaches underlying them, might stimulate a more comprehensive survey of the options for the human future.

China to Others

The momentous experiment going on in China is extraordinarily innovative. But it would not be in character for the Chinese to put it forward as a sort of archetypical model for others to copy. They are quick to caution that they are striking out on a hitherto uncharted course of development, and are learning by error as well as success.

*I am aware of the fact that neither of the terms, "development" or "values," is entirely satisfactory. Development has come to acquire a variety of meanings in studies emanating from "developed" economies and commonly prescribes or implies an externally superimposed set of goals and a change process that bucks or ignores the internal dynamics of liberation in a society. In the Chinese perspective, development is a shedding-creating, breaking-building process, or in Mao Tse-tung's words, a triple revolution—in society, in production, and in scientific research. For an attempt at definition, see Appendix A. In this paper, I am persuaded to use the familiar but somewhat vague social science concept of "values" to substitute for the more accurate and comprehensive Chinese term *cheng chih* (politics), because the latter in English translation is even more prone to misinterpretation by readers of English. It must be remembered, however, that the contest between different value systems is only one aspect of "politics." See Appendix A.

Many innovations, especially institutional ones, are still in an inchoate stage or are experimental and await further testing and perfecting. Furthermore, they add, China must still learn from others, from every possible source of good experience, as they have in the past. However, the method of learning is crucial. Chinese leaders recall how, at times in their own history, they accepted foreign-imposed policy strictures and models of change that proved to be costly detours, if not culs de sac, along the way. Their correct road was no one's sudden inspiration, but worked out painstakingly (and often painfully) in struggle. Its underlying theory, though grounded in Marx and Lenin, was constantly vitalized and enriched by their own struggles, whose advances and setbacks were analyzed and evaluated again and again, pre-eminently by Mao Tse-tung, for clues as to the real parameters of change in the context of China's historical conditions. An example of this approach was Mao Tse-tung's return to the villages of Hunan in the spring of 1927 to seek the answer to the sharply debated question of what the role of the peasantry should be in the actual conditions of China at that stage. Arriving at crucial strategic conclusions later set forth in his famous "Report on the Hunan Peasant Movement", he singled out "landlordism" as the key social force bolstering foreign and domestic oppression and "land to the tillers" as the remedy to unblock the forces of production. He placed great confidence in the enormous potential power of the peasant movement, properly led.

Out of this came a prime lesson of methodology—to marry theory, including imported theory, to one's own specific historical, socioeconomic, and cultural reality. Uncritical, nonevaluative learning must be eschewed, and the correctness and applicability of foreign and domestic experience must be tested by practice, relying first and foremost on the practice of one's own people. *T'ui ch'en ch'u hsin,* "weed through the old, bring forth the new"; *yang wei chung yung,* "adapt foreign things for domestic needs"—these are two of the operational slogans in China today that might well have universal validity for developing countries.

Viewed in this evaluative perspective, China's dynamic society today is indeed an enormously instructive paradigm of fundamental change along lines radically different from those of many other developing countries. The lessons to be drawn from her achievements and short-comings may be crucial, and their human significance is writ large by the sheer scale, depth, and pace of change in China. For what is involved is the metamorphosis of an entire civilisation containing a quarter of the world's people. The very structural foundations and ideological roots of a 2,000-year-old traditional order are yielding to the new in less than one generation. Both the possibilities and the strains are staggering in magnitude.

The Matrix of the Past

What may be particularly instructive for many Third World countries is that, like them, China started with a backward socioeconomic structure that was constrained from basic change by deeply-ingrained, outmoded values and traditional institutions until modern times and was then warped by externally-imposed colonial and semicolonial values and institutions into developmental patterns that served foreign, predator economies rather than the indigenous economy.

But there are certain unique aspects to the Chinese background as well. One is that the radical transformation of society has been and still is directed by a nucleus of leaders who had already run enclaves of power in rural bases for some twenty years prior to achieving state power, accumulating experience not only in fighting but also in social transformation and economic organisation. Some strategies used today were first tested in Yenan and even as far back as 1927-35, in the mountain bases of Chingkangshan and in Kiangsi. Examples are the following principles and approaches:

Participatory mass action in revolution (land reform in the late 1920's, early 1930's and late 1940's) and production, relying on the people to emancipate themselves;

"Serve the People" ethic, politics and discipline for the armed forces and all cadres;

A "Bear Up, Strive On" (*chien k'u fen tou*) spirit plus a "More Production, Less Waste" (*tsen ch'an chieh yueh*) ethic for building a self-reliant economy;

Use of a dual technology (indigenous and advanced) according to need and availability of skills and resources (later to be known as the strategy of "walking on two legs");

A "Serve the Workers and Peasants" orientation to education, combining classroom study with productive labour and with participation in social struggle (Yenan in the early 1940's);

The exercise of rigorous criticism and self-criticism and "rectification movements" (1941-42) to maintain the ascendancy of people-oriented values among the cadres and intellectuals—"the final dividing line between a revolutionary intellectual and [other] intellectuals is whether he is willing to merge and in practice does merge with the workers and peasants" (Mao in 1939).

When the nationwide victory was won in 1949, the leaders who took over the task of steering China's development were no book-learned manager-technocrats, but a leadership steeled and nourished in the vortex of struggle. This was no urbanized elite ideologically emasculated by the infiltration of the politics, economics, or values of a foreign metropolis and alienated from their own people. Most key leaders were relatively untainted by the half-feudal, half-Western life and work styles of the elites in China's treaty port cities from which the Kuomintang officialdom was chiefly drawn, one factor, among many, which unfitted the Kuomintang for leading the population (especially the 80 percent of China that is the peasantry) out of their age-old deprivations and misery.

The Vital Meaning of Starting with Value Perspectives

There was thus a considerable basis for continuity in the leadership of the Chinese revolution between the pre-1949 and post-1949 stages, both in respect of value-orientation as well as of personnel. This was a favourable factor. But what undoubtedly has counted even more heavily in the period since the founding of the People's Republic were the imaginative and firm educative measures taken to prevent the cadres at every level from losing this value-orientation. We shall discuss some of these measures later. When in March of 1949, on the eve of entry into all the cities of China, Mao Tse-tung warned the cadres and the entire army that the bravery they had demonstrated on the battlefield might not be enough to shield some of them from the "sugar-coated bullets" of the bourgeoisie, he was in fact sounding an early warning of the danger of internal corruption and regression leading ultimately to systemic "convergence," to use the preferred parlance of today, with the capitalist world.

At the point of nationwide triumph, the overwhelming psychic relief and satisfaction at final attainment (we've made it!) must have giddied the heads of many a veteran of the long and bitter revolutionary wars. But their weary, sandled feet had scarcely begun to tread the sidewalks of the towns and cities when Mao Tse-tung pulled their thoughts up short. "This is but the first step in a 10,000-*li* march ... a brief prologue to a long drama...." The implied challenge, perhaps fully understood only by the most politically aware at that juncture, was this: Have you made revolution only to achieve power? Or did you achieve power to make revolution? Are you up to the even more arduous responsibilities ahead?

How would the nexus between power and the yet unrealized hopes and aspirations of the people stand up under the rigorous test of history? Here would lie the future judgment of the new regime as genuinely revolutionary, or vulgarly traditional. For the new men and women had won the *old* China, but not yet the new. Nothing less than the thorough excision of the diseased tissues of the old China and the bringing to life of the new China was demanded of them. It was necessary to inculcate in all cadres the perspectives of a long and complex struggle and a sustained posture of integrity, modesty, prudence, and tenacity. The fine styles of work which prevailed in the rural bases must be preserved; and cadres must furthermore be able, under criticism and self-criticism, to shed pernicious attitudes and ways not consistent with the needs of uniting with the people in the task of national construction ahead. To devise ways to keep this orientation alive and vibrant in working, thinking individuals, to build revolutionary values into the new institutional framework in the context of a growing bureaucracy, has since become a central concern in China's development.

The primary problem was to find the right road and long-range strategy for transformation and development. The enthusiasm of cadres and masses, made fully aware of the course ahead, would then become an enduring force for creative change.

The Political Dynamics of Anti-Development

China before 1949 was a tottering colossus of human exploitation and misery, wracked by poverty and backwardness, famine and disease. Under the impact of a hundred years of predatory wars launched from the West and Japan, she was left with only a fragmented sovereignty over her own land, economy, and institutions and little control over her own future. In magnitude and depth, her problems far surpassed those of many Third World Countries today, perhaps equalling those of India if we take into account certain differences. How was one to go about the stupendous task of revitalising the nation and building a strong "modernised" China out of the appalling chaos of the old?

Much depended on the basic analysis and outlook of those who had won power. An obvious answer was simply to plunge into all-out industrialisation. But this simple expedient had also been the promise and exhortation of the "planners" in the Kuomintang regime. They had sought to achieve this through the importation of capital, equipment, and technology. Yet China had sunk deeper and deeper into economic chaos, political corruption, and social injustice, while the masses barely survived a marginal existence.

The new leaders had the advantage of having experienced a close comradeship and common cause with the impoverished masses of China in the civil war. From that vantage point, they had analyzed their nation's problems and come to the conclusion that the accelerating marginalisation of China's economy and culture was due mainly to outright aggression and semicolonial rule, compounded by intervention and the kind of foreign "aid" which aided the aider more than the "aided." Moreover, this external depredation was facilitated by an internal stratum of self-seeking intermediaries in the oligarchy of power, who siphoned off the proceeds left over from foreign profit-taking and left the population in greater anguish than before. The result was not development, but anti-development.

Furthermore, unlike colonial India, China was a semicolony, spotted with many extraterritorial enclaves and exploited by the multiple metropolitan economies of Europe, America, and Japan. The "veering effect" of gravitating China into the economic orbit of different foreign states increased the havoc wrought on the Chinese economy. For example, the railways built by the French in Yunnan and the British in Central China were routed, with utter disregard for China's own needs, to tap the resources and markets of the Chinese hinterland and link them with cities and ports within their respective spheres of influence. They were even designed with different gauges.

Most seriously, the effect of foreign economic penetration was to accentuate the backward conditions in the agrarian system, already the most formidable block to modern development. Over the vast country-side of China, about 75 percent of the land, in the aggregate, was in the hands of 10 percent of the rural population—the landlords and rich peasants. The hard-working producers, the 90 percent, held perhaps a quarter of the land. Over 300 million peasants paid rent to landlords on some 47 million hectares of farmland. The impoverishment engendered by this system of land tenure was made unbearably worse by the destructive effect of imported manufactures on cottage industries, the depression of farm prices, and the increased agricultural tax levies to service mounting foreign loans as well as to service the common venality of multiple layers of officialdom. Every monetary burden and resource drain caused by unequal exchange from the operations of foreign enterprises and subsidiaries in China was inexorably and finally visited on the peasantry through the agency of the tax, rent, and interest collector—usually the landed gentry, the reliable local "cadres" of the system. The first problem for the peasantry was to survive, let alone generate the accumulation necessary for development.

Meanwhile, foreign economic penetration effectively inhibited the growth of national industry. Nor was a reversal of the process possible, as power was in the hands of those who had a vested interest in the linkages with foreign capital.

From the perspective of the people, there could not be the slightest doubt that the problem of development was not primarily a technological one. It was preeminently a political and social issue.

A Schema of Change—Continuous, but Phased

Conceptually, development, like any other aspect of human progress, can be seen as a conscious process of identifying critical tensions and disparities and solving them according to the objective parameters and laws discovered in the course of struggle. In humanity's striving for freedom, it is a continuous and never-ending process. But there are also distinct, though connected, stages.

As we have seen, in the Chinese context two unresolved basic contradictions were ascertained as historically the key blocks to genuine development. These essentially political issues are identifiable, by somewhat loose labels, as the national contradiction and the social contradiction. Both categories of issues had to be solved if China were to advance to a higher stage; but in terms of solutions, each category was the key problem in a sequentially different stage:

Stage I: The National Contradiction. The issue of independence and democracy in the three-decade struggle prior to 1949 pitted China *as a nation* against the "three mountains" pressing on her people, described by the Chinese as imperialism, feudalism, and bureaucrat-capitalism— or in short, the foreign predators and their domestic base of support. Only when power was wrested in 1949 from these social forces and a People's Republic established was the first contradiction considered solved, at least in essential terms.

Actually, to consummate Stage I, there was a short period after 1949 when the agrarian reform ("land to the tiller") had to be spread to the whole country. The effect of this was to detach about thirty million tons of grain from the rent collections of the former landlords, who were now required to work for their own less-than-conspicuous consumption. This grain was then returned to the several hundred million peasants for their use. The reform also had the immediate effect of reducing the size of the two social poles of landless and rich peasants and creating a trend towards swelling the middle peasantry.

265

But what if there had been an extended pause in social change? An inexorable tendency to repolarize would have arisen. For land reform was still based on the small, private landholding. Such a system of tenure would not only be incapable of raising production by critical amounts to break through the poverty-subsistence level but would also constantly generate exploitation, disparities, and the seeds of regression. Hence, organisation of more efficient production based on an economy of scale would be impossible, as would the increased accumulation necessary to support development. The weakness of the petty-landholder economy was shown in 1953 when large-scale industrialisation programmes were launched and agriculture proved unable to cope with the larger demand for commodity grain.

Stage II: The Social Contradiction. The principal contradiction that came to the fore after 1949 was identified not as a technical or managerial one, but as a social one—that between the workers, the producers, on the one hand and the remaining exploitative elements in society, the bourgeoisie, on the other.

To resolve this tension under the changed conditions of political power, however, a violent process was unnecessary. In the cities, the industrial and commercial owners and entrepreneurs were gradually "bought out" by the government, retaining only their returns from investment based on a fixed rate. In the countryside, under the impetus of a powerful thrust for collective organisation spearheaded by the poorest levels of the peasantry, a swift structural reorganisation of agriculture took place. By 1956, some 110 million peasant households, 91.9 percent of the total, had joined the cooperatives. Along with the organisation of handicrafts into cooperatives, the net effect of these measures was to extirpate the socioeconomic roots of exploitation and to lay the basis for large-scale production without social polarisation. This production would in turn speed up accumulation for self-generating development.

But was a structural transformation enough? If it were true, as some theorists have long maintained, that the direction of development depends only on the type of socioeconomic system, one might safely assume that the socialist structure now attained in China would automatically produce socialist development, with the reinforcing values and institutions that go with it. In this case, one need not worry about the problem any further. Indeed, this was apparently the position taken by a cabal of policymakers and senior bureaucrats around Liu Shao-chi, who, seen in retrospect, really constituted a second command organisation moving away from Mao Tse-tung's line even as they paid lip-service to it. This cabal leaned towards the bureaucratic conception of development from above. The new contradiction, they said, was no longer a social or political one, but between an achieved, advanced social system and an incommensurately backward productive system. (We shall have occasion to discuss this further.) After 1956, these officials began to exert strong pulls in the direction of an obsessive emphasis on higher productivity. They followed orthodox lines of policy imported from abroad, with stress on indiscriminately higher inputs of modern expertise, equipment, and technology and on the validity of material incentive.

This counter-trend provoked a severe strain on policy-making and eventually culminated in the Great Proletarian Cultural Revolution. The outcome of the Cultural Revolution was in fact a reaffirmation of the basic value-orientation in development that had been put forward by Chairman Mao. It was a titanic political revolt from below—a revolt which resulted in the removal from decision-making positions of those who espoused regressive policies. Thus the reaffirmed directions of development can be fully understood only when it is seen as the outcome of a fierce and inevitable showdown between two opposed fundamental strategies for China—a struggle which reflected the continuing tension between old and new social forces in a highly kinetic, rapid-transition society.

Development Values

What then are these reaffirmed, guiding values that energize China's transformation and development? They may perhaps be conveniently categorized as *development values,* and *superordinate goals*—the former representing policy norms as well as values in themselves, and the latter representing the ultimate ends of development. The two categories are, of course, interrelated, and the former can be regarded as instrumental values for the attainment of the latter. Without the development values, the superordinate goals would tend to conflict with each other and in the end prove unattainable. We can now list three principal development values:

1. Power to the People, with its corollary, Reliance on the People: A national development strategy can be put into effect only by an independent country. A people-oriented development strategy can only be launched and sustained by a people's regime. In China today, this requires that a hegemony of political power must be held firmly in the hands of the producer classes—the workers and peasants—through every institutional means, formal and informal. But this is not enough.

The concept of people's power has come to mean far more, especially since the Cultural Revolution. It requires the working class, as the most thoroughgoing forward element in social change and economic development, to hold ideological hegemony as well, especially in sustaining the line of development that accords with the people's interests.

The policy derivatives from this value are many, of which some important examples are the following:

a. Leaders must be chosen for their identity with the people and for their adherence to strategies and policies reflecting their interests. To prevent a resurgence of the exploiter mentality, to prevent leadership degenerating into rulership and the consequent loss of people's power from within, cadres must merge with the people, in the celebrated tradition of the "three togethers" (eat together, live together, work together) whenever possible. They must tirelessly re-educate themselves in the strategy of people-oriented development and indeed internalize its whole underlying *weltanschauung,* while shedding regressive attitudes and ways under criticism and self-examination. Rank-and-file working people must have constant, direct, and vigilant supervision over those in authority, using the criterion of the revolutionary line of development.

In this respect, the Cultural Revolution seems to have armed the whole population with a much deeper knowledge of policy and with the experience and analytical tools necessary to distinguish between forward-moving and backsliding orientations of policy. As the situation develops, other "Cultural Revolutions" may even become necessary to decide the major issues of orientation and leadership.

"Power to the people" is thus the prime mobilisatory value for development. Its consolidation is not a mere organisational problem of leadership choice, but a constant struggle against outmoded habits of thought and behaviour. It is worthwhile to note in passing that the current nationwide critique of Confucius (undoubtedly the first in history conducted on a mass scale) concentrates on the residual but tenacious influence of such stratifying and demobilising concepts as the natural right of brain to rule over brawn or the Mandate of Heaven (*t'ien ming*), which Lin Piao evoked to build the theory and politics of great men of virtue and genius playing the decisive role in history.

b. Mass activation, reliance on the people to emancipate themselves, is the corollary approach to development. Mass movements can be effective in economic production as well as in social change. Even technical innovation (or "R and D") must tap the rich source of full worker participation, such as through the "three-in-one" (administrator-technician-worker) workshop teams. People are invariably the most important creative factor. If they are in control and know where they are going, even disadvantageous material conditions can be turned to advantage. This certainly appears to be one of the principal messages of the national models of development—the Tachai Production Brigade in agriculture and the Taching Oilfield in industry, both success stories of human conquest over extremely adverse material conditions.

c. Participatory management. In managerial structures and processes, there must be direct representation from the basic, working level, as occurs in the revolutionary committees now in charge of government and economic enterprises. Concomitantly, there must be debureaucratisation of all decision-making, in favour of what might be described as the "up and down escalator" flow of information and decisions—"from the masses, to the masses," a vertical "feed-in" and "feed-back" mechanism that brings initiative from below into full play.

2. *The Serve-the-People Ethic.* This development value is obviously related to the first. It is the categorical norm for all cadres at all levels of leadership and, indeed, permeates the whole of society.

It is difficult to overestimate its significance for development. In the old China of legalised exploitation and self-serving values, balanced development would have been impossible because there existed hopeless contradictions between the interests of the private entrepreneur and the needs of the consumer public, between "efficient" industrialisation and environmental protection, and so on. These contradictions are being resolved today, in part by public ownership and control. Even more incisively, they are being resolved by starting out from the same serve-the-people value premise in planning and developing both production and distribution, both industrialisation and environmental protection.

Because this ethic is antithetical to the residual individual and family-oriented drives for fame, fortune, and power characteristic of the value system of dominance in the old China, the nurturing and strengthening of this ethic is a process of constant struggle—nothing less than a re-shaping of the human soul. The strain is enhanced if the bureaucracy is allowed to grow in size, power, and routinisation.

To keep this value operational at all echelons, Mao Tse-tung has laid special emphasis on the constant re-identification and re-merging of cadres with the masses. A number of imaginative institutional devices have been worked out for this purpose in the course of the Chinese revolution. In the long-term perspective, they belong in two categories, in-service "re-education" or refresher training for cadres, and the education of the young "successors to the revolution." They include such devices as the following:

Continuing rectification campaigns within the Chinese Communist Party, using the formula "unity-criticism-unity" and instructive paradigms (Chang Ssu-teh, Norman Bethune, and the like) to inculcate the values of selfless service:

The Cultural Revolution;

The "May 7th Road" of personal development—an approach proposed by Chairman Mao on May 7, 1966, calling for service-oriented self-training through the learning of one specialisation but many capacities (in effect, decompartmentalising human activity and preventing alienation from others and from work). One institutional product of it is the May 7th Cadre Schools, in which officials go back to the land or the factory to produce with their own hands and take time out to study and reflect on attitudinal and theoretical issues, especially the question of linking the serve-the-people ethic to one's own work within the grand strategy of socialist development;

Reform of education, directed at combatting elitist training and making the school merge with society and with productive labour, inculcating the prioritisation of collective need over individual need;

The "up to the mountains, down to the villages" movement—a mass movement of high school graduates to settle in the countryside, to help in building up the rural areas where 80 percent of the population live and work;

The *hsia fang* or downward transfer of cadres to basic levels of production and activity.

Systems of managerial participation in productive labour (for example, a factory manager normally spends one day a week working at the lathe).

3. Self-Reliance and Autonomy in Development. It is understandable that Chinese planners are highly sensitive to the need for self-reliance. As we have seen, China has at various times in her history been the victim of destructive economic penetration, of embargo and blockade, of the imposition of inappropriate foreign "models," of the arbitrary withdrawal of contracted technical aid.

This value cannot be operationalised without the optimal use of all available human, natural, and technological resources within the country and within each region of the country. Optimisation of resources calls for a whole set of dual approaches, known popularly in China as policies of "walking on two legs." These are conceived on the principle that two channels of creativity and initiative are better than one. This involves the fullest utilisation of unused or underused resources by resorting to whatever is appropriate and available—both indigenous and advanced technologies; both smaller, low-investment, quickly built plants and big industrial complexes; both mechanised and semi-mechanised technologies, and so on. This has the effect of speeding up a growth pattern geared to sound, common-sense national priorities.

Optimisation of resource use also calls for activating local and regional initiative by "downward transfers of authority" in order to correct bureaucratic overcentralisation. Putting planning and coordination back in the hands of local authorities has the effect of enhancing self-reliance within the over-all framework of national planning. The effect is somewhat comparable to the vitalisation of blobs of self-regenerating DNA everywhere in the living organism.

Self-reliance cannot be operationalised without balanced development of all sectors. Perhaps the more appropriate term here is *congruent* development. "Balance" exists only in a relative sense, while imbalance, which is absolute and recurrent, is precisely what must be identified and overcome again and again to spur healthy, congruent development.

The most critical problem of congruence is that between agriculture and industry. For China, the strategic solution arrived at was characteristically enunciated by Chairman Mao in profoundly simple terms: "Agriculture must be the base, and industry the leading factor." Behind this succinct phrase lies the reality that farm production provides the livelihood of 500 million peasants as well as their food and many raw materials and markets for industry, which must in turn provide the means for modernising and improving agricultural production. But the placing of prime emphasis on agriculture is posed not as a purely economic or technological issue, but first and foremost as a *human* and *political* issue. The relationship between agriculture and industry is in reality the relationship between the workers and the peasants—a vital partnership that would be greatly strained by a different policy stressing lopsided emphasis on industry or continuing the traditional tendency to make the agrarian sector subserve the urban-industrial. The issue then amounted to this: Should the urban working class wholeheartedly support agriculture and the people's communes? Or should they exploit the peasantry for the sake of rapid urban-industrial expansion?

The Chinese answer, reversing the tendency to place priority emphasis on industry, is essentially based on a value preference, that economic policy should serve the whole people, not favouring one sector at the cost of marginalising another. But the policy of "agriculture as the base, industry as the leading factor" has proven to be good growth economics as well. Under the impetus of industry's priority response to the needs of agriculture, the latter sector has grown into a powerful and reliable base for industrialisation. Food-grains, for example, grew from 110 million tons in 1949 to the present level of about 250 million tons. Policy measures to raise farm income (such as price floors for farm prices and price ceilings for manufactured goods) have not only speeded expansion of the vast rural market but also spurred the rate of saving and investment in the rural sector and in the whole economy. The entire set of policies appears to have been mutually reinforcing for both sectors, creating a firm foundation for a self-generating independent economy whose stable growth requires the minimum of external input.

It remains to point out that Chinese self-reliance, while ruling out acceptance of conditional aid, does not preclude normal trade and international cooperation as accessory stimulants to development. As China rapidly expands her foreign trade, she is also ensuring that it reinforces rather than distorts her own pattern of development and that the basic domestic economy is insulated from any disruptive effects of linkage with the world market. My own conjecture is that China will move logically towards setting up a complete export economy (including production facilities) parallel to the domestic, targeted at not too high a ratio to total national income, which would be geared to the competitive international market. The domestic market would draw on the proceeds but would not be caught in the crippling trap of fluctuations in the world market.

Superordinate Goals

The "end" values of Chinese development can perhaps be grouped under four headings.

1. Social justice based on freedom from exploitation, with human relations of egalitarianism, cooperation, and respect for work.

2. Economic welfare for all in a society of abundance, with special attention to raising the level of life of marginalised groups (such as women and national minorities) and regions that have been resource-poor or historically oppressed.

3. Maximum cultural and aesthetic fulfilment. This includes full popular participation in the production of culture.

4. An esthetically and ecologically sound environment. This value is not posed *against* growth, but as *part of* development, fulfiling the same purpose of service to the people as growth.

In a divided society, these goals can be conflicting or mutually exclusive. In a society without basic antagonisms and oriented along the lines of the first set of development values, the goals are interrelated and mutually reinforcing. In specific situations, there may be questions of priority, but never of value conflict. Their common source is the value-orientation of the producer. This question deserves a little further analysis, for which a comparative approach might be useful.

Producer Values, Consumer Values, and Development

In the dominant, profit-oriented economies, production can be influenced by highly manipulable supply-demand variables. Recent evidence increasingly shows that not only rising consumption but falling consumption as well are exploitable levers of corporate "growth" (as distinguished from socially useful economic growth). In these economies, high or rising consumption, based in reality on needless or excessive consumption, particularly in those social sectors commanding high purchasing power, has traditionally been the more useful stimulus of demand. Consumer avidity, induced by promotional techniques and other market mechanisms, has tended to encourage conspicuous waste as the "value" that undergirds the system of maximising investment returns through maximum production volume.

A fall in consumption, induced by short-run real or contrived shortages, without a fall in demand, can also be turned to profit, especially in an era of long-run diminishing availability of non-renewable resources. From the standpoint of the corporations dominating an industry, this fall in consumption is remedied by higher prices. This is rationalised by appealing to the "value" that there must be an "equitable" sharing of economic "costs," including inflationary costs—a "value" that undergirds the system of maximising investment returns in an economy of shortages. The over-all effect is polarisation. In the unequal end-result, the corporation maintains a high rate of return, while the consumer suffers by a kind of double deprivation of goods and money, although he may never cease being a consumer.

The underlying reality is that both waste and inflation are manipulable by the same forces dominating the economy, for the same interests, even though in a relative sense, some may stand to gain and others to lose in the highly complex rivalry among the giants—especially when the economy is in crisis.

Whether in conditions of rising or falling consumption, the worker is individually powerless to change either the policies or the value positions of his employers or his trade union leaders. Indeed, he may find himself forced into a state of value schizophrenia by the symbiotic antithesis inherent in his roles as both producer and consumer. His natural values (social justice for all, use without waste, and the like) are in constant conflict with structurally-induced values (economic survival as a producer, obsessive material acquisition as a consumer), which are all mediated by the maximum-private-gain values of the corporate enterprise on which he depends.

In such a system, it becomes obvious that from the standpoint of those dominating the economy, the "best" results might actually be achieved by an optimal mix of abundance and scarcity, since waste and high prices can both be used, either in parallel or in alternation, to fuel corporate "growth." It is noteworthy in this connection that the degree of acceptability of any "limits to growth" approach must also be understood in the light of these considerations. The essence of the phenomena is that "values" are generated by, and in turn are at the helm of "economics." Operationally, the pattern of unequal power prefigures the pattern of unequal exchange, which in turn further consolidates the pattern of power.

In the Chinese perspective also, "values" (in Chinese terms, "politics") should be at the helm of economics. The fundamental difference is, of course, their answer to the crucial question, *whose* values, *whose* politics?

After a revolutionary takeover of political power, a new socioeconomic system can be established on the ruins of the old, and a new value system can be fostered on this foundation. But neither system can be perfectly reoriented without struggle or at one stroke. To reinforce each other, they must interact over a long period before a final decisive breakthrough is made against regressive forces on both levels. In the current stage, it is the ascendant system of *people-oriented* values that must be made to operate as the decisive factor in setting the parameters for *people-oriented* economic development. In short, "politics must be in command."

This profoundly important strategic principle lies at the heart of the great policy struggles in China, especially in the period since 1956, when the socialist transformation of the economic structure had by and large been consummated. In January, 1957, Mao Tse-tung published his famous essay, "On the Proper Handling of Contradictions within the Ranks of the People." This essay, in fact, set forth the heuristic tenets and even the general programmatic guidelines for change and development throughout the entire period of "socialist transition." A central thrust of the argument was to counter Liu Shao-chi's impatient urge to go the orthodox way of the older industrialised powers, whether capitalist or quasi-socialist. Liu had said that the new basic contradiction, the prime issue that had now come to the fore, was between the newly-established, advanced social system (the socialist relations of production) and the still backward forces of production. Hence, China must now concentrate on the production race with capitalism in terms of aggregate growth rates and GNP per capita, using essentially the same managerial and technological means.

In sharp rebuttal, Mao Tse-tung asserted that there remained imperfections in both "base" and "superstructure" and insisted that the central issue remains the still-unresolved struggle between exploiting and nonexploitative classes—including their antithetical goals, mentalities, institutions, development strategies, and policies. Indeed, he saw this basic tension as the principal content of struggle for a long time to come—for whole generations ahead, right to the day when the socioeconomic and cultural roots of man's exploitation of man are completely extirpated. In the meantime, it is imperative to continue the process of revolutionisation and self-revolutionisation of thought, to bring about a strong and viable people's hegemony in the realm of outlooks and attitudes, habits of work and life, and value-institutionalisation. The strengthening of the new value system can and must in turn energize the growth of productive forces. But the idea that it is possible to go by the reverse process—that is, to let higher production automatically bring about "higher" values—is an illusion, as proven by history, notably the history of the Soviet Union. Even statistically increased GNP per capita has meant in these cases not reducing, but enlarging economic inequities. Without completely transcending the old social system and its values, it may seem possible to achieve higher rates of *growth,* but not balanced, people-oriented *development.*

Indeed, growth under the sole stimulus of material incentive can work like a cancer. Whether on a world or a national scale, runaway growth in one privately dominated part of the economy can at best be a sort of *carcinoma in situ* feeding on only the immediate surrounding tissues of the economy. But when the system is already pathologically weakened, imbalanced growth can become a kind of *invasive carcinoma* that endangers the whole system.

A case in point is the "green revolution," whose results in multiplying productivity have been described as spectacular. Yet in many countries, disillusionment has set in. Spectacular production rises have led not to lesser but to greater inequities. Was the technology at fault? Grave questions have been raised about its appropriateness and ecological soundness. These shortcomings may be *technologically* solvable. Even more serious, however, is the fact that the green revolution was shaped by, and necessarily adapted to international and domestic economics of dominance and dependence. Hence, it was usually superimposed on a system of land tenure that gave enormous advantages to the richer and bigger landowners who were the only ones capable of putting the new agrotechnology into effective use with the requisite economies of scale. They possessed the larger plots of land and adequate financial resources to invest in the artificial fertilizer, irrigation equipment, and the like (much of it imported) that were all part of the high-yield high-technology package. Growth did not automatically lead to better distribution because, it turns out, it was not the technology but the dominant values and institutions that decided the outcome. As a result, in the ensuing, accelerated polarisation, the already marginalised majority of peasants were further impoverished, and more and more were forced to join the armies of alms-seekers in the already swollen cities. Perhaps it is in this manner that, as someone has said, a green revolution might lead to a red revolution. In China's experience, the "chromatic" sequence seems to have been dialectical— a red revolution (the rural cooperative and commune movement) led to a green (the famous "eight-point charter" of interrelated agrotechnologies for raising farm yields summarizing a technology evolved from below), and the green has in turn reinforced the red. The critical factor was a social system that redistributed not only economic but also political and ideological power in favour of the poor but now organised producers, who can be expected, through sustained, conscious action, to carry out long-range planning and development calculated to narrow and ultimately close social and economic disparities at a level of general abundance. In the very long range, the crucial gaps to be closed by upward movement of the system are three: (1) between industry and agriculture, (2) between city and village, and (3) between mental and physical labour.

Of course, to be effective, the new system must be capable of "internalising" in the members of society the primacy of public-service values over those of private gain. But how can a society be built on the denial of such "elemental" characteristics of "human nature" as self-interest and material incentive? The debate over such philosophic issues belongs to another forum. But it is relevant to observe here that the gradual replacement of material incentives (as distinct, incidentally, from material needs) by public-service incentives as motivating factors in production is effective and viable only to the degree that the "adversary" line separating producer and consumer is gradually erased. One might say that the ultimate goal of Chinese social change and ideological struggle is to create a society where in a true sense the producer is the consumer, and the consumer is the producer. The joining of both roles in all individuals enables the people to hold the destiny of the nation in their hands, guided by a common value-orientation.

In such a developing society, how can social polarisation, waste, inflation, and ecological destruction be tolerated, as consumer values are producer values? Similarly, in the effort to emerge out of a marginalised existence, how can a low rate of development be tolerated, since producer values *are* consumer values? Both growth and balance then become firmly entrenched as values.

In such a developing society, the optimal mix of producer-consumer goals cannot be a trade-off between abundance and scarcity. Perhaps the optimal mix at any given point of development can be described as between maximally satisfying the needs of the human body (food, clothing, shelter, mobility, protection from disease) on the one hand, and the needs of the human spirit (satisfying, productive work, non-alienated human relations, cultural development and participation, esthetic environment, and the like) on the other, within the bounds of available resources.

In such a developing society, because the roles of producer and consumer constantly interchange in each person, there are no basic value conflicts arising from antagonistic roles and interests (though other differences and disparities of a nonantagonistic nature will inevitably arise). Hence, it is possible and necessary to mobilize the whole people to take part in the developmental process with the highest degree of common consciousness and motivation. This makes possible the principle of reliance on the people—the "mass line" approach to development.

The Question of Freedom

The question arises as to whether such a mass activation system redounds in the end to the "self-realisation" of the individual, where, it is said, "it counts." This relates to the profound issue of freedom, which can be dealt with only briefly here.

In the Chinese perspective, freedom is not an absolute but a relative entity. It is relative to unfreedom, and in a world of dominators and dominated, exploiters and exploited, freedom resides in a social context, its meaning depending on which of the contending social forces one identifies with. To speak of discrete, individual "self-realisation" outside the context of the real world is neither liberating nor edifying to anyone but those who can afford it, which is definitely not the bulk of humanity. At this stage of human history, freedom for the exploiting minority must mean unfreedom for the exploited majority, and conversely, the long-term trend towards greater human freedom must mean less and less freedom for the exploiting minority, judged by their own values.

In this perspective, the autonomy of a nation, the emancipation of a social class, are stages in human freedom which can be realised only progressively, through the struggles of a wider and wider collectivity of individuals until the whole of humanity is classless and "free"—even including the erstwhile exploiters themselves, now divested of the spiritual self-tyranny of gaining at others' expense! Only then can the largest human freedom—to fulfill oneself in the course of fulfilling the needs and aspirations of one's fellow humans—become a reality.

If the levels of collectivity—family, school or commune or workplace, region, nation, Third World, all peoples—were to be represented by concentric circles with the individual at the centre, the priority of value ascends from the individual to the outermost ring, although the actual sequence of collectivity levels at which specific struggles for freedom occur must depend on the historical circumstances. In any case, the maximum degree of individual freedom results from the emancipation of the largest collective of individuals, not the smallest.

In terms of action, freedom can be seen as awareness of the objective laws of motion in the world of reality and the application of these laws to change reality. In these terms, development is a struggle for human freedom. And in terms of China's approach, the struggle is to be conducted according to a specific value-orientation and strategy that accords with an optimistic view of humanity's future.

An example or two will help clarify this point. In many developing countries, there operate seemingly inexorable pressures toward over-urbanisation. Such pressures are not absent in China, but attempts to reverse them are not carried out by simply proscribing demographic flows from village to city. A reverse flow has been set in motion by appeals to the challenge of building a vast new countryside, of narrowing and closing the economic and cultural gap between town and country, of serving the people where service is most needed. Such appeals, for example, energize the current "up to the mountains, down to the villages" movement of high school graduates.

Similarly, the issue of population growth, so lugubriously stressed by some as the "main" impediment to development, is not exaggerated in China as a scarecrow of hunger to push back demographic pressures on available food and other resources. Rather, voluntary family planning is urged in the positive terms of encouraging all individuals, especially women, to contribute their fullest share to the common effort of developing the production and welfare of their society at a period of life when they are most able to make this contribution. It is also advocated in terms of providing optimal conditions for improving maternal health and the quality of child-rearing. Thus free of suspicious, alienating features as a stricture imposed from above, planned parenthood as a national program can become a self-motivated, conscious movement, as one in a whole set of coordinated strategies for socialist development. Development thus provides the rubric for the discipline of self-liberation.

A Word of Caution

All we have said in this paper refers to basic Chinese *approaches* to the problem of development. It does not necessarily mean that all the intended *results* of these approaches are already a reality, or that China's course will not be again deflected by the strong resurgence of rejected attitudes and values. For example, my own impression is that status-consciousness among some individuals remains a striking contrast to new, egalitarian attitudes and styles of life and work in China. There are other examples. But it is precisely the antithetical coexistence of old and new values that poses the need for a conscious struggle to shed the old and build the new. We are not witnesses to the future. It is not the final outcome, but the condition of health of the metabolism of social change, the direction, vitality and speed of its movement, that we must look at in order to assess the validity of the grand strategies of civilisational transition and development in China.

II

An Interpretation of China's Global Perspectives

The brief observations to be presented here in response to the editor's request, are not offered as an exhaustive analysis of Chinese views on the future of the global system, but only as an attempt to suggest what might be the basic underlying perspectives.

In my view, these perspectives spring from the same fundamental cosmology, historical view, political stance, and over-arching values that furnish the basis for domestic strategies. The peoples, by their struggles, make history, in China as in the rest of the world. The inevitable and principal trend today is revolutionary change, towards the full emancipation of countries, nations, and classes. The human future is bright, although the road to it is hard and thorny.

According to these perspectives, though history is on the side of the deprived and oppressed, the world does not move forward without struggle. To find the correct method of struggle in the short term is to speed up the inexorable forward movement in the long term. This begins with a realistic analysis of the world system, an analysis of the objective dynamics operating in the system as a whole and in its constituent societies. The correct method of struggle then emerges from understanding the necessities and possibilities in the situation and applying the laws and parameters of historical change. Solutions for the global future do not emerge out of intellectual utopias that do not accord with the realities of struggle.

China learned important lessons out of summing up her own bitter experience. It took her an entire century of shake off the fetters of the imperialist world system into which she was drawn after the Opium War of 1839–42. The intrusion into China of the expansionist economies of the industrialized West and Japan did not bring true development but its opposite. They did not destroy Chinese feudalism and build Chinese capitalism. In a sense, what they did was to half-kill feudalism and half-nourish capitalism. A backward agrarian economy still dominated by the rapacious landlord power was shaken out of its self-contained autarchy and further stripped and enfeebled. Superimposed on it was a new, compradore economy of foreign trade and quasi-industrialism in the port cities which acted as extensions and agents of foreign interests and thus served to suck China's economic lifeblood into the metropolitan economies of eight or nine different predatory powers. The whole new political-legal structure making this possible (the "unequal treaty" system) was created and enforced by a series of aggressive wars that ravaged and emasculated the old China, right up to the middle of the present century.

Many historical factors combined to shape the particular course of struggle which finally, in 1949, wrenched China free from the predatory world system. But one paramount principle emerged as a clear lesson: Only through the daring and persistent struggle of an awakened, organised people against seemingly superior military and economic power, winning genuine political and economic independence in this way, could the very first foundations for true autonomous development be laid.

In China's case, this meant waging military as well as political combat. The choice of armed struggle, when it came, was forced on her. Predator after predator refused to relinquish its incursions on China's sovereign rights unless compelled to do so. No appeals to conscience or to the rationality of a more just world order—which in many cases the powers themselves professed to espouse, as at Versailles in 1919 and at Cairo in 1945—would suffice. Indeed, even after the People's Republic was founded in 1949, there was no surcease of armed attempts by the expelled powers to strangle or "contain" the fledgling upstart. Beginning in the 1960s, the Soviet Union did not balk at using force or the threat of force to compel China's compliance and stop her from going her own way.

The Question of International Violence—Whose Question?

With such vivid memories, it is not surprising that the Chinese hold strong views on the question of war and peace in international relations.

The argument runs somewhat like this: To absolutize or generalize the concept of "violence" and "war" into a meaningless abstraction does little to further the cause of peace. The pacifist liberal stand proceeds from certain major premises—that violence is inherently evil; that violence begets violence and therefore is operationally futile in terms of its objectives; that there is always access to a whole range of nonviolent options which should first be exhausted in any dispute.

Serious questions can be raised about each of these propositions, but the most fundamental error is that they evade the key distinction between predator and prey and thereby lose all practical meaning as well as moral force.

Paradoxically, the hortatory apotheosis of peace as the supreme human aspiration does no service to peace as an attainable goal. Not only well-meaning humanists but superpower governments, armed to their bared fangs, indulge in the "anguished search" for peace and invariably inveigh against others as the "forces of war." It is common practice for them to use the phenomena of peace and war not to clarify but to obscure the essence of the problem.

The reality is that in a competitive and exploitative world, peace and violence are both forms of struggle. Political forces choose one or the other depending on the need and possibilities, to the degree necessary and possible.

For all regimes, peace or violence have never been ends in themselves, but instruments of policy for achieving vital interests. It is not peace and violence that are in conflict but these vital interests and the national and social forces pursuing them. When political forces deem it unnecessary or impossible to use force to change or restore the balance between these interests, this situation is dubbed "peace." In fact, however, it may only be a form of congealed violence (or what Johan Galtung calls "structural violence")—a dominance gained by force and sustained by the threat of force while countermovements actually remain at work. Conversely, when political forces believe that it is both necessary and possible to resort to force to prevent unfavorable change or to alter the balance of interests in their favour, then violence will result. In international relations, the supreme expression of violent methods is war. Such wars occur whether we will it or not. Their occurrence will not be finally prevented until predatory social systems undergo profound transformation so that they no longer generate policies which lead to war.

This being the case, there is no moral or practical value in condemning *all* wars. To do so is equivalent to condemning arson without condemning the arsonist, as if the householder victim were equally responsible for having a house which arsonists could set fire to. When an aggression is launched, the usual result is two kinds of war within one war—the war of the predator and the war of the victim against the predator. To then sit in lofty, even-handed judgment against all resort to war on both sides is neither to uphold peace and humane ideals nor to be neutral in the specific situation. No one can be less deluded as to the net effect of such "nonpartisan" anti-war exhortations than the fighting victim. Can there be any objective result other than to help incapacitate the victim and consolidate the aggressor's spoils—in short, to encourage aggressive war?

On the other hand, the position that firmly condemns aggressive war and leaves open the victim's option to conduct a war of resistance does not thereby imply approval of war as an institution or that it is intrinsically to be preferred over nonviolent options. On the contrary, its principal long-range thrust is to move towards the final elimination of war as an institution, on the principle that the aggressive, first-strike war is the beginning of all war, and the most immediate way to discourage it is to defeat it. In the very long run, only revolutionary economic and social change will extirpate the sources of war. In the shorter run, it is only by the very successes of the struggles for national independence and people's power that the weaker countries will be removed from the role of being tempting prey in the war system.

The logic of what must be done is clear. If aggressive war is eliminated, how can there be defensive wars of liberation? To eliminate war then is essentially to eliminate aggressive war. To suggest that it can be done by eliminating liberation wars turns upside down both human logic and human values.

Of course, the principle may be clear, but it may not be so simple in practice. It is not always easy to determine who struck first, and nearly all wars of recent years have begun with mutual recriminations of aggression. Furthermore, the "first strike" can sometimes be identified as one that was launched much earlier, prior to an intervening period of unjust "peace" imposed by force. By a semantic twist, client governments can even claim to be victims of "aggression" from their own people and "invite" foreign intervention. But experience has shown, as in Vietnam and Czechoslovakia, that informed world opinion has little difficulty piercing the screen of propaganda recriminations to identify predator and victim with dead accuracy. The task is made easier once deceptive abstractions about violence are brought down to the realm of concrete analysis.

There remains the question of whether the newly-independent countries might wage war among themselves. Regrettably, there continue to arise armed clashes belonging in this category, caused by a variety of internal and external factors. Chief among these are the legacy of colonialism and continued superpower involvement, which can even lead to proxy wars and protracted half-war, half-peace situations, as in the Middle East. To prevent or halt such conflicts means essentially to combat superpower involvement. Third World countries are increasingly aware of the commonality of their historical experience and the need for cooperation in their present struggles for independent development and against declining but still virulent neocolonialism. Having no fundamental conflict of interests among themselves, there is no reason why they should not, if left to themselves, resort to nonviolent means to resolve their differences.

The idea of exhausting nonviolent means of solving disputes is often posed as a precondition or caveat to approving the just use of force. On its surface, there can be no objection of principle to this. The history of the Chinese revolution is itself full of attempts to use political, nonviolent means to settle issues with the deadliest of adversaries. Some proved disastrous, as in the case of the coup d'etat of 1927, when the armed Kuomintang responded with massive suppression to the political moves of the unarmed Communist Party. Others were eminently successful, as in the case of the Peiping and Suiyuan models of peaceful settlement during the 1946–49 Civil War. Such models could be followed at a stage when the tide had already turned in favour of the People's Liberation Army. They were aimed at minimizing bloodshed and destruction, even though negotiated solutions were expected to leave a more complex aftermath of political and educational problems to be solved.[6] Thus, minimisation of violence was never regarded as

---

[6]An interesting reference to these problems is contained in Mao Tse-tung's Report to the Second Plenum of the Seventh CCP Congress, April, 1949.

equivalent to minimisation of struggle, but only as an alternative channel for achieving liberation, made possible by special historical circumstances. Typically, it requires a situation in which the new popular
forces have already gained decisive ascendancy in a country, although
even in such a situation, their power must be used to maintain the momentum of progressive change and to guard against the inevitable
comeback attempts, violent or nonviolent, of the old forces.

In the foregoing sense, the option of nonviolent means is considered
and exercised from the specific standpoint of the struggle for liberation.
Issued from a different standpoint, however, the "nonpartisan," un-
qualified exhortation "to exhaust nonviolent means" is another matter
entirely. Indeed, it can often convey high irony when directed at still
unliberated nations and peoples for whom the choice of "nonviolence"
was never theirs to make. Some peoples, as in the case of those in the
Portuguese African colonies, exhausted their nonviolent options long
ago in their struggle against the violent destruction and denial of their
rights.[7] If third parties really wanted to stop the violence of the
colonialist war, their duty lay at the very least in supporting *all* the
victim's options for struggle, and decidedly not in trying to deny them
the one option their oppressors seem to understand best. It cannot be a
surprise to anyone that such fighting peoples do not list as their friends
those who spend less energy mobilising opinion against aggression than
trying to persuade people not to fight back.

But Has the Nuclear "Age" Changed Everything?

Is nuclear war "in a different category"? Does its awesome capacity
to "overkill" the world now render meaningless the distinction between
just and unjust wars? Has the proscription of all armed struggle become the highest principle of humanity? Has it, in fact, become the
means of staying the nuclear hand of the superpowers?

To many millions in the intermediate zone between the superpowers,
the dissemination of such ideas strongly suggests unconditional surrender to the total terrorisation of the world by the superpowers. The
underlying threat—pacification or obliteration!—argues that principles
mean nothing if you are burned to a crisp, and docile animal existence

---

[7]In this connection, it is of interest to note Chinese Vice-Foreign Minister Chiao Kuan-
hua's comment in the UN on Oct. 2, 1974: "Both the birth of the Republic of Guinea-
Bissau and the more recent agreement on the independence of Mozambique are in
essence the result of long and persistent armed struggle ... and are by no means favours
bestowed by colonialism."

is still preferable to the nobility of aspiring but immolated peoples—
not a very new threat in the history of human oppression. It is hard to
conceive of a more final execration of humanity in the name of
humanity.

China appears to have taken the view that the development of
nuclear weapons does heighten the urgency of curbing aggression and
war, especially nuclear war. But in her view this purpose is not served
by adding fuel to the nuclear intimidation of nonnuclear nations. The
onus lies squarely on the nuclear powers. The notion that nonnuclear
nations possess the power of choice by choosing between waging or de-
sisting from struggles for their rights which allegedly would involve the
superpowers and trigger nuclear conflict—a notion assiduously spread
by the Soviet Union—has no basis in reality and represents a bald
evasion of responsibility.

Somehow it all conjures up the bizarre image of two rival desperadoes hijacking an airliner, each brandishing a huge bundle of dyna-
mite and professing fear for the passengers' safety unless they obey
commands. Yet the superpowers are not exactly desperadoes, nor do
they have the intention or capacity to skyjack Spaceship Earth to some
distant galaxy. Final, apocalyptic drama is not in the logic of their
existence. Their purpose is neither to commit suicide nor to incinerate
into unprofitable ashes the very objects of their contests for power.
There is therefore compelling logic in the analysis that the threat of
nuclear war is first and foremost a game of political blackmail and only
secondarily poses the possible madness of acting out MAD (Mutual
Assured Destruction).

The nuclear threat is directed at escalating to the utmost all superpower sanctions against attempts to interfere with their reordering of
the globe. As for those who defy this reordering, they must, of course,
bear the stigma of "callous adventurers" who make light of the lives of
their own people in the nuclear age. The Chinese regard this as a twist
of vilification intended to deceive the naïve.

Nevertheless, the prevention of nuclear war is a real issue. But it is
a hopeless undertaking unless we can identify and control the dynamics
of the processes that tend towards nuclear war. There is no basis for
seeking these dynamics in the struggles, armed or otherwise, of the
nations and peoples seeking genuine independence and emancipation.
As we have already noted, these struggles in fact work in the opposite
direction.

The dynamics tending towards nuclear confrontation and conflict are
to be found in the vast, global contest for hegemony between the two
superpowers. The most obvious danger lies in the nuclear arms spiral,

which SALT I, SALT II and Vladivostock try to sustain and codify rather than to wind down and eliminate. The ever-escalating weapons innovation and expansion which this race engenders results, as Herbert York has remarked, in not more but less security. Furthermore, the complex jockeying for advantage which constantly induces either over-commitment or undercommitment in weapons development produces all kinds of intended and unintended political and economic fallout. Because resource limits and political and economic objectives impose severe constraints on weapons development, the arms race is manipulated as much to strain or break these barriers to the detriment of the adversary as to obtain military objectives.

The tense struggle over the number, mix, and deployment of FBS, IRBMs, MRBMs and ICBMs (forward based systems, intermediate, medium range, and intercontinental ballistic missiles) more and more explicitly reflects the immediate preoccupation of the rival superpowers, which is to gain the strategic and psychological heights for political and economic domination over vast strategic areas—especially Europe and the Middle East.

The multifaceted development of these superpower struggles may well be too complex to plot a probability curve on the imminence of nuclear war itself, but the danger needs no calculable proof. It lies in a hegemonic struggle of such high stakes that risk-taking cannot be entirely rational. Hence it is a prime task to continue to mobilize the full weight of world opinion to demand the ultimate and complete destruction of nuclear weapons and the total prohibition of their manufacture, testing, and use. But the integrity of this demand is vitiated by allowing it to be manipulated by those nuclear powers who refuse to take one honest step towards realizing it.

One such honest step would be an unequivocal undertaking by each nuclear power never to be the first to use nuclear weapons. If such a pledge became universal, it would then require the ultimate display of cynical sophistry to argue that "first-strike" or "second-strike" capabilities, on whatever level and at whatever balance, are still necessary. At such a "moment of truth," the collapse of the complex rationale of the Soviet-U.S. nuclear game would make it possible to break out of the fraudulent and self-defeating technological framework in which arms "limitation" talks are conducted. One must surmise that this was the prime intent of the Chinese in repeatedly reaffirming China's unilateral no-first-use pledge and challenging the other nuclear powers to follow suit. There is similar intent in challenging the superpowers to withdraw their forces from other countries as a prerequisite for a genuine "world" disarmament conference. A Chinese saying goes: "To stop the pot boiling, one must pull the firewood out from under."

"National Interest" Versus "Global Values"

Those who have an interest in keeping the pot boiling, however, will not pull out the firewood. On a deeper level of analysis, Peking assumes that an end to international exploitation—and therefore, to war—will not come before the final extirpation of imperialism as a system.

In this perspective, "national interest," as formulated by governments, flows out of the dynamics of the domestic socioeconomic system. Objectively, such formulations inevitably reflect the interests of ruling groups and classes and not necessarily those of the whole nation in whose name they are always enunciated. Foreign policy based on such "national" interests constitutes in reality an attempt to manipulate external relations within the parameters of both the domestic and the international systems, in such a way as to favour those in power in the nation. Whether declared goals are empty rhetoric or genuinely pursued in practice depends in the final analysis on whether such goals ever actually coincide with "national" interest, and this in turn depends on who is in power and the nature of the socioeconomic system they are running.

From the standpoint of those seeking a just and progressive world order, the criteria for judging the foreign policies of states cannot merely be what governments say but also what they do. Even more fundamentally, it is what they inevitably *must* do, as determined by the interests of those in power and the inner drives generated by the political and economic tensions within their societies, tempered only by the leeway they are permitted by other forces in the international arena.

A political system in which power is in the hands of a privileged ruling stratum which seeks to maintain or expand its dominance is likely to behave externally in a very different manner from one in which power is progressively consolidated in the hands of the popular majority. Similarly, an economic system whose inner processes rely in large part on maximation of profits from exploiting external resources and markets is bound to generate attitudes about the world economic order quite opposed to those of an economic system based on self-reliance and maximation of people's welfare. Concomitantly, a cultural system that is chauvinistic in content can provide support for the ruthless imposition of the government's will on weaker nations, support which would be denied in a cultural system in which people-oriented, internationalist values predominate.

Is this frame of analysis too deterministic? Does it not ignore the role in policy-making of other factors, such as the outlook and personality of individual leaders? No, but it does help to delineate the bounds within which such fortuitous factors are able to operate. What it does provide is realistic criteria for judging what maximal and minimal positions can be expected of specific governments, and for projecting what possible ways they may interact with one another and with transnational actors on the world scene.

Such a frame of analysis may also save us from the unrealism of putting our faith in appeals to the conscience or higher rationality of individual government leaders when it is clearly impossible to reconcile the "national" (i.e., class) interest that they espouse with higher global values, and thus help to focus attention instead on the need to mobilize all possible forces for struggle.

Clearly, a deeper analysis of superpower policy must proceed from behavioural to systemic characteristics. For example, in the Chinese perception, it is no accident that the relationship between the Warsaw Pact countries and Moscow should be governed by the imposed strictures of "limited sovereignty" and "division of labour" in a Soviet-oriented, exploitative system of "socialist economic integration." In fundamental terms, this is to be explained by the fact that the Soviet Union is no longer a socialist country. It has suffered a regressive mutation, reflected domestically in the emergence of a profit-oriented economy dominated by enormous monopolies and controlled by a new privileged class. The external expression of such a system is expansionism and hegemonism, supported by huge armament outlays amounting to one-third of the annual budget, which have already created not only a huge nuclear offensive capacity, but also the largest navy in the world. Like its rival, the United States, the Soviet Union inexorably pursues its hegemonic ambitions beyond its real capacities, aggravating its grave problems at home.

The Chinese view of the Soviet-U.S. "detente" follows from the systemic analysis. The two rivals may have a temporary, common interest in spreading the ambiance of detente in order to stabilize mutually agreed-upon, interim patterns of world dominance and to blunt the edge of worldwide struggles against these patterns of dominance. But so long as both imperialist systems exist, their inevitable depredations on others and their mutual rivalries will bring either war or revolution. It is bitter irony to talk of "detente" and "a generation of peace" in the context of a continuing Soviet-U.S. arms race accompanied by frenetic jockeying for strategic position in all parts of the world at the expense of weaker nations' rights. If indeed, as Professor

Marshall D. Shulman of Columbia University writes, "detente" only starts a process of "codifying" the terms of Soviet nuclear competition with the United States, can this be anything but a continued, albeit smiling, cold war? If the game of nuclear arms escalation before "detente" was breeding the danger of a hot nuclear trial of strength, is the danger reduced in any way by setting new "balance of terror" rules for the same game?

Because the alleged detente did not set any new rules banning super-power aggression, expansionism, neocolonialism, and other incursions on the sovereign rights of nations in the intermediate zones, (not even a pledge to respect proposed nuclear-free zones in Latin America and South Asia) these actual and potential victims have naturally in-terpreted the detente for what it is—a temporary bilateral accommoda-tion on nonbasic issues and a brief respite for readjustment and re-deployment in preparation for the next violent test of strength.

In this situation, the Chinese position has been to insist on being counted *out* in the game of superpower rivalry, including its false detentes and to call for maximum vigilance against the superpower game. Again, this is put forward as a long-term policy having a sys-temic basis.

Confucius, Lin Piao, and Superpower Hegemony

On the current world scene, perhaps no country is more relentless in its frank recognition of the nexus between foreign policy and the dy-namics of the domestic system than the People's Republic of China. The logical pursuit of this line of reasoning has recently brought forth one of the most extraordinary statements ever to issue from a govern-ment leader to the world public. In his address to the UN General Assembly's Special Session on Raw Materials and Development on April 10, 1974, Vice-Premier Teng Hsiao-ping said:

> The Great Proletarian Cultural Revolution ... and the campaign of criticising Lin Piao and Confucius now underway throughout China are both aimed at preventing capitalist restoration and ensuring that socialist China will never change her colour and will always stand by the oppressed peoples and oppressed nations. If one day China should change her colour and turn into a superpower, if she too should play the tyrant in the world and everywhere subject others to her bullying, aggression and exploitation, the people of the world should identify her as social-imperialism, expose it, oppose it and work together with the Chinese people to overthrow it."[8]

[8] *Peking Review,* Supplement, April 12, 1974.

Here is the apotheosis of internationalist global values over national-ist principles of power, a declaration as remarkable as the bold expec-tation that future struggles will have to be waged against a possible regressive mutation of China. As a ringing declaration of the primacy of people-oriented values over power-oriented values, the statement is reminiscent of and perhaps represents an extension into the interna-tional sphere of Mao Tse-tung's famous dictum addressed to the Chi-nese people at the beginning of the Cultural Revolution: It is right to rebel against reactionaries occupying the very heights of power! At that time, it was a call addressed to the people from the standpoint of the people, to combat a regressive mutation in the top bureaucratic leadership. Teng Hsiao-ping's near-paraphrase of this call seems to be addressed to the world's peoples from the standpoint of the world's peoples, directed against any new superpower imperialism, no matter where and in what form it reared its head—even if it should be in China. Indeed, exactly *because* it might be in China. For, according to his analysis, capitalist restoration in a country as large as socialist China would mean not merely the re-emergence of another capitalist country, but the emergence of another superpower imperialism.

The degree to which China is serious about forestalling a superpower orientation in her own development must be assessed from many facets. There is evidence of much educational effort being put into inculcating antichauvinist values. One omnipresent slogan that impinges daily on the citizen's consciousness reads: "Dig tunnels deep, Store grain every-where, Never seek hegemony!" Every adult and child is familiar with these phrases. One is struck by the dialectical unity of the three ex-hortations: It is only by not seeking to be a bully in the world that one can rely on the people and be defensively invulnerable. Full civilian involvement in the widespread building of underground shelters and grain silos is a movement of political education as well as of defense preparedness.

That such a posture is possible for China, however, is inseparable from her basic socioeconomic orientations, for all exhortations against superpower roles would be useless if Chinese society were of such a nature that it generated expansionist drives. In terms of both offense and defense, the implementation of the self-reliance principle helps eliminate at one and the same time the urge for external domination of less self-reliant system and the domestic vulnerability of an overcen-tralised economy. Similarly, the rational deployment of small and me-dium industries throughout the rural hinterland, the provision of basic needs and services at the primary level of the people's commune and urban street neighbourhood committee, as well as the preparedness of the regular armed forces for production in peacetime and combat in war are all part of both a sound development strategy and defense planning. The whole set of home policies seems to make possible a strong external posture which is neither arrogant nor subservient on major international issues.

To understand these issues and where China stands on them, it would be necessary first to grasp how the Chinese view the current world situation in the flow of history.

Great and Good Disorder

The current world scene is characterized by great but good disorder.

To Chinese revolutionaries, the present world epoch has been marked by sharp contradictions that have been escalating in scope and depth since the world imperialist system took shape at the turn of the century. It is these contradictions that propel contemporary history, and today they are moving toward a climactic intensity. There are acute struggles unfolding—between the exploiter and the exploited classes within capitalist societies, between imperialist powers and the victims of their neocolonialism, among the imperialist powers (in particular the superpowers) themselves, and between the imperialist powers (including today's USSR) and the socialist countries. The intense fury of these struggles has torn apart the fabric of the old order. The U.S.-dominated world symbolized by the Bretton Woods monetary system is no more, and also demised is the socialist camp, as the Soviet Union assumes the role of a superpower seeking her share of world hegemony. Great storms of change have swept aside old alignments; and in the reshuffle, new alignments have emerged, with even stormier changes in the offing.

In the Chinese perception, the essence underlying all this sound and fury is that the world is moving at a higher metabolic rate in the shedding of the old order and the building of the new. The dismantling of old structures always creates some disorder, but it is "disorderly" for the old forces that are now gradually receding from their all-powerful roles on the world stage, in favour of the newly-independent resurgent forces of the developing nations. The trend is unfettering and moving ahead in the stream of history, and it is in this sense that it is good disorder. In premier Chou En-lai's words,

The universal great disorder throws imperialisms into confusion, arouses and tempers the people, and promotes the development of the anti-imperialist revolutionary struggles of the people the world over.[9]

One symptom of the times has been particularly noted. A turning-point in the history of the United Nations was reached in April of 1974, when for the first time in its three decades of history, the United Nations, under the pressure of Third World countries, convened a special session to air the anti-imperialist views of the long-suffering victims of the predatory world system.

Which World China?

In the global restructuring of forces into the First, Second, and Third Worlds, China has refused to enter the superpower club and has placed herself firmly in the ranks of the Third World. She sees the global future from the perspectives of a developing socialist country. Having emerged only a generation ago from semicolonial backwardness, she is still industrially and technologically behind the advanced industrial countries, like all other Third World countries. But, having also traversed a long road of self-reliant struggle, she is acutely conscious of the fact that while political independence was necessary to gain economic independence, economic independence is necessary to consolidate political independence. Like other Third World countries, China before 1949 was never able to break out of the poverty, low investment, low productivity, poverty cycle, until she found the key to breaking the shackles of foreign domination by relying on her own people and her own resources. Without specifying measures that each nation must adopt according to its own conditions, she sees the Third World's future in terms of all nations winning the right to choose their own social and economic systems and gaining sovereignty over their own resources and control over foreign and transnational capital within their own countries, with self-reliance and mutual cooperation among Third World countries. Having two thirds of the world's population and more than half of its strategic resources, the Third World Nations can change the balance of forces to favour progressive change, provided they join in united action.

Many difficult concrete problems remain to be solved, of course. But the trends are clear in the increasingly united approaches of Third World countries. An example is the vital issue of raw materials. In

[9]*Ta Kung Pao*, Hongkong, April 4, 1974. Premier Chou was speaking at a state banquet for visiting Cambodian deputy premier Khiev Samphang.

March of 1974, the leaders of many developing countries enunciated their common position that

> ... it is imperative to put an end to the exploitation of their economic resources ... (they must) apply the principle of permanent sovereignty of states over their natural resources, support all measures of nationalisation ... to assure control over their natural resources ... and examine the possibility of establishing an equitable relation between the prices of raw materials, primary products, semi-manufactured products and manufactured products exported by the developing countries and the prices of raw materials, primary products, capital goods and equipment imported by them with the aim of improving their terms of trade which are ceaselessly deteriorating.[10]

At the special United Nations session in the following month, China gave broad support to these principles of struggle.

On the planetary scale as on the national, true development means not only aggregate growth but also reallocation of priorities to close the unhealthy disparity gaps. This may call for some sort of "staggered" agenda, but it cannot and should not mean that the "developed" nations should mark time or even stagnate in order that the developing nations can catch up. There are vast areas of underdevelopment in the "affluent" countries too—characteristically shown in the inadequacy of socioeconomic institutions and in the impoverishment of human relations but also manifesting itself in serious pockets of material poverty and backwardness. The emancipation and progress of the Third World may well spur the solution of the inequities and imbalances in the developed countries, and there are immense potentialities in mutual help and mutual learning among peoples in their common strivings. It is erroneous to accept the "struggle for the world product" or "distributional war" theories which put gains in the emancipation and progress of the Third World on the cost side of the developed countries' ledgers, all within the framework of a world of "limited and irreplaceable resources." But this is an enormous issue for further examination and research.

It is increasingly apparent that the strong emphasis on independence and self-reliance in development, such as espoused by China, does not preclude participation in all kinds of useful and non-interventionist international cooperation and aid in bilateral, multilateral and "transnational" forms, especially among countries of the intermediate (non-superpower) zones. Even in the UN itself, a strong trend is growing under Third World pressure, towards turning its agencies into more

---

[10]Final document of the Permanent Bureau of the Fourth Conference of Heads of State and Government of the Non-Aligned Countries, Algiers, March 19–22, 1974.

effective instruments of global cooperation, genuinely geared to the real needs of the peoples. Of more than symbolic significance perhaps was the recent appearance on the podium of a World Health Conference of a "barefoot doctor" or paramedic speaking as a member of the Chinese delegation. This spurred wide interest in setting up a new educative programme on paramedical training as a response to people-oriented needs in many countries.

The closing of antidevelopmental disparities in the world must be guided by systems of value and systems of power. But whose values and whose power? It cannot be imagined that any real breakthrough to a more equitable world order can be made if (1) the effective dominant values are those of the old forces—the few who stand to lose by change—and (2) the process of change itself is controlled and manipulated by these forces. Globally, development is therefore essentially a political struggle of profound depth. To the degree that it turns in favour of the vast majority of the world's peoples, to that degree there will be forward movement. For all who are seriously concerned, the prospectus for the global future is being written, not in neatly schematized "models" unrelated to the real world, but in the portentous struggles now actually taking place between the rearguard forces of superpower hegemony and the rapidly advancing forces of revolutionary order.

We have a choice to make, not for others, but for ourselves.

The future is bright. The road is hard.

APPENDIX A
COMMENT ON THE TERMS
"DEVELOPMENT" AND
"VALUE"

A "definition" of development is useful only as a heuristic device to probe the actual dynamics of change and thus to provide a basis for conceptual guidelines to future development. There has never existed, either in practice or in theory, a developmental approach that objectively accorded with the interests of *all* social sectors. What is regarded as "development" by a dominant sector or class is regarded as nondevelopment or even antidevelopment by the dominated. The reverse would also be true if we were to look beneath the rhetoric to the essence of the issue. There are no value-free approaches and no value-free definitions of development. At best, any attempt at terminological definition is a declaration of standpoint.

Many people are now aware that development, narrowly interpreted in aggregate economic growth terms, can be a stultifying and misleading conceptual tool. However, attempts to define it broadly (e.g., G. Myrdal's "upward movement of the whole social system") can also end up in tautological futility. Of course, development is upward. But which way is up?

It is possible to formulate a concept of development in more normative terms, as for example:

> The movement of the whole socioeconomic and cultural system towards an ever larger measure of power to the people for conscious participation in building their own future, higher production for societal needs based upon non-exploitative relations of production and equitable principles of distribution, and the maximum possible enjoyment by the producers in society of culture oriented towards their own reality, needs and aspirations and of an aesthetically and ecologically sound environment.

Such a statement is, of course, chock full of values. But perhaps it has the advantage of leaving less room for doubt about what is meant and what is not meant by development.

Goulet and Walshok define "value" as "any object or representation which is or can be perceived repeatedly as worthy of desire."[11] They emphasize *perceived* values and inveigh against treating them instrumentally. Change must be proposed in terms congenial to the perceived values of a populace, whose "judgment" must be respected. This is valid. Stress should be laid, however, on the circumstance that there is no such thing as a monolithic populace with a consensus judgment on basic values. In other words, no matter how much we may wish it, there are no universal values, at least not yet in the world. Almost all public leaders everywhere have been shouting "peace, justice, welfare" from the tops of very different houses, often fiercely feuding ones, for as long as we can remember. The problem is not the universality of the terminology, but the particularity of the social vantage points from which the terms are given meaning and fulfillment. Terminology should be used not to obscure but to illuminate the distinction. Differing value systems that exist objectively in society cannot be replaced, displaced, or placed by the purely intellectual judgments of theorists and planners.

The term "values" as used here seldom occurs in the literature of social analysis in China. Values are part of the *weltanschauung* of specific social classes. The contention between different social classes is the principal content of politics. Value-contention is part of the grist of politics.

[11]Denis Goulet and Marco Walshok, "Values among Underdeveloped Marginals," *Comparative Studies in Society and History,* Vol. 13, No. 4, October, 1971.

INDEX